MARK LESLIE LEFEBVRE

Stark Publishing Solutions

Cover Artwork Credits
"Stack of Books in Form of Stairs" © Topgeek, Dreamstime.com
"Rocket education" © Dharshani Gk Arts, Dreamstime.com



**Stark Publishing Solutions**
**An Imprint of Stark Publishing**
**Waterloo, Ontario**
**www.starkpublishing.ca**

Publisher's Note: This work is derived from the author's experience in bookselling, writing, and publishing, and is meant to inform and inspire writers with tools and strategies for success in their own writing path. The author and publisher believe that there is no single magic solution for everyone, and that advice, wisdom, and insights should be carefully curated and adapted to suit each individual's needs, goals, and desires. Be aware that the platforms mentioned are prone to change.

Updates and a list of online resources mentioned in this book can be found at: www.markleslie.ca/wideforthewin

Wide for the Win / Mark Leslie Lefebvre
March 2021

Print ISBN: 978-1-989351-26-0
eBook ISBN: 978-1-989351-27-7
Audio ISBN: 978-1-989351-28-4

*To Joanna Penn.*

*Thank you, Jo, for the friendship, the ongoing inspiration, and your always optimistic outlook on the future of publishing and technology.*

# Table of Contents

# Glossary

This may be a section that you skip and only come back to when needed.

However, if you are new to writing and publishing, then you might be confused by some "insider" terms and abbreviations being used throughout this book as well as by the author community.

This is not an authoritative list by any stretch of the imagination; but I wanted to provide at least a basic high-level list of some terms and abbreviations that are used so you aren't left in the dark wondering what they mean or refer to. While I've done my best to explain these terms as I introduce them throughout the book, for your convenience, they appear here.

Please note that this glossary may include a few terms not actually used in this book, but which are used in other books for writers and within the writing and publishing communities.

The glossary will list a word or abbreviation (in alphabetical order), what it means or stands for (where applicable), then a brief "definition."

**ACX** (*Audiobook Creation Exchange)*
Owned and operated by Audible Inc., an Amazon company that connects authors and narrators. Titles produced through ACX are made available for sale on Audible.com, Amazon.com and iTunes.

**Advance** *(Advance payment for a book)*
Money a publisher pays in advance on a book. Once the advance is "earned out" (where the royalties earned surpasses the money provided to the author up front) the author then receives royalties for sales. For example, if an advance was $1000, and the royalties on a $25 book were 8% ($2.00/unit sold), the advance would "earn out" once 500 copies of the book are sold.

**Alpha Reader** *(Early reader for a book)*
An early reader of a book prior to publication, usually a non-professional, who provides feedback to the author.

**AMS** *(Amazon Ads / Amazon Marketing Services)*
The program is now known as Amazon Advertising, but it used to be Amazon Marketing Service. The name keeps changing, but many authors continue to refer to Amazon Ads as AMS or AMS Ads.

**ARC** *(Advance Reader Copy)*
An advance edition of a book that is sent to reviewers, bookstores, and librarians. This is, within traditional publishing, often done in print trade paperback format, and usually with marketing copy on the back cover specifically geared towards the bookstore/library/trade journal reviewer market. ARCs can be digital. They often are considered "unedited" or "early" proof copies and might be referred to as an "unedited proof."

**ASIN** *(Amazon Stock Inventory Number)*
A 10-character alphanumeric unique identifier assigned to every product by Amazon for every product it sells. Amazon values this identifier over the book industry standard ISBN and will assign a book an ASIN even if it has an ISBN.

**Author Newsletter** *(Also referred to as a mailing list or author mailing list)*
One of the most powerful marketing and engagement tools an author can have, where readers sign up to stay in touch with an author's life, work, new releases, and price promotions. It allows authors to engage directly and share with their readers, rather than relying on retailers and other industry gatekeepers.

**B&N** *(Barnes & Noble)*
An American bookseller that operates the largest number of retail outlets in the United States. Their eBook platform is called Nook, which is also the name of their eReader device.

**B2R** *(Books2Read)*
A free service owned and run by *Draft2Digital* that authors can use to create universal book links (UBLs). These UBLs offer a single URL that contains inclusive links to all the major retailer and some library markets. It also employs geo-targeting to send people who click on a retail link to be brought to their local territory's version of a website.

**BB** *(BookBub)*
A free book discovery web and email service for readers to help them find new books and authors. The company features free and discounted eBooks selected by its editorial team. Publishers and authors can apply to be considered for feature spots they pay for. BookBub also offers a paid advertising program called BookBub Ads.

**BBFD** *(BookBub Feature Deal)*
The inclusion of a title in one of BookBub's targeted email blasts to readers, filtered by genre and retail platform. Getting accepted for a BookBub feature deal after applying for one is a much-coveted marketing tactic for authors and publishers, as they typically earn back the money invested and more in paying for that placement.

**Beta Reader** *(Beta reader for a book)*
An early reader of a book prior to publication, usually a non-professional, who provides feedback to the author. A beta reader often sees a book "later" in the publication process than an alpha reader, and often after a book may have been modified based on suggestions from alpha readers.

**Big Five (The)** *(The Big Five Trade Publishers)*
A term often used to describe the major traditional/trade publishers like Penguin Random House, Harper Collins, Hachette, etc. When I started in the book industry, they were somewhere in the realm of the Big Twelve or the Big Ten.

They were the Big Six for many years before Random House and Penguin merged a few years back. Because of mergers, they might soon be the "Big Four."
(In the indie author community, some might also refer to "The Big Five" as the main eBook retail platforms: Apple Books, Google Play, Kindle, Kobo, and Nook.)

**BISAC** *(Book Industry Standards and Communications)*
Often used as a short term to denote BISAC Subject Codes, which are subject category codes for books from the BISG (Book Industry Study Group) used to denote one or more of the approximately 3500 possible subject categories for a book. Publishers communicate these codes to booksellers and libraries to denote what section of the store they should be placed into. Most stores have their own map from BISAC to an internal subject classification.

**BISG** *(Book Industry Study Group)*
A US trade association for policy, technical standards, and research related to books and book-related products. The goal of BISG is to simplify logistics for publishers, manufacturers, suppliers, wholesalers, retailers, librarians, and others involved in publishing book industry products for print and digital media.

**Chapbook** *(A book format)*
Originally used to denote a small publication of about 40 pages in length. Chapbooks were commonly used for poetry and usually are done to a specific theme. In early

modern Europe it was a type of printed street literature, often saddle stitched and in limited print runs. In more recent times the term "chapbook" is also used to denote short, inexpensive mini-books or booklets.

**Beta Reader** *(Early reader of a book)*
A reader, usually non-professional, who provides feedback on a book after a writer has made revisions inspired by alpha readers.

**Blurb** *(As in "back cover blurb copy")*
Descriptive commentary that appears on a book's item page online and, for print books, on the dust jacket flaps or the rear of the book cover or jacket. A blurb often contains a mixture of plot synopsis and promotional pitch, and successful blurbs are usually ones that act as a promotional bit of "sales copy" to inspire the ideal reader to purchase the book.
*(As in review excerpt or recommended praise quote)*
This term is often used to describe a short line of text, often a single line, that appears on the front cover, or perhaps back cover above or below the book's main descriptive copy, to denote praise for the work; often as an excerpt from a review, or a well-respected author in a similar or complimentary genre. The goal is to assure potential readers that the book in question is worthy of their time and money.

**Box set** *(Known as a boxset or boxed set)*
A set of physical items (books, CDs, DVDs, etc.) traditionally packaged in a box and offered for sale as a single unit. (Within the indie author community authors often say "box set" (or "boxset") without adding the term "digital" to denote a "digital box set"—which, technically, is more like an "omnibus" (see that definition below)

**CTA** *(Call to Action)*
A marketing term for any design to prompt an immediate response or encourage an immediate sale. Authors often include at least one CTA at the end of their book which may include a link to another book, the next book in that series, or an author newsletter sign-up.

**CTR** *(Click Thru Rate)*
A measure for the success of user engagement, typically in advertising campaigns. A CTR represents the ratio of users who click on a specific link to the number of total users who view a page, email, or advertisement.

**D2D** *(Draft2Digital)*
A US company that offers free eBook and Print conversion tools and distribution options for retailers and libraries.

**ENT** *(eReader News Today)*
A daily newsletter that delivers highly rated free and bargain eBooks. ENT, which launched in 2010 is the longest running daily eBook newsletter in the industry.

**ePub** *(eBook file)*
Derived from the .epub file extension used for eBooks. This format is an international standard eBook format as created/defined by the International Digital Publishing Forum (IDPF).

**Erotica** *(Also "erotic fiction" and "erotic literature")*
Erotica is writing with a strong focus on sex or sexual themes, sexual feelings, and actions, with the intention of arousing those same feelings in readers. There are multiple degrees of erotica appearing through much romance fiction. In the "deep end" of that fictional pool one finds more pornographic writing with less focus on character, plot, and dialogue, than on reader titillation. Because of the vast degree (or shades) of erotic literature, and because reader tolerance varies dramatically, there are some retailers and libraries that might automatically choose to filter out certain styles or types of erotica, particularly the ones more focused on titillation. There is a significant double-standard where a trade published title like **Fifty Shades of Gray** is featured prominently, whereas indie publishing books of the same, or even better caliber and quality, are shunted to the "back aisle" or even ignored.

**FFIS** *(First Free in Series)*
Denotes the first book in a linked series that is made free to create a large funnel of new potential readers/fans.

**Funnel** *(A funnel of readers, or a reader funnel)*
Derived from the concept of a "marketing funnel" an author's funnel is a consumer-centric marketing model that illustrates the theoretical customer journey toward the sampling or purchase of a good or service to other relevant content. (IE, a first book in a series for 99 cents or free that drives a large volume of new readers). The understanding is that this large group will self-select to a progressively smaller number of readers more keenly in-tune with that author's specific brand or content, and continue to buy more, adding increasing value back to the investment of bringing them to that first product.

**Hybrid** *(Hybrid Author)*
An author who is both indie/self-published and traditionally published. I have heard some authors, typically those with a very Amazon-centric POV, suggesting that "hybrid" publishing is when an author publishes some eBooks exclusive to Kindle, and others wide. I'm not a fan of the bastardized use of the term in that way, because it's a limiting perspective that doesn't take the larger "hybrid author" model into account.

**Imprint** *(Publishing/Publisher Imprint)*
An imprint of a publisher is a trade name under which it publishes books. Imprints are often used to denote a specific brand to a unique customer demographic. A single publisher or publishing company may have multiple imprints, often using the different names as ways of spotlighting or identifying those brands. Indie authors can define their own unique publishing imprints similarly.

**Indie** *("Indie author," "indie publisher" or "to indie publish")*
A term/phrase that has been adopted by self-published authors to denote a level of professionalism and independence. They are independent spirits taking control of their self-publishing. "Indie publishing" is often used inter-changeable with self-publishing. I tend to use them both and use the term self-publishing quite regularly through this book because the phrase "indie-publishing" might still be confusing or relatively new to beginning authors. Within traditional bookselling the term "indie" is often applied to smaller trade publishers that are not owned by one of the "Big Five" as well as independent bookstores (ie, not part of a national or international chain).

**Ingram** *(Ingram Content Group)*
An American-based subsidiary of Ingram Industries based in La Vergne, Tennessee that offers services to the book publishing industry. The company has the industry's largest active book inventory with access to 7.5

million titles. The markets they serve include booksellers, librarians, educators, and specialty retailers. Ingram offers warehousing services, print-on-demand publishing solutions, and more to publishers and indie authors. The most well-known of Ingram's services to digital publishing are *IngramSpark* and *LightningSource.*

**IngramSpark** *(An Indie-Publishing Solution for POD)*
A user-friendly front-end service launched in 2013 and operated by Lightning Source to cater for the needs of independent publishers and authors via similar tools enjoyed big house publishers but built specifically for independent or smaller publishers.

**IP** *(Intellectual Property)*
A term used to refer to intangible creations of the mind and human intellect. This can include inventions as well as literary and artistic works or designs. The most well-known types of IP are copyright, patents, and trademarks. Authors' rights and copyright are a fundamental component of IP for writers, but a writer's creative expression can be leveraged well beyond the written word and book format.

**IRC** *(International Reply Coupon)*
Often used for international SASEs (see SASE below) commonly used in traditional trade publishing manuscript submissions. An IRC is coupon that can be

exchanged for one or more postage stamps representing the minimum postage for an unregistered priority airmail letter of up to twenty grams sent to another Universal Postal Union (UPU) member country. IRCs are accepted by all UPU member countries. This allows a person to send someone in another country a letter, along with the cost of postage for a reply. If the addressee is within the same country, there is no need for an IRC because a self-addressed stamped envelope (SASE) or return postcard will suffice; but if the addressee is in another country an IRC removes the necessity of acquiring foreign postage or sending appropriate currency.

**ISBN** *(International Standard Book Number)*
A 13-digit book identifier which is intended to uniquely identify a book and the originating publisher. An ISBN is assigned to each separate edition and variation of a book (for example, Hardcover, Trade Paperback, eBook, Audiobook, etc.).

**KDP** *(Kindle Direct Publishing)*
Amazon's direct publishing platform for eBooks and Print (POD).

**KDP Select** *(Kindle Direct Publishing Select)*
An optional exclusivity program that authors can choose to be a part of when publishing directly to Amazon Kindle via KDP. KDP Select terms run 90 days and auto-

renew unless an author de-selects the pre-filled auto-renew button. Being in this program allows for some additional marketing features like making a book free for up to 5 days, Kindle Countdown deals, and having books listed in Kindle Unlimited (KU).

**KENP** *(Kindle Edition Normalized Pages)*
A metric that is applicable to authors with eBooks in Kindle Unlimited (exclusive to Amazon). It measures how many pages of your book have been read by readers who have accessed it through their Kindle Unlimited Subscription.

**Kill-fee** *(Often used in publishing contracts)*
A pre-agreed amount of money a publisher agrees to pay a freelance writer if they decide not to publish their work, or work in progress.

**Kobo** *(Rakuten Kobo, Inc.)*
A Canadian-based digital book retailer owned by Japanese electronic commerce company Rakuten, Inc.

**KU** *(Kindle Unlimited)*
An Amazon eBook reading service that allows customers to read as much as they want from over 2 million titles. It allows readers to explore new authors, books, and genres for what they perceive as "no cost" despite them having

to pay a subscription fee for this access. Indie authors often use this to refer to the side effect of being in Kindle Direct Publishing's "Select" option which locks them into 90 days of exclusivity.

**KWL** *(Kobo Writing Life)*
Kobo's direct publishing platform for eBooks and Audiobooks.

**Lightning Source** *(Also known as Lightning Print on Demand)*
A suite of publishing services from Ingram designed for trade publishers that include print-on-demand, wholesale solutions, drop-ship, short-run printing, traditional offset printing, and full global distribution. An easier-to-use and separate platform meant for indie authors, is called *Ingram Spark.*

**Metadata**
Metadata is data that describes other data. In publishing, metadata refers to any data that describes your book. These fields include title, subtitle, publication date, ISBN, keywords, price, and any other relevant information that readers might use to find your book.

**MM (***Mass market or mass market paperback)*
A format of print paperback mass printed in large quantities for massive audiences at a highly economic price.

Mass market paperbacks are usually smaller in size, (usually 4 inches wide by 7 inches tall), and the text is printed in a smaller font and on less expensive paper. These smaller sized books are often called pocket books, as they can usually fit easily into a purse or a pocket.

**Mobi** *(Often thought of as an Amazon eBook)*
Derived from .mobi, the file extension for "mobipocket" format for eBooks that was purchased and used by Amazon Kindle. The fundamental difference between ePub and Mobi formats is that ePub is widely supported across all platforms while Mobi is predominantly a Kindle format. In early 2021, Amazon shared that they would be deprecating the use of this format in multiple ways.

**More Active Romance** *(Also sometimes referred to as "active romance")*
A cheeky term, first coined by Kobo CEO Michael Tamblyn during a 2013 book industry presentation, to denote erotic fiction in polite company. He was referring to top-selling genres, and listed off Romance, and then, separately "More Active Romance—AKA, erotica."

**NaNoWriMo** *(National Novel Writing Month)*
An annual event where volunteer participants sign up to commit to write the first draft of a 50,000-word book in the month of November.

**OverDrive** *(OverDrive, Inc.)*
An American digital distributor of eBooks, audiobooks, magazines and streaming video titles providing fulfillment services for publishers to libraries and schools.

**PB** (*Paperback - also known as soft cover or softback)*
A generic term to denote a particular type of binding, characterized by a thick paper or paperboard cover, and often held together with glue rather than stitches or staples. Paperback might refer to a mass-market or a trade paperback edition.

**Perma 99** *(Permanent 99 cent book)*
A term coined by indie authors to denote a book that is permanently priced at 0.99 across all retailers. This price point is often used to create a large funnel of potential readers.

**Perma Free** *(Permanently free)*
A term coined by indie authors to denote a book that is permanently priced at 0.00 across all retailers (Note that Amazon KDP never allows this in a permanent way and so authors often have to rely on their whim of when and in which territories they price match to free). This price point is often used to create a large funnel of potential readers.

**PNR** *(Paranormal Romance)*
An acronym used for paranormal romance focusing on romantic love and including elements beyond the range of scientific explanation. PNR titles can blend together themes from across the speculative fiction genres of fantasy, science fiction, and horror.

**POD** *(Print on Demand)*
An order fulfillment method where items (most often books, where authors are concerned) are printed as soon as an order is made, often, and without order minimums. Most indie authors use this method of printing for both author copies and distribution to online retailers and the book market through large wholesalers such as Ingram.

**POV** *(Point of view)*
The narrative eye or perspective through which a story is written. The three main types of POV are: First-Person (told through an openly self-referential and participating narrator), Second-Person (where the reader is made a character), Third-Person (where the narrator is not identified and provides the viewpoint of all characters with third person pronouns like he, she, or they, and never first- or second-person pronouns). There are additional considerations such as omniscient, limited, subjective, and alternating perspectives.

**Reader magnet**
A piece of writing that an author gives away for free in exchange for something such as readers signing up for their author mailing list. The reader magnet is typically relevant to an author's published works and can be exclusively available only for those who sign up.

**RPG** *(Role-playing Game)*
A narrative style game in which players act out the roles of characters. This includes games like *Dungeons & Dragons, Magic: The Gathering* and thousands of others. You might see the term LitRPG which is short for a literary genre combining the conventions of desktop or digital RPGs with science-fiction and fantasy novels where the players are aware they are in such a game. A few popular recent examples of this would be Ernest Cline's novel *Ready Player One* and Chris Van Allsburg's *Jumanji.*

**SASE** *(Self-Addressed Stamped Envelope)*
An envelope with the sender's name and address on it, plus affixed paid postage, that is mailed to a person or company to facilitate quick and "free" return postage. Commonly used in traditional publishing submissions of short stories and book-length manuscripts.

**Self-publishing**
This is an all-encompassing and generic term meant to denote authors that take control of their publishing, by

either publishing directly, through a third-party distributor, or even authors that employ publishing service providers and vanity presses. The term indie publishing is often used by authors who recognize this control and the logistical operation as a professional entrepreneurial business pursuit.

**Slush pile**
A set of unsolicited query letters or manuscripts either directly sent to a publisher or agent by an author. Most larger publishing houses and agents do not accept unsolicited manuscripts and slush piles are usually looked down upon and disregarded as the work of aspiring writers of all levels of skill and talent. The responsibility of sifting through slush piles to find works of potential merit and review, is usually reserved either to editor assistants, or interns often called first readers.

**TP** *(Trade Paperback)*
A specific format of paperback generically used to indicate any paperback book that is larger in size than a mass-market paperback. The term derives from the standard practice within trade publishing of issuing a version of a hardback book in a less expensive form. Trade paperbacks are issued in the same size and format as a hardcover edition of the same book. Unlike the smaller and less expensive mass-market paperback, trade paperbacks often are identical to a hardback book, even having the

same page numbers and same higher paper quality than mass market editions.

**UBL** *(Universal Book Link)*
A web link usually created via a service such as Books2Read that acts as a single share website landing page that is inclusive of multiple platforms, retailers, libraries, often with built-in automated geo-targeting.

**Vanity Publishing** *(Vanity press, Vanity publisher, subsidy publisher)*
A vanity publisher is a publishing house in which authors pay to have their books published, instead of the publisher paying the author. In this model, the author assumes all the risk. Many vanity publishers masquerade as "real publishers" and trick unsuspecting authors into thinking they are getting great value and will be served like a publisher. But these outfits make the majority of their revenue selling services to authors rather than selling books. Before working with any publisher or self-publishing service provider, authors should check resources from *Writer Beware* and the *Alliance of Independent Authors.*

**WFH** *(Working from Home)*
Telecommuting, also called remote working, teleworking, working from home is a work arrangement in which employees do not commute or travel to a central place of

work. This is a common desired experience for writers. Though some writers do find "commuting" to a local coffee shop or library allows for the "transition to work" experience to help them and the people in their lives to take their profession of writing seriously.

**Wide** *(A publishing strategy "publishing wide" or "publish wide")*
In indie author circles, the concept of making one's books (often used to mean eBooks) available on many platforms rather than exclusively to Amazon Kindle. As you'll see, my personal definition of wide goes far beyond that dichotomous perspective. Oh, and there's a hell of a lot more about wide publishing explained repeatedly throughout this book. But I suppose that's why you're reading it.

**WIP** *(Work in Progress)*
For writers, a WIP, or W.I.P is a term used to refer to the current project being written, or in the process of being edited, as opposed to completed and/or published works.

**YA** *(Young Adult)*
A category of fiction spanning many genres and written for readers aged 12 to 18. The subject matter and of YA novels typically correlate with the age and experience of the protagonist. While targeted to adolescents, as many as half of all YA readers are adults.

**ZON**

*(Also referred to as "The 'Zon")*

A cheeky reference authors sometimes use when referring to Amazon, the world's largest online bookstore. I coined the term "world's largest river" many years ago in a tongue-in-cheek "they who shall not be named" during a presentation for Kobo.

# Foreword

I remember the first time I came across Mark Leslie Lefebvre. I had just decided to go wide as an author, because although I didn't know another soul who was wide, I knew I couldn't be KU exclusive any longer. It was grating on my soul to be in KU, and sure, everyone who was making the big bucks scoffed at the very idea of going wide—only a true idiot would give up the kind of money KU authors were making—but I had reached my limits.

I was doing this.

Being both someone who is terribly impetuous, and someone obsessed with learning absolutely everything I can about [next new crazy project], I immediately threw myself into inhaling anything I could find on the topic of being wide. I'm not sure I could've even named the Big 5 storefronts when I decided to go wide (Apple Books, Barnes & Noble, GooglePlay, Kobo, and Amazon, in case you're not sure either), which should give you an idea of how much of a neophyte I was at this stage of the game.

"Clueless" is an understatement.

I found Mark right out of the gate, and hallelujah for that! At the time, he was working for Kobo, and was doing Kobo Writing Life podcasts (which I devoured), along with being filmed at conferences and such doing presentations (which I also devoured). I learned to price lower for the Indian market. I learned it was important to have prices "look right," so I should do research on what was considered a "good price" for an international market. I learned I should never let the currency converter just spit out a random number (7.42) and then blindly use it.

I hoovered it all up. I was stalking the man, and he didn't even know I existed.

And then...he announced he was stepping down from Kobo. My jaw hit the floor. We had yet to even exchange a Facebook message, but still, it rocked my world.

But...but...it's Mark from Kobo! He can't not be from Kobo! Kobo will collapse! And die! And melt into a puddle of nothingness without him!

(I have absolutely no idea why my mother says I'm her dramatic child. I can't begin to see why she'd think that...)

Somehow, Kobo did survive without him (a miracle, in my not-so-humble opinion), and along the way, the two of us actually met—in the virtual sense, of course. (In other words, he finally became aware of my existence).

Let's be frank for a minute here:

I'm just another wide indie romance author. It's not like I'm hitting the USA Today list with every new release, or am winning prestigious awards from the RWA. I wasn't (still am not) setting the world on fire, but I was doing something that—it turns out—was actually quite important:

Paying my bills from my writing. From my wide, indie author writing.

Not by scamming the system or stuffing books full of gibberish and hiring companies to have bots read them. Not by dumping cartloads of money into advertisements on Facebook or Amazon. I was just releasing my books, and then writing more books, and occasionally getting a BookBub, and was focused on being a completely wide author—not just in name, but in action, too—and this set me apart.

By this point, I'd met quite a few authors and was doing multi-author box sets and cross promotions. I was also teaching as I went along—because of course I was—and I started to hear it again and again:

I should start a Facebook group for wide authors.

I should write a book on how to go wide.

Rather than helping authors one. at. a. time, teaching and re-teaching the basics via a method that is completely unscalable, I should start a group and teach everyone at the same time. I should write a how-to and help loads of people. I should build a group that was a safe haven—the only corner of the internet where positive KU talk wouldn't be allowed. Somehow, such a thing didn't already exist, and the cosmos had nominated me to be the one to put it together.

So naturally, I turned to one of my closest writing besties, Suzie O'Connell, and roped her into this project, because of course I did. I was insane enough to think that I could start a Facebook group for wide authors. I wasn't stupid enough to think that I should do it by myself.

Even insanity has limits, it turns out.

It was just going to be a small group of my author friends who I'd help and who'd help me, and it'd never get any larger than, like, a hundred people, at most. But I also decided from the get-go that I'd invite some people into the group who I knew would contribute handsomely to it—people who loved to teach as much as I did.

People like Mark.

By this point, he'd started working for Draft2Digital, but I knew he'd be good at giving advice that wasn't heavily weighted in one direction or another. One of the things you could count on with Mark was that he'd give you advice that was best for you, not best for him or the company he was working at. Although we'd only had scattered interactions at that point, I already knew this was a fundamental part of his personality.

So, in March of 2019, I started a Facebook group called *Wide for the Win* and immediately dove into writing a book with the same name. I was just going to whip this book out and then get right back to writing romance, having done right by the author world by sharing my knowledge with it.

You might've guessed by the name on the cover that I did not, in fact, write the book **Wide for the Win**. (I knew you looked like a smart cookie!) I floundered around, starting and stopping and going and halting and reworking and redoing and then throwing it out and starting again…

It was not pretty. I was not "whipping this book out" and then moving on with my life.

At some point, I started avoiding the group altogether. I couldn't bear to "look 'em in the eye" and admit to my fellow Widelings that I was an abject failure. Whenever I did step foot into the group, someone would excitedly ask me, How is it coming along? So excited! Can't wait!

gulp

In May of 2020, I finally gave up. I surrendered. I threw my hands up and said, "This book isn't going to be written. I'm a failure, and I'm sorry." People reached out to me and were kind about their reaction—they understood. They got it. No one was sticking pins into voodoo dolls (or at least weren't mean enough to tell me that they were doing it). I'd failed, but I'd also found that the Wide community was filled to the brim with wondrous, kind-hearted souls who forgave those of us who were apparently incapable of writing nonfiction books.

About a week or so later, I got a message from Mark. He was just wondering…he had this idea…

What if he wrote **Wide for the Win**? He'd already written **Killing it on Kobo**, and obviously, the alliteration of ***Wide for the Win*** was too good to pass up. No worries if I didn't want to let him take it over—he simply wanted to float a trial balloon. See what I said. Run the idea past me. No stress. I probably didn't even want him to do it, and that was fine, of course.

In case you somehow missed it, Mark is the most Canadian Mark on the planet, and being overly kind and gracious at all times is a part of his DNA. Here he was, offering me the Greatest Gift of All Time, and pooh-poohing it in the same breath.

I do believe (and this is true), I let out a whoop when I read his message. I'd always said, from the day I started working on **Wide for the Win**, that I wished someone else would write it so I could see what they said and learn from them. I'd had no delusions that I was somehow the fount of all wide knowledge. I just figured I was the only one dumb enough to take this task on.

Turns out (and this is also true), I'd found an even bigger sucker than me. Woot, woot!

Between Mark's experience as an author himself, working for bookstores, running professional publishing organizations, starting up and running Kobo Writing Life, and now being Grand Master Liaison for D2D (my description, not his), Mark is better suited in every way to write this book than I am.

I am thoroughly pleased that I took the chance and started the Facebook group, *Wide for the Win* (dragging my writing bestie along for the ride), and even more pleased that it's grown so much (5600+ members as of the writing of this intro), and somehow even more pleased than that, that Mark has written this book in your hands instead of me.

And now, I'm going to shut up so you can actually read something useful.

May you learn how to grow and expand your Wide mindset, and someday be able to say, "I too am a Wideling."

Come join the light side. ;-)

Erin Wright
February, 2021

# Introduction: Prefatory Disclaimers, A Note on Biases, and How to Use this Book

## What is Wide?

Let's talk WIDE.

Yeah, I know. That's why you're here.

But I'm talking specifically of my use of the term "wide" in all caps. WIDE. Like that. I have done it on purpose, multiple times, in fact, throughout this book.

I did it very specifically. And trust me, it provided fruit for animated discussion with my editors and early readers.

It even started off, in an earlier draft of this book, with my use of the term "wide" with a capital letter. As if it were a proper noun. But WIDE is much more than just a proper noun, at least in my book. It's perhaps a proper verb. Because WIDE is an action, isn't it? A philosophy. A way of publishing.

A proper verb is when you convert a noun into an action. It's considered conversion or verbification. When, for example, someone says they want to Xerox® something when referring to making photocopies, or to Hoover® a carpet with a vacuum cleaner.

Despite trying—and trust me, I did try—I wasn't really able to construct any meaningful sentences applying the word "wide" as a verb. They all came out more like adverbs. Perhaps you'll have better luck.

At least Erin Wright was successful in defining a person who adapts a "publishing wide" ethic into their author business as a Wideling.

But let's get back to the word itself, in its existing and known forms.

As an adjective, the word means having a larger or greater distance from side to side than expected, or a more than average width. Such as "a wide road" or "a wide hallway." It can also mean the inclusion of a great variety of things such as "a wide range of options."

As an adverb the word can denote the full extent of something, as in the phrase "her eyes opened wide." It can also refer to something far from a particular point or mark. "The shot went wide, completely missing the goal."

Other definitions of the word involve having a great extent or extending over a vast area.

You get the point.

Plenty of those things are in play when we consider "wide" or even "Wide" or, in the case of the context of this book, "WIDE."

I want to call attention to the word as something big, something larger, something that is its own thing, and not just as the opposite of being exclusive to Amazon Kindle.

Thus, I purposefully use the term WIDE repeatedly throughout this book.

## No, Seriously. Get to the Bloody Point: What is Wide?

In the general sense of the word for most authors, the term "wide" refers to publishing an eBook beyond Amazon Kindle.

But as you'll see demonstrated through the pages of this book, that's a rather narrow view of the word. Because it merely refers to a single decision. A simple and rudimentary "either/or" that's pretty limited in scope.

It takes a viewpoint that there's Amazon, and then there's the rest.

That "entire rest" is much larger, much more significant, much wider than that overly simplistic viewpoint lets on.

Because WIDE is not a single decision. It's an over-arching set of decisions, choices. It's something that is infused into the very core of an author's journey.

To me WIDE is a purposeful set of decisions, actions, mindsets, and behaviors that an author makes and takes in writing and publishing. It is an approach that considers the long-term, considers all options, and considers numerous approaches to cultivating an author career. It is a philosophy, an approach, a way of life for a writer.

And, as you'll see shortly, it's far greater than just looking at it being Amazon versus everyone else. Because if you only see it as that, you, my friend, are limiting your options. You are, in other words, only seeing a narrow choice rather than a much wider set of options.

Or, perhaps, a much WIDER set of options.

## Disclaimers

This entire book is tainted with my own biases, perspectives, and viewpoints. That should be obvious, but I wanted to call attention to it. We'll get into that shortly.

Although the term "wide" is often one used by indie authors, and I suspect that most readers will be approaching from that perspective, I tried to ensure that almost any writer, regardless of where they are on their author journey, can learn from it. To that end, I purposely tried to make it useful for indie authors and traditionally published authors alike, as you'll likely see in later chapters.

I'll often use the terms "self-publishing" and "indie-publishing" interchangeably. Within the self-publishing sphere, many authors take offense to the former term, and have adapted "indie-publishing" as a more accurate description of what they are engaging in. And it's true, because, in successful self-publishing, the only self is perhaps "self-directed." Successful self-published authors might be in control of where and how they publish (that's the "self" part), but they hire and work with others collaboratively. Folks like editors, cover designers, marketing professionals, etc. So, if you are engaged in the more self-directed type of publishing, please don't take offence. I'm using the term "self-publishing" as a way for authors who are new to this space to understand the difference between authors who control their own publishing, and traditionally published authors who sell or license their work to another publisher.

While we're on that topic, I should remind you that a real publisher, a proper publisher, never charges you for your work. So, if you are paying a third party to publish your work, or for a package that includes things like cover design, formatting, editing, and distribution you're using a vanity publisher. Their imprint might be on the spine of the book, but they're not a publisher, or at least, not a **real** publisher. A real publisher is one where the money flows only one way—from the publisher to the author.

I also want to be very clear that this book isn't meant to be a prescriptive step by step for how you can find success in publishing wide. It's meant to help you open your eyes, your mind, and your heart to things that I think will be useful in assisting you on your own path.

This is something that'll be repeated throughout the book; your path, your journey, your preferences, your biases, your perspective are very important considerations. I'm going to share and say things you don't agree with. I'm going to advise things that you might have tried and that haven't worked for you. That's okay. There is no one path. There is no one journey. Even within your own unique and specific writer journey, there will be variances. Something you try for one book or series will work effectively on one retail platform, but flops miserably on another. It will always be that way.

Similarly, you won't put this book down and suddenly be equipped with all the knowledge to dominate and crush it on all the retail, subscription, and library platforms. I hope that you will walk away empowered with some insights, perspectives, and understandings to help you cultivate and curate your own unique and individualized approach to being a successful WIDE author.

I'm not a six-figure-plus author. Nor do I pretend to be. I'm not going to share a "this is what I did and therefore you can do it too" approach. You're too smart to believe that just mimicking what another successful author does is a pathway to success. But, if you do believe that all you have to do is follow some magic step by step plan, or you believe that because I'm not an uber-rich self-publishing success story, you have nothing to learn from me, please stop reading and just put this book down. I will not be able to help you. I'd even argue that nobody is going to be able to help you. Because, as my friend James A. Owen says in his book *Drawing out the Dragons,* "If you really want to do something, no one can stop you. But if you really don't want to do something, no one can help you."

## A Note on Biases

All authors bring their own bias to a book they write. Just like all readers, in turn, bring their own bias. These biases are based on personal experience, upbringing, and the circles one engages in.

I want to briefly share a few biases of mine here so you could apply the proverbial grain of salt to my advice, suggestions, and perspective. I'm sure that many of them will become apparent, but why not start off ensuring you know where I'm coming from.

**Traditional Publishing** is not a dirty word to me.

I started writing in my early teens and started submitting my writing to different markets for short stories when I was fifteen years old. This was in the pre-computer days of typewriters and large manilla envelopes and SASEs (self-addressed stamped envelopes). Self-Publishing existed, but not in the way it does today.

My books have been both self-published and traditionally published and I continue to be open to both, depending on the specific book or project. My bias is that you should also be open. Because, as we'll see, that's part of my larger definition of what it means to be truly WIDE.

In addition, while we're on the topic, I will occasionally use the term "publisher" and "author" interchangeably. For example, if I talk about how a retailer interacts with publishers, I'm using the term inclusive to denote traditional publishers, indie-authors who are self-publishing direct, and third-party distributors who provide indie-author titles to the retailer.

I spent six years working for **Rakuten, Kobo Inc.** in Toronto, Ontario. I was hired to come up with a solution for self-published authors. While there, I worked with an amazing team that developed and launched the platform *Kobo Writing Life*.

By the time I left Kobo in late 2017, *Kobo Writing Life* accounted for one in every four English language sales on Kobo. Since it was regularly the number one selling source of books in English language territories on Kobo, I suppose you could call that a success.

My preferred and default reading device/platform for eBooks is on Kobo.

I'm sharing this so that you are aware of my pretty blatant bias towards having a soft spot for this company and platform.

**Draft2Digital** (D2D) is a distribution platform operating out of Oklahoma City, OK in the United States. Since October 2018 I have been working part-time for D2D as Director of Business Development. Prior to that, even when I was working at Kobo and running their self-publishing platform, I was using D2D for distribution to Apple and Nook and other platforms. And even back then I was using their free Microsoft Word to ePub conversion tool. (Because it was quite a bit better than the built-in one *Kobo Writing Life* uses).

So, while I have attempted to be transparent and open to all perspectives in relation to distribution options, you should be aware of where those biases exist.

Another area where I will probably display a strong bias is in my discussion of **Independent Bookstores**. I have managed indie bookstore operations, have plenty of friends who own and run their own bookstores, and spent a few years on the board of directors and as President of the Canadian Booksellers Association.

When Vice-President and President of the bookseller's association in Canada, I went on national radio and television in several full on assaults against Amazon, their cut-throat business practices, the bottomless pockets of funding they had to send an endless barrage of lobbyists and high-paid corporate lawyers to Parliament Hill, all tactics that were putting independent bookstores at risk of closure.

So, yeah, I'm going to come across as someone with a hearty and strong bias toward independent bookshops.

**Canadian Content** is something I won't be able to avoid. I was born in Canada. I live in Canada. I think Canada is the greatest nation in the world. You'll see all kinds of references to my perspective as a Canadian.

You're likely to catch references to hockey, and poutine, and Rush and The Tragically Hip; to Prime Minsters instead of Presidents, and to provinces and territories instead of states, and to Commonwealth concerns, and to an admiration for the British Monarchy.

I can't help it. I was born this way. (Speaking of which, did you know that Lady Gaga, AKA Stefani Joanne Angelina Germanotta, has French-Canadian roots?) See, there I go, finding Canada in things.

In an oh-so-Canadian way, I'll apologize for those things right now. I might even apologize along the way too. Because, you know, Canadian.

## I Don't Hate Amazon

Given my past (and even my present), struggling against the monopolistic Amazon overlords, you might think that I hate Amazon or have an **anti-Amazon** approach.

I want to ensure you that I'm not anti-Amazon.

But I am anti-exclusivity.

Like many authors out there, I'm able to make a decent income from the tools that Amazon makes available. I want authors to be successful on Amazon. But I want them to be successful on all platforms, or, at least on many platforms, if not all of them.

So, where, at times, it might seem like I'm being anti-Amazon, just remember, I'm not anti-Amazon, I'm pro-WIDE.

Because I'm often critical of some things that Amazon does, like forcing authors to choose between exclusivity to them versus WIDE publishing, people often assume that I hate Amazon.

I suppose, in the divisive world we have created, one often assumes that standing up for something means you have to hate something else.

It's that kind of simplistic thinking that leads people to reflexively reply "all lives matter" in response to the desperate reminder that Black lives matter.

Of course all lives matter. That's a given. But those who take offense to the urgent plea from a demographic of western civilization that continues to suffer from systemic racism are missing the point, the reason why that has to be clearly stated in the first place.

So, because it seems to be the default to think of sides rather than nuances, many people believe that I have a hate on for Amazon.

It's simply not true.

Sure, I've gone head-to-head with Amazon's lawyers in the Canadian parliament and on national television when I was leading the Canadian Booksellers Association, I have struggled against their cutthroat business practices and bottomless pockets as an independent bookseller, and fought their predatory ways of luring authors over to the "dark side" as an eBook retailer. But I don't hate them.

I respect the powerhouse company and acknowledge the incredible disruption Amazon had brought.

Reading Brad Stone's *The Everything Store: Jeff Bezos and the Age of Amazon* endowed me with a deep-rooted respect for the man behind the company.

Having sat on panels with and interacted with many Amazon employees over the years at different writer conferences around the world, people I respect and admire, I know that there are good people who work at Amazon.

And, as an author, I have, of course, benefited from Amazon, both on my traditionally published books and my self-published titles.

So, no, Virginia, I don't hate Amazon.

And no, I don't want to see Amazon fail.

I'm delighted whenever I see authors finding success on Amazon. I just want to see authors have success on other platforms as well.

It doesn't mean I hate them.

But I do hate Amazon's exclusivity program.

I hate the fear that it cultivates in authors, even those who are successful within the program.

*What if one of my exclusive books shows up on another website and they shut down my account? What if they change X or Y about the book item page which removes my ability to buy my way to Amazon success? When will all the things I've studied and learned about how to game the Amazon algorithms to my benefit change again?*

Exclusivity creates a terrifying scarcity mindset that builds anxiety. And I hate *that*.

And I particularly hate the way that Amazon exclusivity regularly forces authors into an unnecessary downward spiral of an "us versus them" mentality.

## An Admission of Exclusivity

It's obvious that I'm partial to a WIDE approach in publishing.

But I'm not going to pretend that I've never taken part in Kindle's exclusivity program.

In fact, I've been participating in KDP Select since it launched.

And, yes, I've had books exclusive to Kindle, and have even launched books into exclusivity on Amazon. In fact, I always have at least one book in KDP Select, and have since the beginning of the program when they first launched it.

I was sitting in the Kobo office as the head of the *Kobo Writing Life* team when Amazon announced their exclusivity program; and within hours I had collected some content I've been considering publishing and put it into the program.

*Why did I do that?*

Well, one, I did it so I could test and explore the program. And two, as someone who helps advise and support authors on their journeys, I needed to understand the program from the inside, rather than the outside.

So, yes, though I'm an advocate for wide publishing, I always have at least one title in the KDP Select program, even if it's something I never push or try to leverage; just to keep me in the loop. Consider it a sacrifice I make for the common good of understanding and knowledge.

I have, as I mentioned, launched books into KDP Select and leveraged the various tools available (free or Kindle Countdown deals) and experimented with them. I've never made serious coin from the experience, but, again, I wanted to learn and explore.

So I'm hoping you don't see me as a hypocrite, but, rather, someone who tasted a specific food and said: "Nope. Not for me."

## My Numbers on Wide

I want you to be aware of where I sit on the wide spectrum, so that you can ensure that I'm speaking from direct experience.

Unfortunately, because my annual numbers aren't just dependent upon online dashboard sales, but rather a combination of self-publishing, traditional publishing, and what I call "mixed" sources, I often don't have the full previous year's "sales" numbers until several months into the year.

And because I'm writing this in early 2021, I don't yet have the full and solid 2020 sales numbers from all sources.

So, instead, I'll share my numbers going back a few years.

And, no, I'm not going to share actual numbers, but rather percentages.

As an author, I'm likely sitting somewhere in the gigantic "mid-list" of author earnings.

I make a modest mid five-figure income from my writing. Enough to make a respectable living. But definitely not enough to break any banks.

I know that there are tens of thousands of authors sitting in that same range as me. Authors who are earning far more than they would be had they just chosen either traditional publishing or self-publishing. Authors who are earning a respectable amount of money and writing books that a specific core group of readers enjoy.

What's important to share here is that my numbers, while modest, come from diverse sources. If any single one of them dries up, sure it'll hurt, but it won't entirely ruin me. I'll have plenty of other legs to stand on.

And that's one of the reasons why I'm such an advocate for WIDE publishing.

Here is the breakdown of my 2019 writing income:

Amazon: 17.89%
Traditional Publishing: 12.07%
Kobo: 6.01%
Audio: 2.39%
Apple: 1.01%
B&N: 0.24%
Google: 0.04%
Smashwords: 0.01%
Other Self-Pub: 28.53%
Mixed Trad & Self-Pub: 30.8%

Despite their percentages being larger, I put the final two categories of *Other Self-Pub* and *Mixed Trad & Self-Pub* on the bottom because they each represent numerous platforms, sources, and streams, which would take too long to break down. The important thing to remember is that, on their own, most of those mini-sources don't really add up to much. But, when you combine them, they really do add up over time to a significant chunk.

If I lost Amazon, sure, I'd lose a hefty chunk of my writing income. Perhaps as much as 20% of that income. But I'd still have plenty of other sources to depend on. And I'm cool with that.

Also, if I only look at my self-publishing eBook revenue for 2019, Amazon Kindle makes up approximately

44% of my income. That's a much larger chunk of money. And, according to a quick snapshot of my sales via ScribeCount, in 2021, Amazon is currently representative of 55% of my eBook sales, with the other major platforms accounting for 45% combined. So, when it comes to eBooks, I have a much larger dependency on Amazon and Kindle.

That's yet another reason, in my perspective, that diversifying one's income as a writer as WIDE as possible is an important exercise.

## Erin Wright's Numbers for Wide

The following is an edited and abbreviated excerpt from what would have been Chapter 2 of Erin Wright's original manuscript for **Wide for the Win**.

I'm sharing it so that you can also have a look at her experience in being WIDE, and more direct words of advice and perspective from this amazingly awesome person I respect and admire.

Please be aware that this draft from Erin's original version of the book was written a long time ago. Her numbers and percentages have likely continued to grow and change. But I want to share it, both for Erin's unique perspective, and, let's be honest, her awesome voice.

### CHAPTER 2: MY NUMBERS AS A WIDE AUTHOR

In case you're wondering how I am *really* doing as a wide author (after all, is it my idea of "success" as a wide author that I make 5% of my income on other storefronts? That's totally a legit question!) I thought it best if I sat down and crunched some numbers so I could share them with you guys. Before I do so, one word of caution:

*Never compare your beginning to someone else's middle.*

Meaning that in the first month, you may really only make 5% of your income from wide storefronts. Your sell-through may be atrocious. You may feel like you could run down the aisle at Kobo naked as a jaybird and yelling, "Look at me! Look at me!" and not get so much as an iota of interest.

*That's okay.*

You have to keep going. Keep working on it. It *will* come.

True story: The first two sales I made on Kobo were me buying my own books. No, seriously. I literally thought that the storefront was broken, and that's why no one was buying my books. Determined to be able to prove this was the problem, I went on and bought them myself so I could send evidence of the website being broken to Kobo so they could fix it.

The sales went through. The website works just fine. I just hadn't convinced anyone *else* to buy my books on there.

*Le sigh.* So much for being able to blame someone else for my nonexistence sales on Kobo…

So yeah, don't compare *my* middle to *your* beginning. What I'm going to show you below is the result of months and months and months of hard work, sweat, and tears, and although you're going to have an easier time of it because you've got this book in your sweaty little hands (whereas I had some wide friends and a total inability to ever call it quits no matter what), it's still not going to be *easy*.

Alrightly, so although I'm not comfortable giving exact numbers, I thought you might find it helpful to at least see some general numbers. Here goes:

- Over the past 20 months I made at least four figures on Amazon all 20 months.
- If I add up the wide storefronts *together*, I made at least four figures on wide storefronts 19 out of those 20 months. (And that $20^{th}$ month, I made $850+, so you know, close).
- If I look at the wide storefronts *individually*, I made at least four figures on a single wide storefront 6 times in those 20 months (and I came damn close another 4 times).

- If I average my Amazon vs Wide income since July of 2017 (which, remember, is that first month where I made four figures), only 55% of my overall income comes from Amazon. Some months, Amazon has been as low as 43% of my income.
- Even more importantly, that overall average is dropping. If I look at just the last six months of my income instead of the last 20 months, Amazon only comprises an average of 49% of my income.
- And I'm not some sort of strange anomaly—for authors who have been wide *for at least a year* (did you catch that caveat? It's important!), it is the norm, not the exception, that a *significant chunk* of their income comes from somewhere else other than Amazon.

So believe me when I tell you: You *can* make a significant amount of money on wide storefronts.

And remember, *I'm making a living wage*. It's not like I'm making $72 on Amazon and $43 everywhere else each month. And no, sadly, I'm *still* not living in a 14th-century castle with a whole army of servants (That fact hasn't changed in the last pages of this book, but I'll be sure to keep you posted if something amazeballs happens in the next ten).

But here's the important part: *I am supporting myself and my family with this income.*

Have I mentioned yet that you can do this, too?

Because you can.

If you can't get enough of Erin's delightful and inspiring voice, make sure you join the Facebook group *Wide for the Win* which you can find at:

www.facebook.com/widefortthewin

## How to Use This Book

As mentioned above, this book isn't meant to be a step-by-step how-to guide for being successful wide. But it is meant to be a companion to help you define your own specific and custom path on your route to publishing success.

This book is divided into five sections: Mindset. Retail. Libraries. Direct & Other. Closing Thoughts.

You'll notice that a significant amount of space is dedicated to mindset, which fewer pages digging into the specific tactics that can be employed. Yes, when I talk through different retail and library websites, I share a few very specific details that I feel would be useful for authors to understand. But trying to keep up with the changes on each of those platforms as they evolve is one of the challenges of creating a book like this. I know it's an issue Erin Wright dealt with when she was working on her version of the book.

The reality is, it's almost impossible to keep up with and stay abreast of changes at a retailer or distributor within the pages of a book.

But what is important is for you to understand the fundamentals of the WIDE author mindset. And that's why you'll find most of the efforts in this book are heavily invested in that area.

Because I want you to invest in a wide mindset. Or, rather, a fully WIDE mindset.

Let's have at it, then, shall we?

# PART I:
## A WINNING WIDE MINDSET

# Wide is More Than Just About Eggs and Baskets

It's inevitable that, whenever someone starts talking about the concept of publishing wide versus being exclusive to Amazon Kindle, there's talk of eggs and baskets.

The phrase "to put all your eggs in one basket" is often attributed to *Don Quixote* (1605) by Miguel de Cervantes. "Tis the part of a wise man to keep himself today for tomorrow, and not venture all his eggs in one basket."

In 1894 Mark Twain wrote, in *Pudd'nhead Wilson*, "Put all your eggs in one basket and WATCH THAT BASKET."

One of the challenging things, of course, in watching that basket, is that's all you can really do.

You can watch it.

But there's not much else to do.

Because someone else owns that basket.

But you own the eggs.

In other words, you own the content that's being placed in that basket, and other baskets. And the great thing about the content you own, particularly in this digital environment, is that you can place a single egg in multiple baskets.

I like to think of this concept as quantum eggs.

We'll get into that in the next chapter.

But in the meantime, let's go back to the original analogy and that sage advice Cervantes shared.

The caution, in his words, and this oft-repeated phrase, is regarding risking it all on a single venture.

And that's what it can feel like.

Sometimes, when advocating for wide publishing, people might toss out the following thoughts or worries:

- What if Amazon goes out of business? Remember Blockbuster? They used to be a dominant company. And even Jeff Bezos himself said that one day Amazon will be disrupted, will fail, and eventually will go bankrupt.
- What if Amazon changes their terms and cuts their royalty in half like they did with Audible? That cuts your sales revenue in half.
- What if Amazon decides to shut down your author account? They've done it with other authors. Nobody is safe from their fickle whims.
- What if Amazon withholds your KENP earnings because you're being accused of [reason of the day] or [whimsical term change you missed]?

You can argue about the legitimacy or likeliness of those things happening. That's neither here nor there. But the important thing to remember is that Amazon Kindle is a retail platform that is allowing you to publish your book content to their platform for free.

It's *their* platform.

They can do whatever they want to, regardless of how you and I feel about it. Regardless of what's in the best interest for authors or publishers.

It's theirs. They built it. They own it. They manage it.

You and I are mere pawns in the grand scheme of things. Our worries, our concerns, our anxieties, mean nothing.

This doesn't mean they are cold and evil. It just means they are a business. They have customers they sell things to. They set the terms on how those sales occur. They decide what to show what customer.

You and I are merely providers of content to sell to their customers.

When the content/customer connection is right, Amazon, and the publisher can both make a significant amount of money.

That can be a good thing. Heck, it can be a grand thing. And it is, for many authors.

But, like the Rush song "Tom Sawyer" states, the wise person knows that things can change, and those changes are definitely not permanent. The only thing that is permanent is change itself.

Things can change.

Things will change.

The question is, are you prepared to adapt to that change? Or, better yet, instead of adapting after the fact, are you willing to be proactive and in control? Are you going to invest time and effort into not having to rely on a single ecosystem that is completely out of your control?

If you are coming from a KDP Select/KU mindset, you might think this argument is all about and only about Amazon Kindle exclusivity.

It's not.

It's about any sort of exclusivity related to your Intellectual Property (IP).

I would argue, if you are coming from the world of traditional publishing, that you also consider opening your mind up to the options available within self or indie publishing.

Conversely, I'd argue that if you're coming from an indie or self-publishing experience, that you consider opening your mind up to the options that exist in traditional publishing.

Being open both ways is going to help you expand your basket options.

But be leery about exclusivity clauses in publishing contracts the same way you might be about exclusivity in direct publishing.

Because the publisher you are working with can decide, at any time, to not offer another contract. Or, if you read the terms of your contract closely, you'll likely find some clause that allows them an out. Sure, there might be a kill-fee involved, but that funding or income source is limited.

That's not to mention that they can go out of business or declare bankruptcy prior to your annual or semi-annual royalty payment coming in.

For me, WIDE is about carefully licensing, offering, and distributing your work to as many different platforms as possible, to maximize your ability to generate revenue from multiple sources.

The question isn't "Why wide?"

It's "Why wouldn't you be wide?"

# Counterpoints to Wide

The entire perspective of this book is about publishing WIDE in all its guises and opportunities. But this doesn't mean I'm close-minded to the fact there are other ways of doing things, other perspectives, or other paths to success.

And I did end the previous chapter with a question: "Why not wide?"

So, I thought it would be important to lay out those reasons here.

As mentioned earlier, and as I will continue to point out, each author is unique in their needs, goals, and desires, and similarly, each book they publish may very likely have their own unique route and destiny.

In addition, I value authors who operate with integrity and transparency, regardless of their own personal stance on the concept of publishing WIDE. Because remember, it's being open to learning, understanding, and attending to new things that's part of the WIDE mindset.

With that in mind, I thought it would be important, yes, even in a book focusing on WIDE, to share some reasoning on why an author might not make that decision. And so, below, I share some high-level reasoning that many authors have shared over the years as well as the perspective from a hugely successful Kindle exclusive author (who wasn't always exclusive) in their words rather than skew it with my own biased tint.

### *Advantages of Being Exclusive to Kindle*

Here are, at a very high level, and in no particular order, some advantages that come with being exclusive to Kindle with your eBooks.

#### *Borrows Count Like Sales*

Kindle Unlimited borrows count like sales in terms of boosting your book's ranking on Amazon. It's often easier for a person to borrow your book "for free" (we know it's not free—they are paying Amazon to have monthly access to read in Kindle Unlimited) than it is for them to take a change on purchasing your eBook.

#### *Borrows Can Earn More Than Sales*

For much longer books, for series titles, and for multi-eBook digital bundles, it can work out that the per page rate reading payout can be worth more than you'd earn in a single unit sale. Epic Fantasy novels of 150,000 to 300,000 words, for example, definitely have this advantage over a 30,000-to-40,000-word novella.

### *Better Organic Reach*

While Amazon has never come out and said this, many authors believe that a book in KDP Select that becomes available in Kindle Unlimited has better organic reach than other titles.

This is based on the assumption that Amazon algorithms will favor titles that promote their ability to advertise the Kindle Unlimited reading program.

But it also is likely due to the fact that not all titles on Kindle are in the Kindle Unlimited program and therefore, the titles exist within a slightly smaller pool. Hence better visibility to KU readers.

Kindle Unlimited books have a little visual tab added at the top of the books, which can be an eye-drawing factor to make a book stand out when it appears on an carousel of titles or in a search result.

### *Kindle Countdown Deals*

This is the only area where you can actually pre-schedule a price change on Kindle. It comes with some automated notifications outlining a bit of a sense of urgency (ie, a temporary price drop) on the Amazon item page consumers see. It also allows you to earn the full 70% (even though we know it's never the full 70% now, is it?) when you drop your price below $2.99 USD.

### *Free eBook Days*

You are prohibited from pricing your book below $0.99 USD on Amazon. However, when you are exclusive you can get up to 5 days within that 90 day period where you can schedule a price change to $0.00.

This counts as the only way you can control the pricing of your book to zero.

(Yes, you can make your book $0.00 on the other major retail websites and Amazon will often price-match. However, they typically only price match in the main territories like the US and the UK, and it's inconsistent and unreliable. It's up to their whims, not your control).

### *Simplicity in Time and Hassle*

It's a lot of work to manage books on multiple websites, and to remember to make price changes on all of them so the title information/pricing can be in sync. If you're only on Amazon, there's less to worry about and it can take less time.

## Why I Am Not Wide: Perspective from Mark Dawson

In late 2020 UK Thriller author Mark Dawson shared to his *SPF Community* (Self Publishing Formula) Facebook group of just under 50,000 members, a most insightful perspective in a post he titled "The Biggest Question for Indies?"

In the post, he outlines his own personal experience within the indie publishing sphere, and also why he decided to be exclusive to Amazon with his eBooks.

If you are not familiar with Mark, here's a bit of a background for you from his website.

*I'm an award-nominated, USA Today bestseller, with more than 20 books published and over 2 million books downloaded in multiple countries and languages. As well as writing, I also teach other authors how to self publish and I speak regularly at writing conferences all around the world.*

*I'm lucky enough to make a good living as a self-published author, but it wasn't always like that. Far from it. I've had a long journey to get to where I am today, spending several years and thousands of dollars learning what works (and what doesn't work) when it comes to getting paid for your writing. It doesn't have to be that way for you. The Self Publishing Formula is everything that I know about writing, marketing and selling books in the twenty-first century.*

*SPF is your one-stop shop for everything you need to know about self publishing. We have a value-packed free weekly podcast, with amazing guests to inspire and teach; vibrant Facebook communities where you can get support and advice from other writers just like you; free writer resources and guides; and our acclaimed courses where I walk you through everything you need to know to help you make a career from your passion.*

Mark gave me permission to re-publish the nearly 1800-word reflection and background that he shared to the group on December 31, 2020. The content has been modified and tweaked slightly from the original post for purposes of clarity, but it has been done with Mark's permission.

For clarity purposes, KU is short for Kindle Unlimited, which authors get their eBooks into by opting in to Kindle Direct Publishing Select, or KDP Select for short. The indie author community seems to have adopted the term KU, one of the side-effects that comes with being exclusive to Amazon Kindle, as the catch-all term to mean being in the KDP Select exclusivity program.

## THE BIGGEST QUESTION FOR INDIES? (Mark Dawson)

I've had a couple of authors reach out to me for advice about whether they should put their books into KU. Rather than answer them individually, I thought it might be useful to set out my thoughts here. It's a little longer than I planned; might be that I was looking for a reason to step away from my WIP today…

The hardest module of the 101 course to record was whether new writers should be exclusive or wide. I think I re-recorded it three times until I came to the conclusion that my difficulty reflected a simple fact: **it is a personal choice for each writer, and dogma is unhelpful.**

I've seen posts describing me as an unthinking advocate all things Amazon and Kindle Unlimited, but that's not true. I am exceptionally grateful to Amazon; the Kindle has changed my life, and it's easy to forget that they took a big gamble in bringing the device and then the store to the market in 2007. They were the first serious players to make a truly popular digital reading device and they deserve the market share that they've amassed in the years since. But I'm not an apologist for them, and there are things about Select that could be improved.

I made the decision to go exclusive a couple of years ago—for reasons I'll set out below—and it has been a successful choice. But it wasn't always the case that I was exclusive; I've been in and out of Select twice, and have also had success wide. Just because I'm exclusive now does not mean that it is the decision that you should take for yours. There is a complicated stew of factors to sift when making a choice like this—political, ethical, financial—and it's not for me or for anyone else to tell you what you should or shouldn't do.

All I can do is to tell you the things that have influenced my own decision and hope that might give you some food for thought.

***At the start:***

I was originally a wide author, although I learned how to sell on Amazon first. It made sense to do that—I could see that Amazon was going to be my biggest platform and I wanted to understand it inside and out before I looked at the others.

Once I had it down, I moved my books onto Apple and Nook and Kobo and Google and did reasonably well. One of the best memories from the first year or two was seeing 100 sales on Nook that I couldn't attribute to any marketing and explaining to Lucy why I was so excited…

### *KU 1—2014*

I don't remember why I originally went into KU. Sales were not spectacular on the wide platforms and, I suspect, I had noticed the success that authors like Hugh Howey were reporting on Kboards. I put my little catalogue into Select and waited for the money to roll in.

Of course, it didn't happen like that.

July 2015 was the first month in KU and I managed 63K page reads. I stuck with it, and saw a very slow increase to around 150K a month. Even with those low levels, I was hitting *All Star* bonuses that served as validation that I must have been doing something right. It did feel good to get those emails at the end of the month telling me that I was one of the top 100 authors on the platform. I've always been a competitive so-and-so, and it was pleasing to get the recognition, even if it didn't amount to much more than a badge on the book pages and a few extra hundred dollars a month.

Those who have been at this for long enough will remember that KU v1 became a haven for scammers who ripped off readers (and Amazon, and other authors) with pamphlets that they pushed hard in exchange for the per borrow payment. I stopped getting those KU bonuses and became frustrated with the platform. I decided to take my books out of Select and to go wide again, but this time I would push it harder.

***Back to Wide***

I really concentrated on building my sales.

Let's take Apple as an example, since I am a MASSIVE fanboy. I made $108K in 2016 and around the same again in 2017. I drove sales that with a mixture of Facebook advertising, BookBub Featured Deals and the occasional promotion that I was able to secure by dint of getting to know the teams in London and Cupertino. I also worked hard to get to know the team at Kobo. This was when Mark Leslie Lefebvre was in post, and, with some promotional assistance from him and his team, I was able to build lifetime sales to around $100k on that platform.

Google and Nook chipped in, too, although not to the same extent.

How did I do it? Advertising. I've seen questions from authors who ask whether the Ads course will be applicable to them. It's a simple yes—while the Amazon Ads module will work best for those in KU (who get twice as much bang for your buck), Amazon will still be your biggest vendor in all likelihood, and you need to know how to use the ads platform to surface your books there. Every day that passes makes that requirement more acute. The days of breaking out as a new author with no advertising are now long gone.

But Facebook and BookBub ads can be deployed to drive traffic to any platform. A great tactic that I employed for months was to take a box set of the entire Milton series, price it at $25 on Kobo where I would get 70% (no $9.99 cap as there is at Amazon) and then advertise the sh*t out of it on Facebook—usually to Canadians, given that is where Kobo is most effective. Conversions are tougher at that price point, but when you make $18 a sale you can swallow lower percentages and higher CPCs.

2016 was a great year—I made over $600k—but, at the same time, I saw an alarming tapering off of my Amazon revenue. I made just $500 in Select in December; that was to be expected, because I only had a handful of books in the program, but my a la carte sales were also declining month on month.

Total Amazon revenue was over $100k in January 2016 and then just $15k in December. I managed to push that up again in 2017 but it seemed clear that the days when I could rely on really big months from Amazon, one after another, were gone. I managed to cushion the blow by selling strongly elsewhere, but I was not happy to see the decline on what had always been my biggest store.

***Back to KU***

Fast forward to 2017. Things were ticking along, and my Facebook ads continued to find new readers and sell books. But I became a little restless. Sales were decent, but not what others were managing. I made $440k on Amazon that year, and, while that's obviously fabulous, the three-year trend was pointing down.

I remember very clearly what prompted my decision to change tack again: John Ellsworth writes legal thrillers, and I saw a post (or it might have been an email) where he set out how well he was doing in KU v2.

Spoiler: It was a lot better than me.

A lot.

I investigated the market carefully before deciding that I would experiment with KU to see if it would work for me as well as it was working for him. Because I am reasonably conservative, I took just the first six books of the Milton series and put them into Select (and, therefore, KU). I thought I would let them ride for a month or two and see how I got on.

The books went live at around 17 December and, by the end of the month, I'd seen 1.7 million page reads for around an additional $7.6K. Contrary to some things I've seen suggested, I had no special treatment from Amazon. No launch promotions. I cheekily asked whether they would forego the exclusivity while I tested the water and they told me where to get off.

It turns out that I needn't have worried. The books continued to do well - much better than I had any reason to expect - and, with the evidence abundantly clear, I decided that I would make the whole series exclusive. It was the right call—I had over 7 million borrows in January and then 10 million in February, and it's grown significantly since then. I had my first seven figure year in 2018. I've been able to replicate that in 2019 and 2020.

***The Future?***

Who knows what will happen next year?

- I'm seeing increasing competition in the US store.
- Ads are more expensive as authors pile in, usually thinking that they need to pay attention to the suggested bid… and thereby making that bid relevant for everyone.
- The UK is a little behind. And newer markets—Germany, for example—would appear to be where

the English-speaking stores were three or four years ago.
• Competition will increase all markets and the smart authors will continue to find new ways to cut through the noise.

As I said at the top of this ridiculously long post, each author needs to make a decision as to what is right for them. I am absolutely not against those tactics and strategies that promote wide distribution.

It might be the case that we have focused on KU authors on the SPF podcast, but that's not been a deliberate decision and, now that I see we have a blind-spot there, we'll see what we can do to bring a little content that will be more relevant to those who choose to be wide.

We don't have any policy in this community that precludes discussion of wide tactics; quite the opposite, I encourage those posts, and, given my experience, there might be some advice that I can helpfully offer.
For those who want a dedicated forum where wide tactics can be discussed I would recommend this one: www.facebook.com/groups/wideforthewin.

I'll see if the founders would like to come on the podcast to talk about their group and the things that they have learned.

> And if you want a podcast with a host who is more slanted towards wide tactics, you need only check out one: Joanna Penn has been talking eloquently about it for years at www.thecreativepenn.com.
>
> What do you think? KU or wide? What factors do you weigh up when making the choice?

In less than two thousand words, you'll see that Mark Dawson mentions multiple times that each author needs to make a decision that is right for them. In my experience, it's always best to make informed decisions, decisions based on learning, and listening, and analysing.

That is something I respect.

Something else I respect about Mark Dawson, despite our differing perspectives on being exclusive to a single retailer, is that he is actually a wide author in a sense of the word that many in the indie author community completely ignore.

In 2019 Mark signed a unique and ground-breaking print-only deal with Welbeck Publishing Group, a globally recognized UK publisher with multiple imprints, decades-long experienced team, and an independent spirit. Unlike previous print-only deals signed by indie authors like Bella Andre (with Harlequin), or Hugh Howey (with Simon & Schuster), the one Mark signed with Welbeck didn't come with a jaw-dropping advance; it came, instead, with a more partnership approach, and a 50/50 split on royalties. Both parties recognized and leveraged one another's publishing adeptness. Welbeck knew that there was no way they could ever out-perform Dawson's nimble eBook publishing expertise. And, similarly, Dawson knew there was no way his print book operations could efficiently reach the global print distribution and network that Welbeck had built since the early 1990s.

If you're interested in learning more about Mark's background and experience specifically related to collaborating with Welbeck Publishing Group, I interviewed him about these things in Episode 100 (Oct 18, 2019), and Episode 160 (October 30, 2020) of the *Stark Reflections on Writing and Publishing Podcast*.

## Counter-Thoughts to Kindle Exclusivity

Yes, as you just read, I wanted to share a broader perspective.

No, I didn't want to try to paint a picture of the world I see without acknowledging that there are other ways of seeing it.

Some might even think it's ridiculous for me to even include a chapter like this one in a book with an overall mission to oppose exclusive mindset thinking.

But I'll be damned if I let the last words of this chapter be all about positivity in being exclusive to a single retailer.

Because that perspective is against my DNA.

And I want you to come away from this book well-equipped to make the best possible decision for you and your long-term author success.

There might be money to be had when you are only thinking about Amazon Kindle. And there might be perks you get from that exclusivity or narrow-focused mindset, that you might not have the same access to when publishing beyond Kindle.

But there are no guarantees for success.

On the flip side, I can guarantee you one thing.

Your absence from other platforms will guarantee, one hundred percent of the time, your lack of success on those platforms.

The only guaranteed winner when you lock yourself into exclusivity with Kindle is Amazon.

I truly, fundamentally, and ultimately believe that if you are looking for more than short-term success and quick fixes, you'll continue to keep your eyes, mind, and heart open to publishing WIDE.

I want you to embrace all that is possible.

I want you to have access to all the potential revenue streams.

I want you to find readers well beyond the shores of that single exclusive river.

Yes, there are perks that come with Kindle exclusivity.

But the question to always be mindful of is: "At what cost?"

I'm confident that you will find the answer that question and more as we continue to explore the options, opportunities, and benefits from being open to publishing WIDE.

# Pet Peeves about Kindle Exclusivity

## The Exclusivity Program is Called KDP Select, not KU

Hearing people refer to Amazon exclusivity as "being in KU" raises my hackles in a similar way when I hear someone refer to the monster Mary Shelley wrote about as Frankenstein rather than Frankenstein's monster. Or those who refer to Shakespeare's *Romeo and Juliet* as a romance rather than a tragedy.

KU is a term many authors use to denote exclusivity to Amazon Kindle, likely because some author who is a major influencer used it and then two other people used it, and so on, and so on, and it became a trend.

If you are logged onto your Kindle Direct Publishing account and look at a book, you'll see, very clearly, that the option (which is blatantly thrown in your face in numerous locations) is to "Enroll in KDP Select."

KDP Select was launched in December 2011.

Kindle Unlimited (KU) was launched in 2014.

I still have the email from Amazon announcing KDP Select. Here's the mention of it from the *Kindle Direct Publishing* newsletter Volume 9: December 2011:

> Introducing KDP Select - A $6M Annual Fund for KDP Authors and Publishers!
>
> KDP Select is a new option dedicated to KDP authors and publishers worldwide, featuring a fund of $500,000 in December 2011 and at least $6 million in total for 2012, giving you a new way to earn royalties, reach a broader audience, and use a new set of promotional tools.
>
> Here's how it works: When you make any of your titles exclusive to the Kindle Store for at least 90 days, those with US rights will automatically be included in the Kindle Owners' Lending Library and can earn a share of a monthly fund. The monthly fund for December 2011 is $500,000 and will total at least $6 million in 2012. You'll also have access to a new set of promotional tools, starting with the option to promote your KDP Select-enrolled titles for FREE for up to 5 days every 90 days.
>
> You can immediately enroll books in KDP Select by visiting the KDP website, where you can also access detailed reporting on the number of borrows for each enrolled title. KDP Select is available for titles participating in both the 70% and 35% royalty programs. For more information about KDP Select, please click here. For more information about the Kindle Owners' Lending Library, please click here.

Amazon later adapted that US-only Kindle Owner's Lending Library into the Kindle Unlimited program which launched in July 2014.

That was, admittedly, a game-changer for many self-published authors. It led to plenty of dollars in plenty of author pockets.

It was also a game-inducer for many as well, with plenty of scam artists seeking to exploit and game the terms of the program.

And it, of course, became a constantly topic for debate in the self-publishing community.

However, since this is my book, and it's my little moment to hold the conch, I wanted to share my pet peeve about the common use of "KU" to denote exclusivity.

It irks me the way that the proliferation of the misuse of *your* where people truly mean *you're* sends me into an over-reacting type of tailspin.

And I know, despite me standing here and stomping my feet in protest, people will continue to take the lazy route for referring to exclusivity.

At least I made my small stand.

But, I suppose, like the creature who is the creation, or side-effect of Dr. Victor Frankenstein in Shelley's classic novel, incorrectly called Frankenstein instead of Frankenstein's monster, the term KU is also a side-effect. Being in KU is a side-effect of being exclusive to Kindle via KDP Select. And it is seen by folks as a monster; when I know that the actual monster isn't a subscription program, it's the program that forces authors to be exclusive in order to be part of that subscription program.

The real monster is KDP Select. Just like the real monster is Doctor Frankenstein.

An ill-fated side-effect of misunderstandings that has proliferated books and literature for centuries.

No different, perhaps, than the way you see people referring to Shakespeare's classic tale of star-crossed lovers as a romance rather than a tragedy.

While we're on the subject, by the way, people also often refer to that play's famous "balcony scene" despite the fact that, in the original text of the play there is no mention of a balcony. Juliet "appears above at a window." The balcony was likely added for some later stage performance which then become immortalized in a painting and is yet another misrepresented part of cultural history.

The way I suspect that one "pundit" in the indie author publishing space used KU to denote KDP Select, and the masses followed suit.

And I'm sure that, despite my "protesting too much" about it, I'm sure that, in time, the use of "KU" to denote KDP Select's exclusivity program will continue to reign supreme.

In the meantime, I'll be over here at the corner of the bar with a huge scowl on my face and opening another beer to mask my frustration when in public.

## My Biggest Pet Peeve about Amazon Exclusivity

The previous segment of this chapter was more of a personal issue that I have with the way many authors in the indie community refer to the Amazon eBook exclusivity program as KU rather than KDP Select.

But here's a more serious one, and another fundamental reason why I'm a loud anti-KDP Select critic.

There are plenty of traditionally published titles available in the Kindle Unlimited program that are not exclusive to Amazon.

This means that Amazon is allowing large publishers to enroll titles in the Kindle Unlimited reading program without the requirement of exclusivity.

And yet, self-published or indie authors publishing to Amazon via *Kindle Direct Publishing* are forced to be exclusive in order to be in and benefit from that program.

Yes, plenty of authors make good money from being in Kindle Unlimited.

But why is Amazon requiring indie authors to be exclusive when they're not requiring the same thing of the major publishers?

That bugs me. It really bugs me.

It's favoritism, and classist, and it's actually preventing indie authors from growing their businesses wide.

When I was running *Kobo Writing Life* I worked really hard to build tools and processes so that a self-published author had access to as many of the resources and opportunities as the large publishers did.

Speaking of Kobo, they have an all-you-can-read subscription program too, which is available in selected regions of the world. At the time of this writing, it exists in Netherlands, Belgium, and Canada. Publishers and self-published indie author alike, regardless of whether they are publishing direct through *Kobo Writing Life* or using a third-party distributor like Draft2Digital or Smashwords, can opt into the program to reach a different customer base without any pre-requirement of exclusivity.

It's a much better option for authors that doesn't back them into a corner.

And a much better potential of available titles for readers who are part of that program.

Because, to me, in an "all things being equal" sort of environment, the reader wins. There's no need to force one type of published book into a program where others can access that program without the same restrictions.

# The Concept of Quantum Eggs

In the previous chapter I mentioned the idea of putting a single egg in multiple baskets.

I called it the concept of quantum eggs.

I'm borrowing it from the quantum physics or quantum mechanics concept of a quantum state or quantum superposition. Very simply (and I'm sure if you have the appropriate background, you'll be shaking your head at my oversimplification), a quantum system exists in several separate quantum states at the same time.

I'm adapting that to the concept of eggs and baskets to illustrate that one egg (your IP) can exist in many baskets (revenue sources) at the same time.

But before I explain, let me credit the source of this train of thought.

I go to a lot of writing and publishing industry workshops and conferences. I'm always learning. And I'm constantly paying attention to those who are also always learning.

Take Kristine Kathryn Rusch and Dean Wesley Smith, for example. This power couple of publishing have hundreds of books each, been on the New York Times Bestseller lists numerous times, and more than eight decades of writing and publishing experience that include traditional and indie publishing between them.

And yet, they both continue to expend a tremendous amount of time learning, listening, watching, and reporting their observations back to the writing community to help other writers.

I've been a long-time attendee of several of their annual workshops and have learned and re-learned so many things about the craft and business of writing from them over the years.

One of those things, which they shared in one of their Las Vegas masterclass workshops a couple of years back, is what inspired this quantum egg theory.

And it comes down to you and your author IP.

If you're an author, you likely approach this realm with the concept that as authors we write. We write books, stories, and articles.

Sometimes as authors we expand our horizons when it comes to books, stories, and articles, and we think beyond a single format or maybe a couple of formats. We have paper and all its formats (hardcover, trade paperback, mass market, large print), and then digital and its many formats (ePub, Mobi, audiobook, PDF, and a multitude of RSS, subscription, blogging, and other app-distributed formats).

But even that is limiting.

Let's walk it back a little.

Where do these stories, articles, and books come from?

From you.

From your mind.

From your creativity.

You are the ultimate source of all of these wondrous imaginative entities that are ultimately your Intellectual Property.

And the idea of funneling them into a book is merely one way of channeling that IP.

A "book" is merely one stream of sources for revenue based on your IP.

As Kristine Kathryn Rusch writes in her book **Rethinking the Writing Business**:

> "The *book*, the published book, is *not* the holy grail.
>
> "The *story*, the thing that the writer has created, is the holy grail. Before publication of any kind. Because publication is *a license*. Whether you do it yourself and upload to Amazon...or whether you go through a traditional publisher...you are *licensing* a tiny portion of your copyright to make distribution of some product (in this case a book) possible."

Kris, Dean, and a handful of other experts from multiple industries, spent an entire day at the aforementioned Vegas workshop digging into details on numerous licensing opportunities for an author's IP.

I won't get into them in detail, but I do want to share the concept so that you might start thinking less about the limited discussions about Kindle exclusivity versus publishing wide to other eBook platforms and more about opening your mind to the multitude of opportunities when you start to value your work at that higher IP level.

This is not to say that there isn't plenty of money to be had in the eBook selling space, or in the book area. But just remember, it's only one source. And if you want to be thinking WIDE, don't limit yourself in that way.

Another thing that Kris suggests is perhaps change your thinking from "story" (which can be confused with storytelling, which can be limiting) to "property."

What are the many ways that your property can be split off, licensed, adapted into different revenue streams?

I'm going to share a few unique examples below from my personal experience and observations from the industry. My hope is that, in seeing just a handful of examples, you might better grasp the concept and perhaps adapt your own ideas/stories/properties into ways you might exploit your creative talents in WIDE ways.

## Stuck in My Limited View

Near the beginning of the Covid-19 pandemic in 2020 I was filled with an underlying anxiety. Pre-planned business and personal trips were canceled. Life was dramatically changing. Needless to say, I was anxious and stressed, and perhaps even in the early stages of grief, like millions upon millions of other people.

I had a slew of writing projects I had lined up with expectations of working on them in 2020. But nothing was "flowing from my pen." At least not in the way I had originally planned.

I felt blocked. Stuck. Stagnant.

I had long been a fan of writing parody lyrics. It was a writing warm-up ritual that I had often used to get my creative juices flowing. There's something about forcing my creative and writing mind into matching a syllabic beat and even sound or rhyme structure that, for me, lubricates those creative gears in fascinating ways.

So I wrote a set of parody lyrics one morning to the song "Stuck in the Middle with You" by Stealers Wheel. Normally, when I write lyrics like that, they go into a folder or just get lost somewhere. They're like doodles or scribbles. But I thought these ones were pretty good.

I read them to my partner, Liz.

Here is how that parody song opens:

*Well I don't know if I'm up for this fight*
*I've got the feeling I'm trapped—it ain't right*
*I'm so scared, this nasty bug in the air*
*And I'm wondering how I'll soon dye my hair*
*Cat hair to the left of me*
*Dog fur to the right*
*Here I am: Stuck in this house here with you*

She smiled and laughed appropriately. Then I suggested that this could be turned into a duet. I was remembering how, the previous year, we'd seen *Bat Out of Hell: The Musical* based on the Jim Steinman lyrics in the Meat Loaf *Bat Out of Hell* trilogy of albums. In the musical, the 1977 power ballad "Two Out of Three Ain't Bad" was adapted into a duet instead of, like in the original 70s classic song, being sung by a single performer. Seeing that really opened my eyes to the way a set of lyrics could be interpreted.

She laughed again, and shook her way, almost mimicking the lyrics of the Meat Loaf song in saying: "There ain't no way I'm ever gonna sing this."

But a couple of days later, she mused that she had some ideas on how that song could be adapted into a funny video. Liz had long been a maker of fun video shorts. But she was often one who preferred to stay behind the camera.

This time, however, she agreed to singing the song with me in duet fashion, then making a video of it based on her ideas.

And that's how we spent Easter weekend 2020.

One day we spent recording and mixing the song itself. The next day we spent running around the house, changing costumes and settings numerous times, and recording the video.

It was the perfect distraction from what would normally be time that we spent with our extended family, her adult children, and my teenage son all gathering together for meals, drinks, and interactive games.

I published the video to my YouTube channel and, though it got nowhere near to anything that would be considered viral, it took off. Friends and colleagues found it and loved it. So did thousands of others.

And a local CTV television affiliate in Ottawa, Ontario picked it up and featured it in a segment called "The Lighter Side." Shortly after, a Sudbury CTV affiliate also covered the story.

No, doing that parody video did not make us famous or rich.

But it did something better.

It opened my mind to the fact that, though I've defined myself as a writer, an author, for decades, that I'm ultimately a storyteller. In multiple formats, in multiple mediums.

And it drove home those concepts that Kris and Dean had been sharing when talking about an author's IP and licensing.

I went on to do multiple other video shorts, mostly humor. Some were stupid dad jokes turned into parodies of genre films like *Under Attack* (thriller), or *You Better Knock First* (horror). Others were adaptations of a single strip Rubes comic, *Dramatic Exit*. Others were further song parodies: *Mark's Tavern* (parody of Cheers), *There is No Mash* (parody of "The Monster Mash"), *Nano-Chameleon* (parody of "Karma Chameleon") and one made specifically with the concept of this book in mind: *"Got My Mind Set on Wide"* (parody of "Got My Mind Set on You" by George Harrison).

No, not much money has been made from these pursuits. Not yet, at least. I'm shy of the 1000 subscribers needed for that at YouTube. But I'm working my way there.

(In fact, I see that as not all that different than how I started when writing—selling my short stories to markets, first for payment in copy, then small payments, then, eventually professional pay).

In the meantime, my YouTube channel has had over 162,000 views and over 2,500 hours of watch time. (Pay attention to that; I'll be bringing up how a far more successful author than me has leveraged YouTube to make money from her books).

Despite this not being a money-making venture for me, it does satisfy one of my motivations for writing. I write to share stories, to connect with people, and to make them feel something. My experiments with video and audio satisfy that part of who I am and fulfill me intrinsically, in the same way that I am fulfilled when sharing information and inspiration to help fellow writers.

Starting to create this other content removed the blocks I had previously placed on myself, and the words, as before, again started to flow. That flow wasn't just my writing, my ability to string words together in a book, story, or article. That flow was an all-inclusive output for my creativity.

Yes, I know, that was a pretty self-indulgent moment. But I hope it helped to illustrate that some reasons, some whys, go deeper than your pocketbook.

## When Weir Things Happen

Andy Weir had been publishing content on his website for years before **The Martian** became a blockbuster success. He shared web comics and stories, and his 2009 story "The Egg" inspired the Logic rap album *Everybody*, has been translated into 30 languages, and was adapted into an animation on the *Kurzgesagt—In a Nutshell* YouTube page that has had 19.7 million views since September 2019.

Weir wrote the first draft of **The Martian** on his website in serialized format. He did it in an interactive and engaging way with readers offering him scientific advice and suggestions. His readers requested he make it available on Kindle and he sold it for 99 cents, moving more than 35,000 copies in a few short months. He sold the audio rights to Podium Publishing, and shortly after sold the print rights to Crown Publishing, an imprint of Random House. The book was optioned by Ridley Scott and turned into a blockbuster movie of the same name.

Of course, for every Andy Weir there are other examples that are far more likely to happen. In 2006 I serialized a story about a suicidal teenager suffering from a death curse in blog format over the course of 9 months. It picked up readers from around the world, and I even leveraged the story's popularity to raise money for a local literacy group in Hamilton, Ontario.

A UK publisher purchased the rights for the novelization of this blog, with the first third of the book being adapted from the blog. That publisher folded before publication, but it got picked up by a Canadian imprint which was eventually folded into another Canadian publisher, *Edge Science Fiction and Fantasy Publishing*. That book, **I, Death** was released in print and eBook in 2014. I maintain the audiobook rights. I also maintain the intellectual property of the characters and the universe and have further books in that world on my long-term writing plans. I released a 10,000-word short story featuring the novel's main character, and it is available in eBook, print, and audiobook format.

So, no, there's no Andy Weir "Cinderella story" with **I, Death**. It's more of a modest property that makes me revenue via many streams of income in multiple formats.

There are concepts that I have adapted and re-adapted in numerous ways over the years. For example, in the early 90s I started thinking about what might happen if, like in that classic Christmas Carol, a snowman actually came to life. What would that life actually be like? That became the short story "That Old Silk Hat They Found" which I sold to a magazine, and then have re-sold and re-printed many times over the years.

An adaptation from that same concept "a snowman being alive" was used in another short story "Ides of March" which has also been an extra stream of revenue over the years.

Years later, I wrote a story for a YA anthology edited by Rebecca Moesta called **Sparks**. That story "Impressions in the Snow" hasn't yet been reprinted; but

I do have plans for it. As well as more ideas based on, yes, you guessed it, snowmen that are alive.

My mini chapbook **Snowman Shivers**, which runs 64 pages in print, is available in eBook, paperback, and audiobook versions. I've also earned revenue from live readings of the stories from that collection, and even earned revenue using those stories in examples of workshops teaching young writers the craft of writing.

In another example, which I like to call re-print, re-use, re-cycle, you can leverage your ideas and stories multiple times over the years for increased revenue.

I sold a short story called "Browsers" in 1999 to a magazine for semi-pro rates of 3 cents/word. The rights reverted to me. I re-printed the tale in my 2004 story collection **One Hand Screaming**. I used it in a 2006 marketing sampler handed out at literary events. In 2008 I sold re-print rights for it to appear in the beautiful leather-bound edition of **Bound for Evil**. In 2009 I re-printed it in a chapbook called **Active Reader: And Other Cautionary Tales From the Book World** on an Espresso Book Machine. In 2015 I published it in eBook format. In 2017, I published the audiobook edition using the narrator Eric Bryan Moore. This collaboration with Moore led to a far greater number of new readers to discover me, because he, as a narrator, had a huge following. I even had a book club pick up this book, and another one of mine, to read, because they were fans of his. In 2008, the story appeared, as part of **Active Reader** in a BundleRabbit volume with 9 other books called

**Books Gone Bad**. In 2019, I released a revised print edition of **Active Reader**. In 2020, I performed an excerpt of the story as part of a video series for Hamilton Public Library *Virtual Storyteller* series.

My good friend Kevin J. Anderson, who has decades of experience as a New York Times Bestselling author with hundreds of books published both traditionally and through indie-publishing, has had more than his fair share of experience leveraging his creativity, stories, and properties in multiple formats.

Kevin's openness to licensing and publishing options, and to multiple formats and special editions has led to plenty of incredible opportunities for multiple streams of revenue. But I'll only take some time to share a couple of them.

In conjunction with the release of his Terra Incognita series, Kevin and Shawn Gordon, musician, and ProgRock Records owner, created a crossover project called *Roswell Six*.

They released the album "Terra Incognita: Beyond the Horizon" with Erik Norlander for Book 1 (**The Edge of the World**) and "Terra Incognita: A Line in The Sand" with Henning Pauly for Book 2 (**The Map of All Things**). The albums combine progressive rock with science fiction lyrics written by Kevin and Rebecca Moesta, his wife.

Kevin became friends with Neil Peart, the drummer and lyricist for the Canadian rock band Rush after sending the band three copies of his first novel,

**Resurrection, Inc**. Kevin had been listening to their newest album *Grace Under Pressure* while writing the novel and paid acknowledgement to the band, even infused Easter Egg-style references to the album and the band's work. Peart read the novel, loved it, and the two began a written correspondence that blossomed into a lifelong friendship.

They collaborated on writing projects, but the biggest project they co-authored would be *Clockwork Angels*.

Decades earlier, the band had produced a concept album called *2112* which was partially inspired by the novel **Anthem** by Ayn Rand.

Peart had some ideas for another concept album based on a single character's story in a fantastical imagined world he imagined. Via a series of back-and-forth correspondence and long mountain hikes where the two collaboratively mapped out characters, stories, and scenes, they came up with ***Clockwork Angels***.

The lyrics for the album were written by Neil Peart.

The novelization of that story was written by Kevin J. Anderson.

This is, of course, an example of a single story idea becoming two very distinct, yet complimentary, products. An album, where Peart collaborated with fellow musicians Geddy Lee and Alex Lifeson. And the book, which he collaborated on with Kevin.

**Clockwork Angel**s was released as a novel in conjunction with the band's album release and world tour. An audiobook (read by Neil Peart) was also released. A comic book series and graphic novel were also produced.

Then Neil and Kevin collaborated on a follow-up novel **Clockwork Lives**, and, though Peart passed away in Jan 2020, Kevin is, as of the writing of this chapter in early 2021, working on the next book in the series the two had discussed at length, **Clockwork Destiny**.

Kevin has long been involved in multi-media and non-book licensing of his work, and also benefits from some of the book work he does via the recognition that his collaborations and solo writing projects offer. He has written in the *Star Wars, X-Files, Dune, DC Comics,* and *Star Trek* universes, among others, and is continuing to pursue utilizing his passion for creativity and storytelling in fascinating new ways, all of which bring in new readers, and new revenue streams.

## The Egg's the Thing

We have just spent some time exploring different examples of how eggs can be placed in multiple baskets.

But we haven't even taken that analogy further by exploring the various things that you can do with an egg.

One of the things that we know about eggs (at least the bird eggs alluded in the "eggs and baskets" analogy) is they are organic vessels containing a zygote in which an embryo develops within that protective shell until it can survive on its own. It's an entire world within a world.

Eggs, on their own, are a veritable super-food. Packed with protein containing all nine essential amino acids, healthy fats (two-thirds of the fats in eggs are unsaturated), and many nutrients like iron, vitamins A, B-12, D, E, folate, choline, selenium, and lutein.

But eggs can also be used as vital ingredients in cooking other products. The egg is a strong coagulator. It helps to thicken and emulsify sauces, mayonnaise, and custards, it creates structure and stability within a batter. It adds moisture to baked products such as cakes and pastries, and it can act as a glaze or even a glue.

Your quantum eggs can not only be in multiple baskets, but they can simultaneously be cracked and used in numerous recipes for your author success. As we will see in the next chapter.

# Wide Beyond the "Kindle Exclusive vs Other eBook Retailers," Argument

In plenty of author circles people say that the **biggest** debate in the author community is "Exclusivity vs Wide."

That is such an extremely limited world view.

As if that's the only thing an author should be thinking about.

As if "wide" is just a handful of other eBook retailers.

In some ways, to me, that's like watching two people discussing the merits of the different slices in a single pie while they are in the middle of a bakery.

And that's usually where writers find themselves today. There are more opportunities, more options, more pathways than are often ever really considered by most writers.

Because we often limit ourselves when we focus only on eBooks. Even if we expand our thinking to multiple formats of books (print, eBook, audio), we're still only looking at a single pie in a world of so many other dough and pastry products.

When Amazon launched *Kindle Direct Publishing* in 2007 concurrently with the release of the Kindle eReader it began a change in the path authors could consider.

I was there in those early days, having "grown up" within a pretty singular publishing path that existed for writers, and I saw the writing on the wall.

The ability for authors to self-publish without the restrictions of managing physical inventory was a major game changer.

It opened up opportunities beyond the dreams of most authors.

That power and dominant presence might also prevent some authors from seeing the much larger world of publishing that exists. And, again, beyond just the world of "books" there are some significant opportunities that draw back to the previously mentioned concept of quantum eggs.

## Traditional Book-Related Revenue Sources

Because much of this book is focused on helping self-published/indie authors learn how to publish beyond just thinking about Amazon (heck, the term "publishing wide" is one that was born within that indie author space), I want to take some time to remind authors that there are more ways, beyond just self-publishing that authors can earn money.

Within the realms of traditional publishing, there are ways that authors sell or license their work to a publisher, who, in turn, provides them an advance and royalties on sales of those books. Authors can also earn revenue from selling sub-rights to their work either through a publisher they have signed with or via direct sales to other markets if they have held onto those rights.

There are, of course, thousands of books written on this topic, but I thought it would be handy to outline some of the various ways that authors can earn money from within this realm of publishing.

When I was first starting, I would always buy the annual Writer's Digest books **Writer's Market** and the **Novel and Short Story Writer's Market** guides. While the last published version of the aforementioned title I could find was **Writer's Market 2020** published in November 2019, I know that Writer's Digest still maintains a web presence with plenty of articles and links to resources where authors can send their work for consideration by publishers.

Below are lists of various activities that might involve selling or licensing the rights to your work to a publisher. Please note that some of them might also lend themselves to self-publishing opportunities. The control over that, of course, is all yours.

**Short Stories**

- Selling original and re-print rights to works
- Foreign language translations

**Poetry**

- Selling original and re-print poetry

**Articles**

- Writing original articles, columns for magazines, websites
- Re-selling and compiling articles into book format

**Novelist**

- Full-length books published under contract with an advance and royalties
- Full-length books published with royalty share

**Story Collections**

- Original or re-print (or a combination) stories collected together under a theme. Sometimes the author is the "theme"

**Non-Fiction Books**

- Full-length books published under contract with an advance and royalties
- Full-length books published with royalty share

**How-To Writer**

- Full-length books published under contract with an advance and royalties
- Full-length books published with royalty share

**Textbooks**

- More academic-oriented books on a specific subject area that aligns with the education market

**Memoirs**

- Personal memoirs, some of which might be based on pre-existing articles and essays written and sold to different markets

**Travel Writer**

- Opportunities not just to licensing books and articles to different markets, but sometimes these come with paid travel by book and magazine publishers for specific assignments

## Ghost Writer

- Working with a personal who has ideas for fiction but not the means to write it out in long form
- Working with those who want to tell their memoir/personal story and writing it as if it were them sharing the tale
- Working with those who have expertise in an area but not the means to write it into book format.
- This work is paid up front and usually a flat fee in advance or at publication.

## Media Tie-in Books

- Typically, flat fee payment in advance to write a novelization of an existing property (movie, television show, popular video game)

## Screenwriter

- Adapting existing books/stories into screenplays for television and movies
- Creation of original content for film and television

## Playwright

- Original content meant to be produced on a stage
- Adaptations of existing properties (books, stories, movies, or television shows or stories) for the stage

**Lyricist/Songwriter**

- Even if you aren't musically inclined, there are some opportunities for selling lyrics to musicians and bands

**Speech Writer**

- Public figures, celebrities, and politicians often have someone behind the scenes to write or co-write speeches for them

As mentioned, those are just some different ways that writers can sell or licence their work to publishers and other entities for earning revenue.

Just remember that each is an opportunity for diversifying your revenue, and I'm hoping that within that rough outlined list you might have found something intriguing enough to spark an idea that is unique for you and your writing goals.

## Discovering a New Spirit

When I was first started off on my writer journey back in the mid 1980s, you needed to submit your type-written manuscripts in a specific format to publishers or agents, then wait for them to either make you an offer or reject that submission.

The popular advice to writers was to first build up a name for yourself through short fiction. You'd start to submit your stories to magazines and anthologies, get some stories in print, and that would, over time, eventually catch the attention of an editor, agent, or publisher.

An author might start offering stories to local and small press publications, often for "payment in copy" (which was basically the publisher sent you a copy of the book or magazine your story appeared in), or some token flat fee of a few dollars, or even a per word rate. Semi-pro rates were often considered 1 to 4 cents per word. Where 5 or 6 cents a word were considered professional rates.

The idea was an author needed to "work their way up" through the submission slush piles of various markets, and earn their way to potentially work with regional and small press publications, and maybe even one day the big New York publishers.

I worked my way up through those ranks, earning my first $5 and contributor copy in 1992 with a YA humor story in a digest sized magazine called *Chapter One* from a micro press in Ohio.

I eventually worked my way up through the ranks, beginning to earn semi-pro and pro rates for my short stories.

I had one such story called "Spirits" which was 6000 words long. It was a strange genre-crossing piece, written in a more literary self-reflective style, but it contained elements from horror (a ghost), as well as a love story.

At the time, I felt it was my best story, and I received many rejections from different markets I'd sent it to. Some of the best rejections came back, with notes from the editors that they'd enjoyed the story, but it "wasn't quite right for them" because of the genre-blending nature of the tale.

A horror market would enjoy the story but say that it was "too tame" for their needs.

A romance market would enjoy the story but tell me that the love story wasn't strong enough and the ghost element wouldn't appeal to their readers.

A literary market would enjoy the style and writing, but find no merit in the ghost and romance.

I had pretty much exhausted my options for that story, because I had reached a plateau in my writing career where I wouldn't send it to any market paying less than 5 cents a word.

Which would net me about $300.

I'd had, in my mind, the idea that this story would be worth somewhere in the realm of $250 to $300. But I was stuck. There were no other markets paying the rates I'd been seeking.

I had already self-published back in 2004, in print, a collection of previously published short stories. Years later, I adapted that into eBook format for Kindle and to other retailers through Smashwords.

So, I thought I'd try the same thing with this story.

In June 2011 I launched "Spirits" in eBook format on Kindle via KDP and via Smashwords for 99 cents. I earned a resounding $4.90 from Amazon and $2.80 from Smashwords.

But that $7.70 wasn't a slap in the face, it was evidence that there was something new afoot here. A new opportunity for writers. I estimated the hundreds of dollars spent on postage and self-addressed stamped envelopes for the rejections I had spent trying to sell this story to earn the $300 I'd been seeking for this story, and shook my head.

A small investment in the cover and editing on this story was now a onetime fee, with residual earnings, though not major, now starting to stream in.

By the end of 2017 the 99-cent story had earned me $270 in revenue. And it has since earned me more, both as a stand-alone short story still out there, and in the mini story collection **Literary Haunts:** ***Nocturnal Screams Volume 4***.

I stopped trying to calculate how much that story has earned because of the way its earnings are now blended into other collections. The math on that is too hard.

But I learned a valuable lesson, and a new spirit of publishing.

## Thank You, Apple

I think that any author who is either currently earning a living wage off of their eBook sales or is even earning any revenue from self-publishing eBooks, should pause and say "thank you" to Apple.

Pause for a moment, right now, and say it with me.

*Thank you, Apple! Thanks for your generosity that makes this possible.*

If it weren't for Apple, the 70% royalty rate paid out to publishers and self-published authors wouldn't be the standard.

Kindle launched in 2007. So did KDP.

But when the Kindle first launched, Amazon kept 65% of the retail price, and only 35% went to the publisher. Or to the self-published author using KDP. I had a KDP account in those early days and remember seeing the royalty rate of 35%.

That didn't change until three years later, in 2010.

And it was all thanks to Apple. Apple was offering publishers 70% on royalties, keeping a mere 30% of the retail price.

So, Amazon fired back, and announced they would be giving publishers and authors 70%, along with several conditions that included the eBook price had to be 20% below the list price of the print book, and also priced between $2.99 and $9.99 USD.

So, again, if you're sitting on earnings from any of the major self-publishing platforms out there that easily top or double the previous standard of 35%, pause with me one more time to say: *Thank you, Apple.*

## More Than Just Books

In summary, here are some high-level categories and options that exist within them you could consider when thinking about those quantum eggs you are laying as a creative:

**Books**

- eBooks and Print (Hardcover, Trade Paperback, Mass Market, Large Print)
- Comic books, graphic novels, illustrated editions
- Special or limited-edition/exclusive releases
- Foreign language translations
- Audiobooks/etc.

**Audio**

- Audiobooks (regular narration read, enhanced audio, audio drama, multi-cast performance, radio play)
- Podcast (serialized chapter by chapter) and other RSS
- Radio
- Foreign language translations
- Music and songs

**Art & Paper Products**

- Paintings, posters, transferable images to merchandise and clothing, imprinted onto jewelry (see merchandise below)
- Stationary, calendars, bookmarks, greeting cards, sticky-notes, notepads

## Video

- YouTube, Vimeo, TikTok, Instagram, Facebook, other social media

## Film

- Hollywood, Indie films, foreign markets, made-for-TV movies, theatrical releases, serialized releases, online streaming, consumer-direct

## Television

- Local, network, cable, online streaming, foreign markets, serialized programming, episodic content, filler material on existing programs

## Merchandise

- Toys (action figures, dolls, novelty, plush)
- Collectibles (coins, cards, bobbleheads)
- Apparel (t-shirts, hats, costumes, and cos-play, underwear, pajamas, masks (costume or covid-19), convenience (purse/fanny-pack)
- Jewelry (buttons, pins, rings, earrings, necklaces, bracelets)

## Games

- Table-top-games
- Role-Playing games
- Card games

## Consumables

- Food and beverages, bubble-gum trading cards, recipes, candy, chocolates, beer, wine & spirits

### Lifestyle & Home Décor

- Mugs, cups, classes, dishware, utensils
- Furniture, bookends, bedding, sheets, curtains, blankets, wallpaper, pillowcases, stencils

### Experience

- Live performance (theatre, stage plays, musicals, live readings, book club discussions, monologues, GPS-enabled audio)
- Escape rooms, dinner/evening/party experience packages, themed cruises, conferences, conventions, walking-tours
- One-on-one (mentoring, workshops, Cameo)

### Electronics

- Games, apps, software, slot-machine themes
- Accessories for smartphones/tablets

### Education

- Adaptations for educational use, teacher guides/models, book club editions/guides, learning resources

# Hybrid and Traditional Publishing for the Win

In the previous chapter we explored a multitude of opportunities when you look at splitting your IP, and the importance of thinking "beyond the book" when leveraging your multiple income streams from your creative works.

In this chapter I'm going to narrow that focus back to books and the publishing industry.

I'm not going to get into any overviews of traditional publishing in general, because, in the same way that there are hundreds of books out there about publishing on Amazon, there are also hundreds of books about the book publishing industry. But I do want to share the benefit of being open to traditional publishing opportunities.

If you are looking for a book recommendation about the traditional publishing options available and how the industry works, one of the most comprehensive books I have ever read in my three decades of working in the book industry is Jane Friedman's **The Business of Being a Writer**. It contains a great overview of the industry and has a solid understanding of the indie publishing realm. If you wanted to balance the traditional side with a solid indie-publishing side of overview and the main concepts, a companion with a much more solid indie-publishing perspective in mind, but one that recognized options outside indie publishing is Joanna Penn's **How to Make a Living with Your Writing, Third Edition** which was released in March 2021.

What I can tell you about being open to traditional publishing opportunities is that in the past it has allowed me to typically double my writing income most years.

Lately, particularly in the past couple of years, my self-publishing income is significantly higher than my traditional publishing income, but in my earlier years the split between self-publishing and traditional publishing revenue would toggle back and forth with a 60/40 split. Regardless of the larger growth in self-publishing revenue, I will always still welcome the money that comes in via traditional sources.

Earnings from traditional publishing sources might include include:

- Short stories.
- Non-fiction articles.
- Reprints (of shorter works—stories and articles).
- Books (fiction or non-fiction).
- Editing (as in story curation from submissions, not developmental or line-editing).
- Editing (traditional freelance editing work).
- Work for hire writing.
- Ghost writing.
- Speech writing.

# Publishing Contracts

If you only remember one thing when it comes to publisher contracts, remember this: a contract is a negotiation tool and can be changed.

Most publishers have a boilerplate contract that is designed as a catch-all "rights-grab" to leverage as much of your IP as possible. But they'll often make changes to the default terms when requested. And, if they can have all the rights they request, why wouldn't they ask for them, even if they don't currently have plans to exploit them. They're like, in some ways, rights hoarders. Grabbing everything and piling it around them in case one day they might be useful.

But, as I said, a contract is a negotiation tool. It's flexible and can be changed. You just have to ask.

After reading the 2013 book **Dealbreakers: *Contract Terms Writers Should Avoid*** by Kristine Kathryn Rusch (Please note that this has been updated into the 2016 book **Closing the Deal...on Your Terms: *Agents, Contracts and Other Considerations***) I looked at a contract that was offered to me by Dundurn Press, and replied with 12 things that I wanted changed. They modified the contract for me, making 10 of the 12 changes I requested. But they would not have made those changes had I not asked.

And I learned to ask thanks to advice from Kristine Kathryn Rusch.

Without getting into specifics of contract negotiation, here are some ideas of the different things you can request changes to:

- The advance amount—*Advances have plummeted in the past ten years, and they typically start in the $500 to $1000 realm for most first-time authors.*
- The royalty percent—*Please note that, unless you are a big-name author, you're most likely going to be getting an offer of 8%. You might be able to get as high as 12 to 15% or 20% but that usually comes with a proven track record.*
- Reversion of rights clauses.
- Right of first refusal.
- Competition clauses (that might prevent you from selling to another publisher or self publishing).
- Kill-fees.
- Cost of author copies.
- Audiobook rights.
- eBook rights.
- Other non-book related rights.

Not every publisher is going to be amenable to changing any of the things above. Some might be flexible on one, and not another. But the key thing to remember is that this is a negotiation, and if you don't ask you definitely don't get it.

# Ten Tips for Going Wide

The following is a slightly modified/edited version of a June 2020 article that Erin Wright wrote and shared on the Hidden Gems Books blog.

Some content and tips that appear in this list will be repeated throughout the book, but if you haven't already guessed it, I'm a fan of Erin's writing style and I figure it never hurts to hear excellent advice more than once, or from more than one perspective, in order to help it really sink in.

Erin's percentage of sales is quite diverse, and Amazon typically accounts for somewhere in the range of about 40% of her author earnings. In 2017 Amazon sales represented nearly 75% of her author income.

The original article appeared on the following URL:

https://www.hiddengemsbooks.com/top-10-tips-to-going-wide/

## Top 10 Tips to Going Wide

Howdy, y'all! *waving* I'm Erin Wright, a USA Today bestselling author. I write contemporary western romance and am a dedicated wide author. Although I didn't start out as a wide author, I quickly became one as Amazon went through one upheaval after another, stripping page reads from authors, shutting down accounts without warning, and in general being the massive gorilla in the room, willing and able to stomp any author's career to pieces at the drop of a hat. Being completely dependent on them seemed like the quick road to insanity, so I went wide at the end of 2016 and haven't looked back since.

### 1. Stop jumping in and out of KU…

…like a kangaroo hopped up on sugar. You might think that this will help you increase your sales or page reads or whatever, but what it ends up doing is making everyone upset with you. **KU readers** get used to getting your books via KU and are now upset that they can't every time you pull them to go wide. **Wide readers** get used to being able to buy your books on their preferred storefront and are now upset that they can't every time you pull them and go into KU. **Wide storefronts** take one look at your record (in, out, in, out) and wonder why they should waste their precious audience on you, and instead pick another author to promote in-house who's been consistently wide for years. (And if you think they aren't paying attention to things like that, you're deluding yourself. They *absolutely* do. Amazon and Google Play don't, but Apple, Kobo, and B&N do. It plays a significant part in their decisions of which authors to include in their in-house promos).

Pick a lane and stick in it, for at least a year if not for the rest of eternity. You'll be so much better off for it, promise.

**2. Stop giving away Amazon gift cards or Kindle eReaders.**

When you give away prizes, give away prizes that work for ALL storefronts, not just Amazon. When I give away gift cards (I give away a $15 gift card every single week in my newsletter), I let my readers choose from any of the five major storefronts (Amazon, Apple, Barnes & Noble, Google Play, or Kobo). This tells my wide readers that they matter. Instead of saying, "You only count if you get your books from Amazon," you're saying, "Every one of my readers matters to me, and that means you too, Google Play reader." This makes a difference to them, I promise, and it also makes a difference to the wide storefronts. Again, do you think they don't notice when you run a big promo on Facebook and the grand prize is a $500 gift card to Amazon? I *promise* they do, and the next time they go to pick an author for a specific promo, are they going to pick you? I doubt it.

Oh, and I only give away iPads, Nooks, or Kobos when I give away an eReader as a prize. I *never* give away a Kindle. There are enough Kindles in the world. I don't need to add to the number.

In the weekly drawing for prizes that I include in my newsletter, I and also link to the survey online so people who haven't taken it before can take it, which will enter them into the drawing from there forward. Any submission to the survey by someone who isn't subscribed to my newsletter will automatically get discarded, and ONLY the people who open and scroll down to the bottom of each newsletter can win.

It's quite simple—the US winner of the week simply has to hit reply to claim their gift card. I ask them which storefront they shop on; they tell me; I send them a $15 gift card for that storefront. For international readers, all the same applies but they're choosing an eBook of mine to win as their prize. I use BookFunnel to deliver their prize to them. All in all, a cheap way to ensure that my readers are reading my newsletters every week while also working no matter which storefront a reader prefers.

**3. Stop advertising in paid newsletters that only include Amazon links.**

(This is one of the reasons why I love Hidden Gems, by the way! They're one of the "good guys," who link to ALL storefronts, not just Amazon. I've been using Hidden Gems as a way to reach new readers for years now and have never been disappointed by their results).

I've actually unsubscribed from author newsletters from paid newsletter companies where they only link to Amazon, and dropped them a quick note before I did so, explaining why I was unsubscribing. I will no longer pay for an advertisement in a newsletter where they only link to Amazon. Period. I've also emailed companies that link to multiple storefronts, and have told them I appreciate that, and that I pay attention to that fact. If they're reconsidering this policy in the future, I want them to know that I'm specifically using them because they allow me to link to all storefronts, and maybe this will cause them to choose to keep in the links to all storefronts. It doesn't hurt, anyway.

**4. Stop linking to just Amazon...**

...on Facebook, in the description of a book trailer on YouTube, or on any other social media platform. People get frustrated by looking at an ad for a book and thinking, "Hey, that looks great!" and then when they click, they're brought straight to Amazon. This means that either they take the time to look the book up on their preferred storefront (not likely) or they just click away, that sale lost forever. Stop making your wide readers work harder to make a purchase than Amazon readers have to.

**5. Stop buying your books on Amazon**

I know this sounds slightly insane, but it can be done, I promise. This has all SORTS of bennies connected to it: You're no longer supporting an entity with your dollars that is actively hurting authors every day, *and* you're using another storefront regularly, which means that you learn how that storefront works. Instead of only paying attention to how Amazon works, you're learning the bestseller charts of the other storefronts. You're learning their marketing strategies. You're learning how their search engine works. All of this gives you an edge in gaining new readers on that platform.

If moving your business to another storefront seems just this side of nuts and there's simply no way you'd be willing to do it, at least take the step of cancelling KU. Cancel Prime. Quit your Audible subscription. Stop supporting Amazon through subscriptions to their services. I used to have KU, Prime, and Audible credits every month. I now have none of them.

It can be done.

**6. Stop cross-promoting with other authors who are KU exclusive.**

Everyone knows it: KU readers are not loyal. If a reader found you through KU and then you stop offering your books through that program, they won't start buying your books, at least not at the $4.99 price point. They *might* buy your books if you run them on a super sale but otherwise, they're dead weight on your newsletter list. Not all subscribers are created equal, and you only want the ones who are willing to pay the higher prices. Not to mention that if you promote an author in your newsletter who is in KU, you're telling your wide readers once again that *they don't matter*. I will not advertise an author in my newsletter who is exclusive. Period. I don't care how good of a friend that author is. I just won't do it. I refuse to tell my wide readers that they aren't worth thinking or worrying about.

**7. Stop targeting KU authors in your ads.**

Again, this brings in the wrong audience. *Only ever target wide authors*. I will target someone who has part of their books in KU and part of them wide, but never someone who is all in with KU. This is true no matter what platform I'm advertising on (Facebook, AMS, or BookBub ads).

**8. Stop spending money on AMS ads.**

Try not to have a heart attack with this one, lol—I'm being serious. Use Facebook or BookBub ads. They both allow you to target a wide audience. I get Amazon clicks; I get wide storefront clicks. I get them all. Instead of spending my money to grow my audience on one specific storefront (a storefront I personally cannot stand), I spend my money growing my audience on *all* storefronts.

**9. Stop having an ARC team that only reviews on Amazon.**

As a wide author, you want reviews *everywhere*. Readers on Barnes & Noble or Google Play want to know that your book is awesome before they click "Buy," just as much as a reader on Amazon wants to know this. When I add new readers to my ARC team, I will only add readers who will review on at least two storefronts (and it can be any two storefronts that they want. They can review on Apple Books and Kobo. Or Amazon and Google Play. Whatever combination works for them). If a reader currently only gets their books from Amazon, that's okay. It's free to set up an account on all other storefronts (although do bear in mind that you need an Apple ID to review on Apple Books). But none of the other storefronts have a $50 minimum purchase amount before people can review there, like Amazon does. So I tell potential ARC readers to pick another storefront, set up a free account there, and review. I don't care which one, but they do have to pick one.

And later on, if that reader is thinking about switching away from Amazon and to a new storefront, do you think they'll be more likely to pick that secondary storefront? You betcha. They've spent months or even years at that point, writing reviews on it. That increased comfort level will play a big part in their choice.

**10. Stop trying to learn from authors who are KU exclusive.**

There are authors who choose to teach classes, run Facebook groups, or even write books to help their fellow authors, and they have their own biases, just like everyone else. They might say that their books (or classes or groups) are applicable to all authors but the strategies for success on wide storefronts is so diametrically different from succeeding on Amazon that this is quite literally not possible. Stop reading or learning from sources that are focused on the wrong thing. It's like trying to learn how to become a vegetarian by taking a Paleo cooking class. It's just not gonna work.

If you can't tell, being wide is as much of a mental shift as anything else. It simply isn't enough to throw your books up on wide storefronts and call it good. If you're putting your books up on all storefronts but otherwise running AMS ads, giving away Kindle eReaders, linking to Amazon in social media posts or in your newsletters, and collaborating with a bunch of other KU authors…Well, don't be surprised when your wide sales never really take off.

**One Last Thought**

Wide sales take a long time to build up, at least compared to Amazon. But they also take a long time to die down, at least compared to Amazon. Amazon is your bipolar friend—a lot of fun when they're up and a whole lot of no fun at all when they're down. Wide sales will stay a lot more steady over the long-term, although of course they also go up and down. The swings simply aren't as wild (in EITHER direction!) So, when your sales are slow to take off on wide storefronts, keep plugging away. Make sure that you're wide in more than just name, and don't give up after a week or a month of poor sales. The sales will come, I promise…as long as you actually follow the tips outlined above.

I hope this helped! If you'd like to start collaborating and learning from other authors who are also wide, be sure to check out the Facebook group *Wide for the Win*. We have over a thousand authors in our group now, and we're getting bigger by the day. We've also got reps from a wide variety of companies that are on-hand if you have questions, including D2D, Smashwords, Hidden Gems (of course!), IngramSpark, Google Play, and lots more! We're the largest wide-centric group on Facebook, but there's always room for more, I promise.

# Wide Mindset for the Win

It's important, when looking for success as a WIDE author, that you don't just "do the things" that make you WIDE. You need to also "be the things" that make you truly WIDE.

The former is a lifeless prescriptive set of tasks.

The latter is a way of thinking, a way of seeing, and a way of behaving.

One of the fundamental lessons I remember learning when I was in the process of first getting my driver's license was that we often, by default, drive in the direction that we are looking.

I remember an excellent driving instructor reminding me that, when driving, especially when driving on a highway where the speeds are fast, that you not spend your time looking at the road immediately beyond the hood of your car in front of you, but at a point much further ahead.

That broader, further-reaching way of driving allows you to see and anticipate the turns and obstacles on the road ahead.

A wide mindset is similar.

Do you merely publish wide, or do you actually think wide?

Be honest with yourself.

If publishing wide, to you, means getting your title listed in as many places as possible, that's merely just part of the process.

The more important part is behaving in a wide manner.

Just putting your books up on all retailer platforms and then only focusing on Amazon is not going to come with any benefits.

You need to understand and nurture your relationship and understanding of those other platforms.

Remember, you likely didn't just put your books up on Amazon and not do at least some work on optimizing your cover, description, and the keywords, not to mention running Amazon Ads, or sharing links to your book on Amazon.

So why would you expect to sell anything if you're not willing to put in at least the same investment in those other platforms, or those other methods of people discovering your books?

Because I'm pretty sure that your goal isn't just to publish wide, it's to be selling your books wide.

Perhaps the title of this chapter should have been "Wide Behavior for the Win" instead of "Wide Mindset for the Win."

But we have to start somewhere.

Because it's often a wide mindset that can lead to wide behaviors.

# Wide Strategies Versus Narrow Tactics

Although this might have been said in different ways already, I wanted to spend at least a brief moment highlighting something that I think is critical for long term author success.

Exclusivity to a single retailer is a narrow and single-minded focused short-term tactic.

Considering all the options beyond that single source of revenue takes a significant amount of work, learning, and effort. That's more of a strategy.

Let's briefly consider the words themselves and what they mean.

A tactic is concrete, often focused or oriented toward small steps and within a shorter time frame. A strategy is a long-term path that comprises of planning, an overall mission statement or goal, and can include numerous tactics along the way.

It's like the difference between looking at a tree, or looking at a forest.

It's like considering a single battle, versus a war.

A tactic is a single move, or maybe even a combination of one or more single moves in a chess game. A strategy is the overall approach taken to the match, or series of matches in a chess tournament.

When you narrow your focus, when you narrow your mind, when you only look at a single target, you're engaged in the tactics.

But when you take a larger view and perspective, when you consider the place of where each tactic fits in the overall grand picture, you're engaging in strategy.

This book may contain some tactical insights and information. Of course, many of those tactics are likely to change. In fact, they're almost guaranteed to change.

That's why much of this book is more focused on strategies and strategic approaches.

Instead of outlining a "you must do this one thing here" I try my best to share a "here's how this thing is currently working and I'd like you to understand it."

One of the reasons I do this is that I can't know your overall ultimate goals and the things you're most familiar or comfortable with. So I do my best to lay out the groundwork for you, to help you see the landscape, the chess board, the multiple chess boards in this grand tournament.

If you find yourself feeling cheated at times throughout your reading of this book, that I didn't outline any sort of blow-by-blow prescriptive checklist, I hope you pause to step back and look at why you're feeling that way.

Ask if you might have been looking for some quick-fix tactic. Or, better yet, ask why I chose to talk about or share something? And is there something in there that you can take and apply into your own situation?

There's a movie from 1984 called *The Karate Kid* that comes with the tagline: "He taught him the secret to Karate lies in the mind and heart. Not in the hands."

In the story, Mr. Miyagi teaches Daniel that martial arts training is as much about guiding and training the spirit as the body.

There are moments such as the "wax on, wax off" style scenes, where it appears that Mr. Miyagi is exploiting Daniel's desire to learn by leveraging him as an unpaid employee to perform chores, such as waxing his car or doing his painting. But we learn, later, that the master was helping his student to learn through muscle memory, because of the movement associated with the phrase "wax on" that is one type of critical defensive block.

Some of the repetition that I purposely scattered throughout this book is meant to be like that muscle memory. It's repeating things that I believe are important to sink into a similar type of "muscle memory"—particularly that all-important brain muscle that comes with a wide mindset.

But I encourage you to not merely blindly follow the tips, suggestions, examples, viewpoints, tactics, and strategies that are outlined here.

Take these ideas and perspectives. Consider them within the context of your unique location within your own author journey and re-adapt them into your own long-term strategies for success.

# Pre-Orders for the Win

Most of the pundits who focus on Amazon will tell you that pre-orders on Amazon aren't important. And let's be honest, the leading pundits in the self-publishing space focus on Amazon almost exclusively—no, I'm not judging, I'm just stating a fact.

First, a bit of a word on pre-orders themselves, and how they work with traditionally published books, and how they have "traditionally" worked within the indie author community.

I'm sharing this because I want you to be as fully aware of the entire landscape as possible so that you're making decisions for your book within the full realm you are operating within, and not just the indie author realm. Because every time you only operate within that realm, you're limiting your perspective. And, since you're reading a book on WIDE publishing, I'm already under the impression that you're all about expanding your perception to make the most informed decision you can.

## Traditionally Published Books—Overview

In the traditional publishing sphere, a book goes through many gatekeepers (agents, layers of editors) and multiple rounds of curation, editing, and design that result from mining for those diamonds and gems in the overflowing slush piles of manuscript submissions.

The process of cultivating the title from submission into "ready for publication" can take anywhere from six months to a couple of years. And typically, about six to nine months before a book is put up for actual sale and exchange of money for product, it is placed into a seasonal catalog of titles.

Depending on the size of a publisher's offering, and the different imprints that they manage, there might be a single catalog, or a number of smaller catalogs created.

The catalogs are created in print (yes, even in 2021), and many are also created in a digital online format. PDF for download, and also as part of a browsable and searchable part of the publisher's website.

The catalogs that are printed are mailed out to bookstores and regional and national buyers for chain bookstores. They are sent to libraries. They are given out from giant stacks at book industry trade shows like Book Expo America (BEA) in the United States, London Book Fair (LBF) in the UK, and Frankfurt Book Fair (FBF), in Germany. There used to be a book fair in Canada, called Book Expo Canada, which died more than a decade ago. And the end of BEA was declared in 2020, with the global pandemic having dealt a final death blow to it after the industry watched it dying a slow and painful death over the past five or so years.

At these book fairs, publishers spend a significant amount of money for a booth and fancy display and to send staff to work long days in those booths, meeting with booksellers to discuss their forthcoming titles and take orders for those titles. Orders placed at book fairs like this often came with additional discounts and bonuses. Booksellers would often also gain access to early advance reader copies of books (ARCs) and sometimes get to meet big name authors to get those free copies signed.

BEA took place in late May, and the titles being pitched and sold to bookstore buyers were usually ones coming out in the late summer and fall of that year.

Regional sales reps, either from the publisher, or via a third-party company that might represent numerous publishers and imprints, would travel to meet with chain buyers and bookstore owners and managers, usually with a stack of catalogs, where they'd walk through the catalogs, highlighting titles they feel might be relevant. Those buyers would place orders as they planned out which books would be placed in their stores, and, at that time, special placement, and potential co-op opportunities (where the publisher would pay the retailer for specific prime-visibility placement in the stores, typically with a minimum required purchase number or dollar value from the bookstore).

At the same time, as all this is happening the publisher would send their metadata feed either directly or through a distribution mechanism or partner, so that the books could be listed as pre-order on the different customer-facing bookstore websites where consumers could place their direct orders.

When it comes to online bookstores or digital bookstores, such as eBook and Audiobook sites, there would also be sales calls and even printed ARC copies of books sent out well in advance to a group of people who are like buyers—only, they are often called merchandisers. Since, in most cases, the entire digital catalog is imported, so there's no buying, but there is definitely strategic merchandising placement of those books, specifically with retailers like Apple Books, Barnes & Noble Nook, and Kobo.

Publishers also send ARC copies of their books to reviewers and trade magazines like Kirkus and Publishers Weekly, knowing that bookstore owners, buyers, managers, and employees, as well as librarians, also subscribe and read these trade publications, looking to stay on top of new and interesting books to acquire or merchandise.

They also use services like NetGalley that allow for digital ARC versions of their forthcoming titles to be accessible by booksellers, librarians, and reviewers.

Much of the work and effort placed by publishers throughout all of these significant expenses is directed at a small core group of each season's release. Those large name authors and blockbuster titles, the ones in which there was a significant advance paid out, are ones in which the publisher wants to make sure earn back from that investment.

And this happens, typically, on a seasonal basis. There are the four main seasons for catalogs, with the fall catalog (released in the spring) typically being the major one, as the Christmas season, or, at least, September through December, is, for the retail world, the most dynamic and active selling time of the year.

## Indie Published Books—Overview

One of the significant benefits to being an indie author is that you're not bound to the four-season selling cycle of traditional publishing. A book's release isn't dependent upon a sales rep meeting with a buyer in New York, London, or Toronto in the spring to sell titles for the fall season. Instead, a book's release is dependent upon whenever the author wants to release it.

There is power and might in that.

But there's also a draw-back.

Many of the large retailers out there evolved from traditional bookselling. Even Amazon adheres to plenty of "tropes" from the days of warehousing and shipping dead trees around.

Amazon, of course, is mostly algorithm driven. But the other players have a lot more human interaction, human intervention, and human curation taking place. They have internal merchandisers who plan out promotions and features and spotlights for different seasons, themes, world news events, etc. And many of them are used to working with a catalog where they can plan 6 to 12 weeks before a book's release date.

Which means that lead time can become important for a book's visibility.

Particularly when you think of that book as competing with all the titles out there, and not just competing with other indie author titles.

Because ultimately, consumers and customers don't care where and how a book is published. They just want to read the entertaining, informative, and excellent books that they want to read.

And most them are searching for their next read in a vast sea of books.

Yes, there is an advantage to rapid release. Write, edit and polish, publish the minute it's ready to go.

But there's also an advantage to rapid release with a longer lead time to publish date. Write, edit and polish, publish with a future release date.

Below we'll get into some of those advantages.

Just remember, it's not necessarily for everyone. But it's good to be aware of.

All too often, even wide publishing authors tend to only focus on and share screen shots of their Amazon ranking, as if that's the only ranking that matters.

And, in adherence to the old mantra that I learned from Erin Wright, that it's more important to focus on bank over rank, having a high ranking on Amazon doesn't pay the bills. Sure, it feeds the ego; but rank isn't going to directly put any extra dollars in your pocket.

But, seriously, if it's all about ego, then go focus on Kobo's website and their ranking.

For perhaps 1/10th of the sales on Kindle (maybe even a smaller percent) you can easily be in the top 10, or even number one in more than one category on Kobo. If you're all about satisfying your ego, stop looking at Amazon, and pay a bit of attention to Kobo.

## Pre-orders by Storefront

Here's a bit of a breakdown on how pre-orders work for the major storefronts, listed in alphabetical order.

It's also important for you to understand that it doesn't matter how a book is published to the platform. Whether it's traditionally published, self-published direct, or through a third-party distributor, the effect is still the same. This means that if your book is traditionally published, you can still leverage marketing activities to take advantage of the pre-order bonus you get on some of the major players.

### Amazon

Every single customer pre-order for your book will immediately increase the sales ranking of it on the day the customer places that order, giving it a ranking boost. There are some who have claimed that an Amazon pre-order also results in a slight boost on the day of launch, or that KDP Select exclusive books (books in Kindle Unlimited) get an extra "bonus" elevation that non-exclusive titles don't get. All of this is complete speculation, since Amazon never shares anything useful to the author community and keeps their constantly changing algorithms and methods firmly guarded and locked.

### Apple

Every single customer pre-order for your book will immediately increase the sales ranking of it on the day the pre-order happens, giving it a ranking boost.

A second ranking boost will happen on the launch day for the book.

This gives you player advantage early on, and player advantage on launch day. It's like a double bang for your buck. It's a 2 times bonus. Once on the day of the customer order, once on the day of eBook delivery.

### B&N (Nook)

Every single customer pre-order for your book will immediately increase the sales ranking of it on the day the pre-order happens, giving it a ranking boost.

That seems to be it. Like Amazon, there's no additional benefit. However, authors like Erin Wright leverages pre-orders at Nook and swears by having long pre-orders (they allow up to 12 months in advance) which have been hugely successful for her. For some, it seems, there is some sort of systematic reward for having long pre-orders.

### Google Play

Pre-orders on Google Play are given an undisclosed algorithmic boost. The specifics of it (much like Amazon's) are unknown and have not been shared by anyone at Google. And because there don't seem to be the same number of analytics experts analyzing the Google

Play store, that information is likely to remain less known. At least for now.

### Kobo

Every single customer pre-order for your book will immediately increase the sales ranking of it on the day the pre-order happens, giving it a ranking boost. But (and this is important to note), you get a 2X ranking bonus for every pre-order sale. (IE, consider whatever the normal ranking increase would be for a single sale, and multiply it by two on the day the customer places the order).

This means that every time you get a single pre-order, Kobo applies a 2 times bonus to the regular ranking boost you would get. For anyone who is familiar with Dungeons and Dragons, that's like having a magic weapon that inflicts twice the damage to a monster for every direct hit.

The reasoning behind Kobo doing this is that if a customer is that eager to lock in a sale prior to the book's release, it's a book worthy of additional attention.

## Pre-orders and Merchandisers

This information is generic, but does apply to most of the main retail platforms that aren't Amazon. Kobo and Nook were born out of retailers, and they modeled their organizational structure and behavior after a similar structure that those big-box chains employ. And, even though Apple and Google were not evolved from physical retailers, they also employ similar merchandising and curation strategies.

Buyers, or merchandisers, are usually assigned to manage books based on particular category groupings. There may be anywhere from three or four to a dozen or more merchandisers tasked with their custom categories.

In the way that buyers for a bookstore sort through marketing catalogs sent to them from publishers, deciding which books are going to be ordered in which quantities for the store, the merchandisers decide which titles from the catalog will be added to feature spots on the website as well as targeted marketing emails to customers.

The merchandising calendar is planned out anywhere from 6 to 12 weeks or more in advance. That planning usually involves dependencies on other departments within the company, such as the marketing, web layout, and email teams.

The merchandiser decides which titles get selected for what spots on the website, and which are included in marketing, monthly, or seasonal messages to customers.

Some of those decisions are informed by the catalogs and ARCs (Advance Reader Copies) of books they are sent from publishers upwards of 6 to 9 months prior to a book's release. Yes, even at a place like Kobo, which is a 100% digital book company, every day boxes of books and catalogs are received that go to the merchandising department.

Those decisions are also informed by running daily, weekly, and monthly reports. Some of those reports are to spot titles with a release date in the future that are already capturing the interest of customers.

Indie authors might want to consider what they can do to stand out among the gigantic digital slush pile of hundreds of thousands of other indie-published books.

One of those things is long pre-order periods.

The other is submitting ARC and review copies.

If you have a large reader based, one of the things your readers and biggest fans can do to help you and your forthcoming book get some visibility and perhaps extra attention at those retailers is by placing their pre-orders as early as possible.

A pre-order suggests, to the retailer, that there's a significant demand for a title. And they do pay attention to such things.

Of course, a handful of pre-orders is not likely to get anybody's interest, but the more pre-orders flowing in on a consistent basis, as much as a month or two or three ahead of the publication date, is certain to capture the attention of those looking at such reports.

There are, of course, also algorithms and dynamic merchandising tools that automatically find books within specific categories and populate them to carousels and lists.

Leveraging pre-orders well in advance of the release date can help you and your books be seen and recognized potentially by both the humans and the systems at many of these retailers.

# Breaking the Bank with Box Sets

Digital box sets are an extremely valuable commodity for eBook publishing. They come with so many different uses and perks for authors and readers that they become a very valuable asset and tool with respect to enhancing and expanding your revenue streams.

But before we get into the perks and joys and wonders of this most magical creation, please allow me to demonstrate my historic experience within the book industry.

## A Word about Box Sets

You have likely heard the word "box set" being tossed about the author community, and it's an extremely valuable commodity, especially when you are publishing wide.

The term "box set" is common within the indie author community. It is used to denote a single ePub file that contains more than one book. These books were originally and also still published as multiple separate volumes of an eBook.

Indie authors liberated and re-adapted that term from the book industry.

A "box set" in the bookselling and even music retail worlds, normally denotes a set of related items or multiple volumes packaged together in a box and sold as a single unit.

In the book world specifically, one would regularly see multiple volumes of a physical book (often a series, but they didn't have to be; they were usually just related in some thematic way—all by the same author, or in the same genre) that come in a cardboard box sleeve.

The traditional term for a single volume edition that contains multiple books in the book industry is called an omnibus or omnibus edition.

An omnibus edition is defined as a creative work containing one or more works by the same or different authors. In an omnibus, it's common that two or more components have been previously published as books. In addition, a collection of shorter works, or shorter works collected with one previous book, may be considered or denoted as an omnibus.

Technically, if indie authors want to more accurately portray the multi-book single volume ePub file, they should be using omnibus.

But I suppose authors have an understandable desire with wanting to see a 3D rendition of their books as if they were print volumes packaged in a neat little cardboard box on display on a table at the front of a bookstore plainly visible as valued treasures for all customers to see.

I merely want to ensure that you weren't confused or misled about the use of the term. This is especially important to be aware of because if you're talking to a bricks-and-mortar bookseller and use the term "box set," they're likely thinking of a very specific physical item and not the digital product that you're wanting them to think about.

This is why I prefer to use the term "digital box set" to distinguish the eBook version from the physical book world product.

With that brief history lesson about book industry terms aside, let's get on to the value of this magnificent product.

## Discoverability

Plenty of authors use digital box sets to compile themed collections of their eBooks all published together in a single volume.

These can not only provide great value for readers, but they also allow authors cross-promotion opportunities with the other authors in that bundled product. Authors who participate can gain new readers.

For example, let's say there are five authors who write urban fantasy. They each have an average of 500 subscribers on their author newsletter and some of them have significant social media followers.

Any one of those authors can do promotions, send out a message and reach a certain number of subscribers and followers. They might even purchase ads to target more ideal readers.

But imagine five authors pooling their marketing. Their newsletters, if they publish a volume collaboratively, can reach 2,500 subscribers. Those with a large social media following might reach even more potential readers.

Themes for digital box set collaborations are only limited by author imagination. Authors can all take their "free first-in-series" books, for example, and offer them as a value sample pack for either $0.99 or free. The goal is to get as many new ideal readers into your author funnel as possible so they invest in your series and your author catalog.

Just make sure, if you are participating in such things, that all the books and authors match the expected theme. You don't want the wrong readers picking up your book if it's not in the wheelhouse of what the theme promises and they should reasonably expect.

For example, if I'm invited to be in a military science-fiction multi-author digital box set and I try to slip in a splatterpunk horror novel, I'm going to get the wrong customers who'll end up hating me and my book, and I'll likely annoy and let down my fellow authors.

One of the downsides to multi-author collaborations is that it becomes the responsibility of a single author to manage. They have to do all the work publishing and managing the title and then have to take the money from the retailers, then calculate the split and re-distribute that money.

It's even worse for authors across geo-territories. I'll use myself as an example. If I were to lead a project like this, I'd be taking in money from multiple US sources into Canada. The conversion from USD to CAD is always at a bit of a loss (because the Bank of Canada always wins there). Then, once I have the money, I have to translate most of the split revenue back into USD for any US contributors, and again I lose money on that conversion.

While *PublishDrive* has a tool called Abacus to help with this process (it's free for the first title, then every other title costs $2.99 USD per month), it only offers a calculation, not an actual payout. In my situation, they solved a simple spreadsheet calculation, but not the handling of the money. And it's also optimised for Kindle. So it's likely more useful for authors who are exclusive to Amazon Kindle.

I have preferred to use both *BundleRabbit* and *Draft2Digital* to solve a major issue for collaborations.

First on the scene with the technology, *BundleRabbit* is a platform that offers single entry collaborative publishing to multiple eBook retailers, and print books to KDP Print and takes care of the payment split for you. They also offer some flexible built-in tools that will automatically merge different author uploads together into a single bundled ePub file. It comes with reporting so that authors can see how a bundle they are participating in is performing.

In the fall of 2020 *Draft2Digital* announced payment splitting for eBooks and print books that does the same thing. And since then, this has been my preferred platform for collaborative publishing.

Within *Draft2Digital* payment splitting, a single person is determined to be the publisher who then collects the content and metadata, publishes the book and assigns, upon creation of that publication, a custom split for eBook and/or Print book for each author. Each contributor needs to have a free account with *Draft2Digital* so that D2D can collect income, pay appropriate state and country taxes, and then pay the shares direct to each of the authors. Along the way, authors can run reports to see how the collaborative title is performing.

I launched an anthology, *Obsessions*, exclusively through *Draft2Digital* in the fall of 2020, with each of the 16 authors involved getting an equal split for eBook and print sales. D2D Print, which is in beta release at the time of the writing of this book, offers extended distribution, which is virtually the same as what an author would get using Ingram Spark for wide print distribution.

## Banking on Digital Box Sets

Kindle has a price cap at $9.99 USD for the 70% royalty rate. Apple Books, Google, Kobo, and Nook do not.

At Kindle, if you take 3 eBooks that each retail for $3.99 USD and put them into a digital box set that sells for $9.99 USD, you've created a single purchase item that saves the customer about $3.00, which is almost the price of one of your books.

It's almost like a "buy two, get one for 99 cents" type of deal.

But if you have three eBooks at $4.99, the original price for those is $14.97. The customer saves even more, and you earn the exact same amount of money.

If you walk that price up just one penny on Kindle, to $10.00, your royalty is cut to 35%.

Instead of earning $10.47, you're earning $3.50. That's the same as selling just one of those eBooks individually.

So, if your regular price is a bit higher, or you want to collect more than just two or three books in a digital box set, then you'll be cutting your margin and revenue stream significantly.

It's good for the customer, but not good for the author.

However, the wide platforms allow you to keep more of that margin and revenue in your pocket.

So it makes sense to offer more expensive or digital box sets with multiple volumes on Apple Books, Google, Kobo, and Nook, but not on Amazon Kindle.

Many authors, particularly those who still only think of Kindle all the time by default, might consider this a sacrilegious thing to do.

But just remember, I'm not suggesting that you DON'T publish your eBooks on Kindle, just that you only publish certain, more expensive products on the other retailers.

Readers on Amazon can still get all your eBooks individually, but they can't leverage additional savings from larger digital box sets. It's not your fault. If anything, it's Amazon's doing. They're the ones who set the price cap.

Romance author Lauren Royal was the first author to break into this strategy on Kobo in a major way back in 2015, and I'm liberating part of this story I'm about to share from my book **Killing it on Kobo**.

The Kobo Writing Life Blog has a September 21, 2015 article by Lauren entitled "How my $19.99 Boxed Set Became a #1 Kobo Bestseller."

In the article, Lauren explained her reasoning behind creating a digital box set of 8 books. "I felt I'd gone too long between releases," she said. "But I had nothing brand-new in the works that would be ready for release soon."

All of her full-length books had already been in 3-book digital box sets that had been selling quite well. She decided to experiment and merge two digital box sets into a single volume and also add in a few shorter bonus titles in order to sweeten the deal.

That is how her "Complete Chase Family Series" digital box set was born. She priced it at $19.99 USD, and her only additional costs were the price of a new cover and the time spent to format the new eBook.

Her $19.99 box set of 8 titles, which was a great value to her readers, hit #1 on the overall best-seller list on Kobo. It wasn't only the top-selling book on Kobo (outselling one of that year's biggest hits, **Fifty Shades of Grey** sequel **Grey**), but she also earned $14.00 USD per unit sale.

Lauren also submitted the eBook to several promotions via the *Kobo Writing Life* author dashboard. The tipping point came when the book, which had already started to trend, caught a merchandiser's eye and ended up being hand-selected to be featured in the top of a "read the entire series" email blast sent to Kobo customers at its regular full price of $19.99.

I'm sure you can imagine that earning $14 per unit sale and selling enough to be the number one book on Kobo is an extremely more profitable venture than selling even 10 times as many books priced at 99 cents and only earning 35 cents per sale.

It's not unreasonable to guess that Lauren had to sell upwards of 500 copies of that book in a single day to hit that best-seller stat. (FYI, I'm making that number up. While I did know the number while I worked at Kobo, I can't remember her actual unit sales, and, even if I did remember, that information is confidential and isn't something I would share).

At 300 sales, she would earn $7,000 in a single day. On a non-Amazon retailer that has a significantly smaller market share than Kindle in the US and UK.

She would need to sell 20,000 units at $0.99 to earn the same amount.

## 3D or not 3D, that is the Question!

As previously mentioned, authors are keen to have a 3D version of their digital bundle collection of multiple volumes, making it look like a physical cardboard box of physical books.

It's fun, it's thrilling, it's exciting.

But not all retailers like that.

Two, in specific. Apple Books and Kobo.

So, go ahead and load your 3D cover digital box set to Kindle. But be aware of how the other might look at such things.

Apple Books will outright reject your 3D image book cover. You must remember the DNA from which they built Apple. It's all about look and feel with one of the strongest and most powerfully recognized brands on the planet.

They are consistent in everything they deliver. And 3D images in place of where a rectangular or square 2D image are supposed to be is obvious a violation of the promise they deliver to their customers.

So, no 3D covers at Apple.

Kobo will accept them, but they won't necessarily like it, and unless they're backed into a corner, you're not likely to get a manually merchandised feature there. (They regularly do include 3D covers, but they don't like it, because, like the good folks at Apple, it makes for a less than ideal browsing customer experience.)

Tara Cremin, who heads up the *Kobo Writing Life* team at Kobo, explained it this way years ago in an effective way that still resonates with me.

The eBook realm of Kobo's website was designed to display book covers as 2D images with a 6:9 ratio. When you create a 3D image, you're creating an image that has to fit inside of that, leaving plenty of white space around that 6:9 ratio box. When looking at the book as a thumbnail in search results, it makes the image even harder to make out. And most savvy authors know the value of an on-brand and on-target cover that resonates as both a full-sized view and as a thumbnail.

Another thing about a 3D "smaller space occupying" cover like that is, when the book appears in a carousel on a Kobo merchandised display, it can look out of place, like that "one of these things is not like the other" bit on the old Sesame Street segments.

Of course, some authors like "standing out" but it can also rub people, particularly any merchandisers who might be a little OCD in their approach, the wrong way. And why would you want to give any retail merchandiser any easy excuse to not include your book in a promotion carousel?

In addition, a startling thing sometimes happened at Kobo, which is a digital only platform: Customers would contact us, confused and angry, claiming their book never arrived in the mail.

Let's forget the fact they paid maybe $0.99 for that book. Let's forget the fact that nowhere on the website does it indicate you're getting a physical book (because it doesn't even let you know if it's paperback or hardcover). Let's forget that nowhere was the customer asked to enter or confirm a shipping address for that order. Let's forget the fact there was no shipping fee added to the order (or some "bonus free shipping offer") Despite all those seemingly clear indicators, some customers would still be confused as to what they were getting.

I'm not making fun of those customers, because I know that, even in early 2021, most people who read are still reading paper books and not digital books, so their assumptions automatically ignore some data or fill in the unknown blanks with known things. (We all, after all, suffer from significant confirmation bias that can allow us to believe some pretty outrageous things merely because they align with our personal beliefs or understandings about the world). I'm just asking you to consider how a person who is already confused on a website like Kobo about physical books versus eBooks, might interpret that product image that looks like a physical 3D rendition of 2 or more beautiful printed books bound inside a lovely cardboard box.

# Important Pricing Wide Practices

Price is an important element of publishing, particularly when you are taking the reins and controlling the publishing yourself.

We should see pricing not just as a noun, but as a verb, because of the way you can dynamically change and update your pricing in order to leverage different marketing opportunities, especially when it comes to eBooks and digital audiobooks.

I'm putting this brief chapter early in the book because there's a small but important contractual pricing clause that authors need to understand, but regularly don't realize.

## Your Contractual Pricing Obligation

I'm actually shocked at how many authors, even authors who have been indie publishing for a long time don't understand.

It's likely because most people never bother to read any of the terms and conditions of the retailer or distributor they are working with.

But I've read them.

In extreme detail.

And I want you to understand something really important about pricing.

In fact, I'm going to make sure that this is mentioned a few times here in this chapter and in other parts of the book to help undo some of the misinformation and misunderstanding.

**YOU HAVE TO HAVE THE SAME EBOOK PRICE ACROSS ALL RETAIL PLATFORMS!**

It's true. Trust me. I had to create one of those "Terms and Conditions" documents from scratch when I was devising a plan to create *Kobo Writing Life*. And before creating that document, I had to read all the ones on the other platforms to understand the existing landscape and create something that I felt was compelling and progressive.

And then I had to work with a legal team to make sure it was contract ready.

And then I had to re-write, and change, and craft those terms to help make them as non-lawyer readable as I could.

Prior to being hired by Kobo to come up with a solution for making it easier to get self-published books to the platform, I barely skimmed through the terms and conditions of virtually any app or platform. Yes, like you, I clicked the button on the disclaimer asking me if I read and agreed to the terms of the giant multi-page documents that I either skipped, or begrudgingly had to scroll through, without reading, to get to that "I agree" button.

For most new platforms and retailers, I did at least look at three areas in the contract. The part about money, and how much I could get, and what the payment cycle was. I also looked at what rights I was giving up, or offering, and what rights I maintained.

Most people don't read the contract they are signing.

And chances are that, even though you are reading this entire book, you still won't go back and look at the contracts you've already accepted. And chances are that on the next platform you sign up for, you'll perhaps give the contract a cursory glance at best before accepting and getting on with the business of uploading your intellectual property to some strangers who most likely will never meet.

So, let me repeat something that bears repeating, because, despite me having been screaming this from the rooftops since 2012, it's a common misconception that I want to ensure I have spent enough time and attention on helping you understand.

**YOU CANNOT HAVE A CHEAPER EBOOK PRICE ON ONE RETAILER OVER ANOTHER.**

This means that:

**YOU HAVE TO USE THE SAME EBOOK PRICES ACROSS ALL RETAILERS.**

Which means that if you do a price drop to participate in a promotion on a retail platform, even if the promotion is only being run on a single platform, you are obligated, under the terms of your contract, to have the same price drop on all of the platforms.

*But Mark,* I can see you already responding. *Nobody ever talks about it. It can't possibly be true.*

It is true.

Please trust someone who painstakingly read these contracts in detail.

And it might seem like I'm beating a dead horse, but I actually feel that I've been flogging this horse for close to a decade and the word isn't properly sinking in. So, I'm taking this opportunity to use this space in my latest book to do my best to help you understand.

And if that means constantly repeating the same information hoping the word can be spread, even if I look silly by doing it, I'll do it.

**YOU HAVE TO HAVE THE SAME PRICING ON ALL THE MAJOR EBOOK PLATFORMS.**

Many authors are, of course, familiar with the fact that Amazon has this clause, even if they've never read it. That's because Amazon uses auto-bot price matching and is viciously brutal in their practices of upholding these terms.

They've become efficient at automating those price matching terms. It comes from their adherence to always putting the customer first. This is something they are remarkably good at.

But just so you don't take my word for it, here are some examples of the terms from different platforms.

And, since I'm talking contract and looking at contract terms, in case I lose you, please make sure to meet me back later on in this chapter where I share practices for ensuring you're not in violation of this contractual landmine.

Oh yeah, before I share the terms, one more reminder: ***All of the retailers have a clause stating that your eBook may not be priced lower on any other platform***, or they reserve the right to price-match.

**Amazon Kindle Direct Publishing**
*Last Updated: August 14, 2020*

**5.3.1 Providing Your List Price.**

The list price you provide to us is referred to in this Agreement as your "List Price." For some marketplaces, you will provide us a List Price inclusive of value added or similar taxes that are included within the customer purchase price of a product ("VAT"). Where your Royalty is calculated based on your List Price, it will be calculated based on your List Price exclusive of the VAT applicable to the customer.

5.3.1 also has a link to specific eBook pricing page (https://kdp.amazon.com/en_US/help/topic/G200634500b)

*Clause D. Matching Competitor Prices. 35% Option*

The price at which we sell your Digital Book may not be the same as your List Price. For instance, we might sell your Digital Book at a lower price to match a third party's price for a Digital or Physical edition of the book. Or, we might match Amazon's price for a Physical edition of the book.

Additionally, from time to time your book may be made available through other sales channels as part of a free promotion. It is important that Digital Books made available through the Program have promotions that are on par with free promotions of the same book in another sales channel. Therefore, if your Digital Book is available through another sales channel for free, we may also make it available for free. If we match a free promotion of your Digital Book somewhere else, your Royalty during that promotion will be zero. (Unlike under the 70% Royalty Option, if we match a price for your Digital Book that is above zero, it won't change the calculation of your Royalties indicated in B above.)

*Clause D. Matching Competitor Prices. 70% Option.*

The price at which we sell your Digital Book may not be the same as your List Price. For instance, we might sell your Digital Book at a lower price to match a third party's price for a Digital or Physical edition of the book. Or, we might match Amazon's price for a Physical edition of the book.

If we price-match your Digital Book, your Royalty will be:

The Royalty Rate indicated above, multiplied by the price at which we sell the Digital Book, less taxes and Delivery Costs, for sales to customers in the Available Sales Territories.

Royalty Rate x (Amazon price - taxes and Delivery Costs) = Royalty

By "price-match" we mean where we sell the Digital Book in one or more of the Available Sales Territories at a price (net of taxes) that is below the List Price to match a third party's sales price for any Digital or Physical edition of the Digital Book, or to match our sales price for any Physical edition of the Digital Book, in any one of the Available Sales Territories.

If price-matching your Digital Book results in the Amazon price falling below the minimum 70% List Price requirement, you will earn 35% royalty.

**Rakuten Kobo, Kobo Writing Life**

*Last Updated: June 15, 2020.*

From SECTION 4. PRICING, PAYMENTS, PROMOTIONS, AND OTHER FINANCIAL MATTERS.

4.1 **Price.** You shall provide Kobo with the Suggested Retail Price ("SRP") for the Work, which shall be exclusive of any goods and service, sales or similar taxes ("Taxes") and shall be inclusive of any of any value-added (VAT) taxes within VAT inclusive territories. Kobo shall, in its sole discretion, set the actual selling price paid by the User ("ASP") for each Work and may also display or add any Taxes to the ASP as separate items or included in the ASP.

**4.2 Payment Terms: eBooks**

**(b)** Additionally, the eBook must be priced at least twenty (20%) percent below the SRP of all physical editions of the book, if available.

**(c)** The SRP for your eBook provided to Kobo must be less than or equal to the lowest price provided by you to any third party. In the event that another retailer is selling your eBook with an SRP that is less than the SRP provided by you, Kobo may elect to adjust the SRP of the eBook to match the lower SRP and substitute this as the price used in calculating and remitting payment during the period where the price discrepancy exits. Kobo's determinations regarding SRP matching are at its sole discretion and are not subject to review.

**(d)** Subject to Section 4.2 (e) below, if the eBook does not satisfy the criteria in Sections 4.2 (a) and 4.2 (b), Kobo shall pay the Publisher 45% of the SRP for each eBook sold.

[NOTE on 4.2 (b)—This is in line with terms that are offered to traditional publishers, whose pricing practices on eBooks are not as generous as the pricing practices of most indie authors. And it leads to eBook pricing windowing. If a traditionally published title is first released in hardcover, the eBook price is supposed to be 20% cheaper. As that title moves on to paperback, and a lower price, the eBook price is typically also reduced. "Windowing" with respect to pricing and formats are covered in another chapter of this book.]

When you publish to a retailer through a third-party distribution platform like Smashwords, Draft2Digital, PublishDrive, or StreetLib, you are doing so under similar terms and conditions that exist in the direct author publishing terms.

This means that if you are running a price promotion, even if it is one that is run by one of the retailers and you are publishing direct to that retailer, you must drop your price on all the other platforms.

If you don't, you violate your contract terms.

So if it's a Kobo-specific price drop where you make the book $0.99 USD, you need to make that book $0.99 USD on Amazon, Apple, Google, and Nook.

This is why, as we'll discuss when I talk about specific retailers, if you ever participate in a promotion where you aren't required to change your retail price, where the retailer provides a coupon to allow their consumer to get a specific percentage off the retail price, there is no price-change involved, and you are not in violation of any contract terms.

Fortunately, several of the self-publishing platforms allow you to schedule price changes. While KDP does, platforms like Kobo Writing Life and Google Play, and Draft2Digital do allow for this type of pre-planning.

But the most important thing that I want you to walk away from understanding when reading this chapter is knowing that your pricing should be consistent across all retailers at all times.

# Tips for Authors at Different Stages

Over the years I have been approached by authors at different stages in their own author journey looking for advice. They often ask me if it's too early, or too late to adopt a proper WIDE mindset.

My answer is that it's never too early or too late to start thinking and acting WIDE.

How's that for being open and inclusive?

In my world, it's not just the Prodigal Son who wins the parental heart. So too, does the Loyal Daughter, and the Newborn Child. And let's not forget the Adopted Older Child. A parent's love isn't finite. Love itself isn't finite. The same goes for a reader's love for consuming more and more books.

We live in a world where no single writer will ever be able to produce enough material for their most passionate readers. A world where those readers aren't all in the US and UK. A world where digital and eBook publishing is still at the very beginning of a long journey into digital reading. (This is based on industry stats that show most book lovers have yet to adopt eBooks into their reading diet).

So, it's good for authors to remember that there are more readers in heaven and earth than are found along the shorelines of the world's largest river. And on the shores of those other rivers, streams, lakes, and bodies of water sit readers, eager to soak in your words, stories, and unique insights.

Your specific introduction to WIDE is typically more complicated than the four segments outlined below. And, while I'm sure you can find helpful ideas and perspectives within each one of them regardless of where you sit, you might approach WIDE from one of these four areas: *At the Start of Your Indie Writer journey; Coming out of a Tour of Duty in KDP Select; Returning to WIDE;* and *You've Been WIDE and You're Not Selling.*

## At the Start of Your Indie Writer Journey

Common advice for beginning writers is to start with Amazon because there is so much to learn. The idea of having to understand the five main retail platforms, not to mention dozens of other retail, library, and subscription models of digital reading, can be overwhelming.

From a logistical and perhaps even business standpoint, this makes sense. Amazon is, after all, the world's largest bookstore. Why not start with the largest body of water that contains perhaps the biggest number of fish?

But that approach might not be the best for properly adopting a WIDE mindset. Because, if you first focus on Amazon, learning all there is to know about that platform, your mindset, and your approach, is going to be obfuscated with their preferences, and how things work on that platform.

And all of your understanding of other platforms will be tainted with the scent or echoes of Amazon. Even if you are starting off on Amazon because it's the biggest pond, but aren't clicking the KDP Select checkbox that will put you into a 90-day tour of duty with Amazon Kindle, it's good to be aware that you are coloring your perspective in a Kindle-centric way.

It might make sense to consider one of two approaches.

Start with a different platform, or perhaps start with two platforms. Amazon (they are the largest, after all), and another one.

Let's take the example of launching on a non-Amazon platform first.

I've known authors who have decided to launch either a book, or even a series, on a non-Amazon platform first, and then, after learning a little about publishing in general, moving to Amazon and other platforms. This allowed them to experience what a book launch is like, especially one in which pre-orders really do matter, and then apply those experiences to the other four major platforms for the launches and releases there.

Consider a parallel to this approach from the indie music scene. If Amazon is the biggest platform for authors, launching and learning there first might be compared to launching your first performance at Royal

Albert Music Hall in the UK, Sydney Opera House in Australia, or Radio City Music Hall in the USA. Indie musicians usually cut their chops at a local bar or tavern, and then work their way up to larger and larger venues. There might be a benefit in getting to learn and understand the retail and digital reading environments through other or smaller venues first. There might be less pressure; not to mention the opportunity to make a few mistakes on a stage in front of smaller audiences.

Let's also consider the 30 day "cliff" common to Amazon. Imagine having a five-book series already launched on one or more of the other WIDE platforms that took time to produce. Picture all you'd learned about launching WIDE and then introducing it to Amazon in the "rapid release" approach that can work well there? I'm not suggesting this as a strategy, merely exploring it as a potential option. Remember, most readers stick to the single platform they read on. It's often discussed from the WIDE vs exclusive perspective, but it also can apply to benefit you when moving TO Amazon from the other retailers.

While I'm not suggesting that Apple, Kobo, or Nook might be looking for their own versions of exclusivity, I have known each of those platforms, over the years, to be open to a "[*platform name*] First" type program, where a pre-order is only available on that platform, or perhaps the eBook is available there for a limited time, even if it's just 30, 60, or 90 days. These are sometimes done collaboratively with authors in exchange for promotional consideration. Again, I'm not suggesting that a first-time author consider that as a strategy, particularly because the platforms are usually looking for authors with an existing audience, or large reader following. This strategy might depend on an existing relationship with contacts at those platforms. I'm merely sharing it as an example of a trend I've spotted.

Something that might be more realistic, because it reduces your learning to two platforms from learning them all at the same time, is launching on Amazon and a second platform. The benefit is that you aren't first conditioning yourself to always be thinking Amazon first and everything else second. Like growing up learning two languages in the familial home, you're likely more adept at speaking and even thinking in both languages rather than first learning one, then having to uncomfortably shift your thoughts and re-learn a second language, while having to force yourself to unlearn the rules of the first language.

For example, if you're a Canadian author, and you know that Kobo has a significant presence in Canada, you might consider learning Kindle and Kobo first. Then, once you've comfortable, introducing yourself to the other platforms is done in a way where your mind was already open from the beginning.

When setting up your book, let's say you're using Kindle Direct Publishing and Kobo Writing Life. Try to do so on both platforms simultaneously, in either two windows, browsers, or tabs, while toggling back and forth. Pay attention to the differences between the two platforms, the required fields, the optional fields, the steps.

- How they differ in terms of how on one you can use a WYSIWYG editor for entering your synopsis, while the other requires entering basic HTML code to get specific formatting.
- The way one of them allow entering keywords, while the other has no such field.
- How one allows for global territorial pricing in NZD, while the other doesn't.
- The manner one provides the ability to set different EUR prices by country, while the other has a single universal EUR price for the entire continent.
- How one has a cap on 70% at $9.99 USD while the other offers 70% for any eBook priced $2.99 USD or higher.
- The scheduling of price changes and promotions in advance that one platform offers while the other only allows those changes to be done live.

Those, of course, are just in the setup of your titles. You will, in parallel, learn much more about each platform. You'll learn the different customer bases, the countries where each retailer is prominent. The fact that one is driven by automated algorithms whereas the other relies more heavily on manual human curation.

Instead of assuming all things Amazon, you "grow up" learning that there are plenty of differences and perspectives.

Hopefully, you'll also learn something that I'm continually shocked most long-term indie authors still don't properly understand: The fact that the contracts with all major retailers include a clause that your retail pricing has to be the same on **every single retail platform**, and that you can't have a lower price anywhere else. (The common mistake most authors make is they're aware of this clause on KDP—and Amazon is the most aggressive when it comes to enforcing this price-matching—but they haven't a clue that all the retailers have this same clause).

## Coming out of a Tour of Duty in KDP Select

Some think I'm being cheeky when I refer to the 90-day cycle of exclusivity in KDP Select as a tour of duty. But I'm not. The term "tour of duty" is derived from when a military person commits 24 Hours a day, seven days a week, on active duty to serving in combat or a hostile environment.

When you are exclusive to Kindle, you are committing to a dedicated service. You're serving Amazon's eBook platform and its customers. And you are sacrificing other things in order to do so. You are giving up freedom to publish eBooks to other platforms, giving up all customers from other eBook platforms, and giving up on the ability to offer library sales.

I won't even get into the parallels to shell-shock and PTSD I regularly see sketched onto the faces of authors leaving a KDP Select tour of duty. Let's suffice it to say that, with very few exceptions—and this would mostly be authors who are already independently wealthy or perhaps already have multiple income streams—when authors leave exclusivity, it's often with some sort of emotional scars, anxiety, even bruised egos, or perhaps the feeling of being rejected, betrayed or let down by something they gave a good part of themselves to. Also, they are returning to a world that differs greatly from the hostile and cut-throat "pay to play" conditions they've become accustomed and conditioned to.

So, in many ways, it's not easy to integrate into the environments of the broader global e-reading communities. And it might even be harder for you than for a beginning author. Because, as I mentioned in the "At the Start of your Indie Author Journey" section, your perspective has become tainted significantly in favor of Amazon.

Take keywords as an example. Amazon is the only platform that truly leverages keywords very specifically that is used to "game" Amazon's retail store algorithms for placement in certain categories and maximizing ranking. Most other major retailers don't even have a specific field to manually enter keywords in your metadata. And yet entire businesses have been built upon understanding and leveraging keywords for Amazon.

How, then, would you understand that Apple, Kobo, and Google mine other metadata fields and even the content of your ePub file, to derive a similar effect to what those seven fields entered in Kindle Direct Publishing can provide? It's simple. You wouldn't. Because you "grew up" learning Amazon.

I would advise that you start in the same way that authors are advised to learn about eBook publishing. Pick at least one of the WIDE platforms and spend some time trying to learn and understand it. And not just the publishing side, but the consumer, the reader, the retail browsing experience.

How much time do you spend looking at your book's item page on Amazon and worrying about the category ranking? Do you spend even a quarter of that time looking at your book on other platforms? Do you even know if they have and display a ranking, or how it even works? Have you ever browsed, shopped, purchased, or read an eBook on any other platform? What is their customer experience like?

Stephen King said that if you want to be a writer you need to read a lot. I would argue that if you want to be a WIDE author you have to understand WIDE platforms a lot. If you begin to see how your book looks, how it shows up (or doesn't) in search results on the other platforms, what internal and third-party promotion tools work best for elevating your sales and ranking and discoverability on those other platforms, you'll begin to properly cultivate your sales there.

One thing I can guarantee is that it won't be fast. And it won't be easy. Consider the term "cultivate" from the horticultural origin of the word. Plants prosper differently under specific conditions that are unique to each. They require careful attention, training, study, and time. Your books, and the platforms they grow in, are no different.

Oh, and one more thing that I think is important for you to be aware of: You might need to re-condition or re-approach your existing customer base. If you've been exclusive to Kindle and making good bank on Kindle Unlimited page reads, chances are you've conditioned a good portion of your reader base that your books are "free." You might need to ensure they know that, when you are truly WIDE, your books will be available to millions of MORE readers and also now free to even more people through numerous library programs.

## Returning to WIDE

While this realm is similar to one's first introduction to WIDE, it also comes with its own challenges. The first is recognizing that, every time you delist your titles to go exclusive to Amazon Kindle for 90 days of multiple tours of duty in KDP Select, you are re-setting or wiping out the ranking and temperature of your books on the other platforms.

I liken it to falling off the wagon of sobriety. (And yes, if it's not already blatantly obvious, I have a deep personal bias about exclusivity that seems to result in using negative anecdotes for describing KDP exclusivity, such as *tour of duty* or *addiction*. But let's follow along.) Every time you give in and take another drink, you give up the right to hold a sobriety chip and the counter goes back to zero. The same holds true when you delist from other platforms. The rank of your book goes back to zero. Any systematic benefits from being wide are gone.

Perhaps the only thing that is likely to still be there when you return would be the reviews. Because, if you publish using the same ISBN/edition of your book that was delisted, most of the WIDE retail systems retain a connection to a customer review. That is, at least, one saving grace.

But you might have lost the faith of your readers along the way. If you were, for example, releasing a series and then disappeared for those promises of the "greener pastures of the Kindle Unlimited fields" any readers who had been avidly following you might have been put off and moved on to other easily available books and authors. You may have lost them. You may even have insulted them. You might be able to win them back. But in many cases, you're often having to start from scratch with each re-entry.

It can take as long to return to success on the WIDE platforms as it took to first build up your sales there in the first place. Maybe even longer, depending upon some of the emotional scars and damage that might have been inflicted when you left.

Just be aware that when you play the "in again and out again" game of Kindle exclusivity vs WIDE, you're doing yourself no favors on those WIDE platforms. You might, in fact, be harming your reputation as a reliable and professional author with any of the people who work for or with those platforms. Think of the spouse whose partner has had an affair and cheated on them numerous times. How likely are they to ever fully trust that person again? If you think I'm being overly dramatic in that perspective, just remember, I spent several years at one of those retail platforms, and had to play the doting and loving Betty who always took that fickle Archie back in no matter how many times he dumped me when the rich and privileged Veronica batted her pretty little eyes at him. I'm sure I'm not the only one feeling the side effects of that blatant rejection.

So, when a promotional opportunity comes up, just remember if you might be seen as the spouse with a history of "stepping out of the relationship" or the reliable constant one whose faith and commitment has never wavered.

## You've Been WIDE and You're Not Selling

If you haven't already guessed, I enjoy drawing parallels to other life experiences. This one reminds me of what can happen in a long-term personal relationship. At the beginning, everything was new and fresh and exciting. As you were getting to learn about one another, there was a unique high in each new experience. There was hope for a bright future; the romance was strong.

Then, as the newness and thrill of discovery gave way to normalized and systemized patterns, the luster and shine faded, and you found yourself in a comfortable routine of taking that partner for granted. You already know, or think you already know, everything about that partner. There's no newness, no freshness, no dramatic fanfare.

But here's the reality. People are always evolving. Always changing, learning, and growing. We notice it in friends we haven't seen for years, but rarely notice it in those closest to us. Because the change, the growth, the differences, are subtle, and are things we don't often consciously perceive. So it's important to pause and step back and take a fresh look at this long-term acquaintance. Give them the respect and attention you would give to a new prospect.

In a relationship situation you might ask yourself things like this:

- When was the last time you actually looked at your partner? Really looked at them?
- When was the last time you asked them how they felt about something rather than assuming you already know their feelings about it?
- When was the last time you tried to do something new with them or explored new opportunities you could do together?
- When was the last time you attempted to seduce or woo them, like you did back in the early days of your relationship?
- When was the last time you purposefully let them know they were a priority?

I'm sure you see the parallels I'm getting at here. Are you taking this platform you've had a long-term relationship with for granted? When was the last time you bought it flowers or cooked it their favorite meal, or crafted something unique, by hand, because you knew they would appreciate it? When was the last time you prioritized spending quality time together?

When was the last time you focused on listening to them, observing them, watching how they performed in their element? Recognized their strengths and unique talents and abilities? Do you even know what those things are? Have they developed or grown new ones?

Talk to them. Listen to them. Pay attention to them. Be willing to re-learn, re-appreciate, and re-cultivate things with them.

Or, if you can't draw your own parallels, here are some ideas:

- Where are they speaking, sharing, or communicating with authors? And are you actually there and attending to what they say?
- Is there an opportunity to network, connect, and interact with them in any way? Relationships are far more critical on most of the WIDE platforms than they are on Amazon's algorithm-centric platform.
- What other authors have had success on the same platform? What are they doing? How are they doing it? Are there any similarities between their books and what you write?
- Reach out. Talk to them. Ask for feedback. Engage with them.
- Offer them something. Is there something that would be valuable to them you can assist with? A blog, podcast, other content they would find helpful for their authors or readers?
- Speaking of readers, are there tools you can leverage to offer something for their readers? Do they have their own unique eReader that can be offered up to your own mailing list/reader base? (Most authors think about offering an offer of a free Kindle as a prize? But that's so specific to one retailer prominent in the US and the UK? What

about the rest of the world? What about readers on other platforms?)

The whole idea is not to take the WIDE platforms for granted. Treat them the way you might treat a budding new relationship. Attend to them the way you would attend to a new friend, a new romantic interest. Yes, it takes effort, and it takes time. And chances are that you'll have to focus on one at a time, because each of the platforms is unique in their approach. But you'll likely find that if you attend to what's special, unique, and important about each of the platforms, you'll find an approach that can work to strengthen your own presence with their customers.

I cherish the quote because it reflects my lifelong love affair with books, with writing, and, for my entire post-secondary education life, working in the book industry. But one thing that writers can often forget, when thinking about the romantic notion of a room filled with books, is that bookstores and libraries are businesses, each fulfilling a specific need within their communities.

# Thinking Narrow When Being Wide

By now, we've gone through numerous details regarding the power and benefits of WIDE thinking and behaving.

But there's one area where I think it's critical to NOT be thinking wide, but rather, in a tight and narrow fashion.

And that's when you're thinking about your reader.

Your idea reader.

This is where it makes the most sense to not think wide, nor big, but consider them, as your target audience, in the narrowest way possible.

I know it might seem counter-intuitive to being and thinking wide, but focusing in on your ideal and target reader as much as possible will lead to larger success.

Bear with me.

In a general sense, while there are major blockbusters and viral-style sales patterns that can happen to a book, it's usually because of one really fundamental inciting incident.

The reader really connected with that book.

Yep. One reader. One connection.

That's the magic and power of books.

And that's what it's all about.

You've created something that truly resonates, truly inspires, truly entertains and impresses a single reader.

If that connection is powerful enough that's where the next level of magic can happen.

Because they'll suddenly be wanting to share the great thing they experienced with other like-minded people.

What happens when you find a book, television show, movie, or joke that brings a positive reaction and experience? You often immediately think of the people in your life who would most appreciate that. And you tell them. You might not just tell them about it, but you'll do it in such an enthusiastic and compelling way that they have no choice but to check out whatever it is you're selling them.

That's what you want.

And, while, yes, when that becomes big, because they tell two friends, and they tell two friends, and so on, it always starts with that single person.

You might notice that in his notes at the end of his books, Stephen King addresses "constant reader." Did you ever notice that he addresses a SINGLE person, not the millions of people who are adoring fans? It's an intimate, one-on-one experience, or at least, that's the way he's writing it, like he's sitting on the other side of a campfire and there is an intimate relaying of the tales he is telling solely to you.

There are theories about King's writing that suggest his "Dear Constant Reader" is his wife, Tabitha King. He has expressed thoughts and feelings that would lead to that.

In *On Writing*, for example, he wrote:

> "Someone - I can't remember who, for the life of me - once wrote that all novels are really letters aimed at one person. As it happens, I believe this. I think that every novelist has a single ideal reader; that at various points during the composition of a story, the writer is thinking, 'I wonder what he/she will think when he/she reads this part?' For me that first reader is my wife, Tabitha."

So, considering that Tabitha King is Stephen King's single ideal reader, it could be that his use of "Constant Reader" to talk to his fans is an endearing way of being inclusive in his approach to his fan base. Because he's really just addressing Tabitha, but doing it in a way that nobody else feels left out.

It retains that critical, and important intimacy.

He's writing that book for a single reader.

And you, as the reader, get to sit in Tabitha's spot if just for that moment.

Fortunately, millions of people are pleased when Tabitha is pleased.

But consider how your writing, your books, the things you share, might best be focused. Who is *your* ideal reader, and how can you express your story in a way that is most intimately meant for them?

Because, chances are, if they are enamoured with it, so too, will many more others.

That's thinking about the work itself and who your audience in. And it's an important overall strategy that I think is a critical part of any marketing exercises you become involved in.

But let's take that same time of narrowed in and focused approach to each of the venues, outlets, and platforms where your book exists.

Because they each have a unique approach, look and feel, atmosphere, and customer base.

And though you are wide and available in multiple places, consider how you can move about and change your focus, where required, to each of those platforms.

Think about a touring musical act that you've seen perform live.

During at least one point in the middle of their act, they called out something to the effect of: "We love you, [*current city they are in*]!"

In response, the crowd likely went ape shit!

They screamed in delight. *This band loves us! They really, really love us!*

We all know that the band said the same thing the night before in a different city. And that tomorrow night, they'll say the same thing to a different crowd about their hometown.

They love all their fans. So they're not two-timing. They are being authentic. They're being authentic and grateful, and appreciative, of each hometown crowd in turn, as they tour.

While in New York, they focus on The Big Apple. While in Detroit, they focus on Rock City. And so forth, and so forth.

They attend to and nurture each audience in a very focused way.

Because you can be sure that, if they come to Toronto, Ontario, Canada, they'll have a positive thing or two to say about the Toronto Maple Leafs hockey team. And then, when they're in Oklahoma City, Oklahoma, they'll be raving about the Oklahoma City Thunder. And when in London, England there'll likely be cries of "God Save the Queen."

They are focused, on their audiences, on giving them what they want and what they signed up for when they bought a ticket.

Just like you should make sure that your books and products are effectively addressing your audience, and even acknowledging the specifics of their audiences.

I remember reading one horror novel from an indie author many years ago on my Kobo eReader, and there was a scene in the book where the light from the Kobo was an important element that saved the main character's life in that moment.

I suspected that the writer customized each version to the platform, having that device be a Kindle eReader for Amazon, a NOOK device for Barnes & Noble, and an iPad for the Apple Books platform.

A brilliant and subtle play on the author's part to make the readers of each of those readers regardless of their platform feel connected with the chief character.

And, yes, there's going too far. Because that was a significant amount of work.

But think about other elements that aren't embedded in the book itself, but in the end matter you compose that's meant to directly connect with the reader.

Are you asking them to leave a review on Amazon despite the book being published everywhere? How does that make the reader on Apple, Kobo, or Nook feel? You've just pushed them away at a time when you should be pulling them closer.

Again, don't forget those small things, those tiny yet powerful touches, that can make a significant difference in your reading audience.

It comes when you focus on that reader, that platform, just like those musicians who are, when they're with that audience, focusing directly on them.

# Who is Going to Promote my Book the Best?

If you want to save time and skip to the quick answer, here it is: **Nobody**.

That's right. Nobody. Well, nobody but you, that is. Unless, of course, you don't do anything to promote your book and you think that someone else out there, some publisher, some retailer, some distributor, is going to be standing with a gun in hand loaded with some sort of magic bullet that is going to skyrocket your book to success.

For anyone who has already stopped reading because the answer isn't the easy one they were looking for, I'd wager a bet they will not be a successful author. But the fact you are still reading is a sign that you see the mountain and realize that nobody is going to climb it for you.

Kudos to you.

Keep reading.

Because I'm going to share the reality with you: The mountain is bigger than it looks. The terrain is tough, it's brutal, it's nasty. There are plenty of places to get hurt, fall down, break a limb, get lost, or even perish. But then again, you've already written a book. You've already succeeded where millions of others have failed. You've already climbed a significant mountain. So what if there's another mountain before you? You're not going to let anybody tell you that you can't do this.

And trust me, the view from this mountain is spectacular. And I'm not even talking about the top. Because few very of us will make it to the summit; we'll never have that view. It's a narrow peak, and there isn't room for that many up there. But that's okay; you'll notice this mountain has a glorious peak, but it also widens out dramatically and has plenty of outcrops and plateaus that offer all kinds of magnificent views for plenty more of us. And it has multiple sides, too. Different areas, regions, landforms, and vegetation; each offering a unique and fascinating panorama.

If you want a different view, you need to find your way there. There are guides along the way to point out options, paths, and even pitfalls to avoid, but nobody is going to do the work for you. It's ultimately up to you and the very custom map and plan that you are the master of.

You get out of this treacherous climb what you put into it.

Just don't forget, there are plenty of amazing views all over this mountain—not just at the top.

*But what about the old days of publishing?* You might ask. Or: *Isn't there an option where I just hand my manuscript to someone and they do all that stuff?*

Sorry to dispel that illusion. But that's all it is, an illusion as powerful in some people's minds as their rose-tinted glass visions of the "good old days" in either traditional or indie publishing.

Authors used to think that having a publisher would remove the hard work and effort of promoting and marketing and selling a book. And many avoid self-publishing the book not because of the stigma that is still prominent, but because there is an underlying belief that having a publisher means not having to do any marketing or promotion.

There's also this misconception that "back in the day" all a writer had to do was write a book and the publisher would do the rest. That might have been somewhat true for some higher-end mid-list and bestselling authors. But the reality is that has never truly been the case. If anything, publishers do far less promoting and marketing than they used to, and the majority of those efforts, time, and money, are spent on a small handful of books they produce.

I've known plenty of authors over the years who would be considered successful authors, with at least a handful of titles on the shelves of virtually any bookstore you walk into in North America. The New York Times Bestsellers with millions of copies of their work sold, who regularly received advances from publishers for books that were enough to make a decent full-time living off of. (Remember, of course, that receiving an advance of $100,000 typically means three payments of $33,333, usually spread out over a year or more. One third upon signing the contract, the second upon turning in the manuscript, the third upon publication).

Those authors never had the luxury to just sit back and let their books sell. They had to go on tour, do readings, book signings, interviews, go to book fairs and meet with booksellers and librarians who might remember them and order in their books, might even actively try to hand-sell their books to the right customers. Yes, in some cases, the publisher had a publicist who organized and helped arrange these tours. If the author was huge enough, or successful enough (ie, Stephen King, Danielle Steel, Nora Roberts, James Patterson), the publisher would also pay for lavish events and shuttling them around the world.

But most authors, even some authors whose names you might recognize, were midlist authors within a publishing house, and mostly paid for their own hotels, airfare, and expenses, to get out and do book signings, readings, and even sit at a table in the front of a bookstore for hours spending most of their time not signing copies of their books, but directing people to the nearest washroom, or pointing out where the latest bestseller display was, or maybe even where the "non-fiction" books in the store might be located.

Nobody promoted, or marketed, or sold their book for them.

The onus was on them.

Something to also remember about those so-called "glory days of yore" in publishing, is a fact I realized when I was managing a bookstore and buying books to put on my bookstore shelves.

Most books published rarely sell many copies. Industry statistics show that the average traditionally published book sells anywhere from 250 to 500 units. Many sell less than that, because the outliers that are selling millions of copies skew those numbers up.

I got into bookselling because I love reading, and I love books, and there's nothing quite like connecting the right reader to the right book. But let me walk you through the process of how a book gets to the market in the traditional realm. This is a high level "average" look, but it's not atypical.

First, millions of manuscripts are submitted to publishers that go into what's known as a "slush pile." At larger publishing houses, editorial interns open and look at the submissions, and often read no more than the first five pages before rejecting them. Those rejections are often form rejections. A slip of paper that says "thanks, but no thanks," or "not for us" or something pretty vague because it is, after all, a form and impersonal rejection.

An exceedingly small percentage of those books gets passed along to the appropriate editors. Each editor then rejects most of the manuscripts they are given, and some might offer a rejection form with a checklist for why they might not have accepted it, or, even, if the editor found merit in the work, a hand-written or typed personal note. That same editor also likely has manuscripts from several agents whose submissions go into a much smaller slush pile. And, while those manuscripts may have bypassed the initial "entry-level" intern or assistant-editor reading, (even though they did go through a pre-screening and slush pile of their own at the agency) they still have to get through that editor's decision before it makes it to the editorial board pitch.

The editors get together in a board meeting, each with their selection of titles. For the sake of numbers (which I'm completely making up here) maybe there are, for a specific imprint, 100 available spots that season, with 10 editors that have brought 30 titles each to the table. That's 300 books deemed worthy via all those levels of curation. 200 of those titles will then get rejected, and this is where the rejection often will come with a much more detailed personal response from the editor.

Then those 100 books get signed to go through the production cycle with publication being as much as one to two years out on average. They are scheduled into a seasonal printed catalog with book cover, possibly other images (for the larger titles), and marketing copy meant to appeal to the book buyers at chain and independent bookstores. The editorial and/or marketing teams review those titles with the sales reps. The catalogs are mailed to bookstores, chain buyers, librarians, and the regional sales reps then schedule meetings with some of the booksellers.

During their sales call meeting (which might be one hour or perhaps a half hour), the sales rep takes that catalog of 100 titles and will typically spotlight or highlight maybe 10 to 25 titles they think will perform well for that bookstore. Or, when pitching to a chain buyer, they might identify which titles will do well in different regions/sizes/formats for their stores. But rarely do they highlight or spotlight all 100 titles.

From that sub-set of highlighted titles, and perhaps one or two others not highlighted that the bookstore buyer finds on their own (if they have the time to peruse, which is rare considering they usually have a seasonal stack of hundreds of catalogs), an order is placed with the publisher or distributor. You must remember that there is limited space and budget, that maybe, of those 100 titles, only 15 may actually be ordered in.

Then, 3 to 6 months later, the books arrive and are shelved in the store. If the order quality was over 3 copies, the books will be faced out in its section in the store and potentially even featured for a week, maybe even as long as a month, in a more prominent section of the store. In the case of many larger and chain stores, the majority of those feature spots might only be due to paid placement (sometimes referred to as co-op space) from the publisher or wholesaler.

Paid spots are often for a small percentage of those 100 titles that the publisher has put most of its faith into. Often, it's those titles from existing big names with a track record of already selling millions, or where the author was paid a significant advance. Those titles would also get larger feature spots in the publisher catalog and usually appear on the catalog cover too. The publisher, after all, wants to earn back their investment in the authors who were paid the biggest advances. They are putting most of their chips on those spaces on the board for when the roulette wheel of publishing spins.

In addition, the publicist at the publisher is more apt to be actively looking to support those new titles in the one to two months leading to publication, and often in the first month or so of the book's release. Like the co-op placement, they're likely to apply most their focus to the big-name authors, or the titles where there was a major advance paid out. If you're not that big name author, you're almost like an extra on the set of one of those last couple of Avengers all-star blockbusters movie shoots. You help fill the scene, but everyone is focused on the major actors like Robert Downey Jr., Brie Larson, Don Cheadle, Chris Evans, Scarlett Johansson, or Chris Hemsworth. If a newer or lesser known or mid-list author is local or regional, the publicist might try to help set up bookstore appearances and local media engagements. Press releases might be sent out to local media and advance reader copies (ARCs) might also be sent out. Again, ARCs are often only created and sent out for the major titles.

(Major ARCs, by the way, look different than the final copy. They often get sent out 6 months prior to the book's release, sometimes further back. Some might not even have the final artwork on the cover, and many have a back cover that includes marketing information about the book. These are designed to highlight just how hard the publisher is working to make the book a success.)

One publisher I worked with asked me to provide a detailed spreadsheet of contact names of media, bookstores, influencers etc. associated with the forthcoming book that included phone numbers, addresses. I had been under the impression they were going to be sending advance copies of the book to all of those contacts, but only found out, many books later, that rarely is the case. I stopped investing so much time in creating lists like that for them and ended up sending out my own copies to the booksellers and reviewers/etc. that I wanted to ensure saw the book. They never created special early ARCs of my books. I was never a big enough name for them. A special ARC edition of a book has its own ISBN and the back cover copy is marketing info about the book directed at bookstores, libraries, and media. When they did send out advance reader copies for any of my books, it was merely the final edition of the book sent prior to the book's release.

After 6 to 9 months, as many as 50 to 80% of those titles ordered on bookstore shelves will be returned back to the publisher, unsold. Because remember, that buyer has limited space for new titles, which they are constantly looking, and so has to look at sales reports to determine the titles that aren't moving and should be returned. Books that sell quickly are often re-ordered. Some others that sell fall through the cracks, because plenty will sell a single copy that get missed in those daily, weekly, monthly reports. Trust me, I did this for years. I missed great titles all the time. I had limited time and so often attended to the quickly moving or high-volume selling titles. Sometimes a staff member would alert me to a title or author that sold out, and would suggest bringing it back in. But that was rare. Many get overlooked.

Yes, this is just an example, and a high-level view at that. But I'm using it to illustrate how elusive marketing can be within traditional publishing.

Even if a publisher picks up your title, the marketing and promotion you receive is often going to be caught somewhere in the mix. Unless the publisher paid a significant advance for your book, you're flying coach economy, not business class, not first class, as you're jammed in right beside that sweaty guy with putrid B.O. who makes funny noises breathing through his nose. They might even run out of those little bags of pretzels by the time the service comes around to you.

This means that the onus of rising out of that catalog comes back to you.

Are you just going to have the title listed and available? Or are you going to do what you can to help the right readers become aware that your book is out there on those physical and virtual bookstore shelves?

That's the reality of what it's like for most traditionally published authors. That's the reality of what it has always been like for most traditionally published authors.

So, let's stop pretending and dreaming of some mythical magical times. It was only magical for the authors at the front/top of those catalogs. Everyone else was flying economy or maybe even in the cargo hold. And I suppose they felt lucky when they started to think about the millions of authors stuck at the airport looking at a cancelation board and wondering if their flight might never arrive.

Things are different now.

Authors have the option of bypassing those slush piles and the myriad of gatekeepers and curators and can get their books into the catalog either directly or through third party distribution services.

And, yes, in the digital environment especially, with fewer gatekeepers, and people taking slices of the distribution pie, an indie author can keep upwards of 70% of the retail price of a book that sells, compared with the 8 to 15% that's more typical in the traditional publishing realm. Yes, even on eBooks, where there are far fewer people with their fingers in the pie, the publisher still keeps the majority share. Because, for most of them, their contracts and numbers are based on systems where the publisher usually only keeps 30 to 40% of the retail price, and, in there, has to pay for editors, marketing, sales reps, and their expensive New York and London based office buildings before they pay the author.

But, if you thought it was a packed flight of flying sardines in traditional publishing, once you get into eBooks, you're now looking at a flight that has room for several folks who will fly first class. That's where you'll see folks from the indie publishing scene whose names you might immediately recognize. The next section, business class, is far larger on this flight, with thousands more earning high five figure and six figure incomes from their writing. You'll never know the names of most of these authors.

But ultra-economy coach is where you'll most likely find yourself. And there are millions of authors impossibly jammed in there. Crammed in even tighter than you ever thought possible, in a gigantic marketplace that the industry never imaged could take flight.

What you find truly stunning is that stuck in that uber-economy section are some of the best writers you'll ever read; truly marvelous talents with phenomenal books, sitting right beside tired hacks and lazy first-draft wannabes who slap anything and everything they write up without any sort of editorial consideration.

It seems like a dismal picture. And I painted it because I want you to see the reality. Yes, there aren't as many hurdles and gatekeepers to get past in order to get your book out there. But at least you have your book listed and available, ideally, if you're truly a WIDE author, in at least 170 countries around the world.

Now that it's in there, you're actually not all that different from the mid-list or newbie author with a single title on the shelves of a massive big-box bookstore. Of course, your book is in virtual stock, and doesn't have the threat of being returned. (So there's a minor perk right there). And your fight to be seen is perhaps harder, because you don't even have the tactile and in person experience of holding and touching a book and seeing the cover art in its full 6 X 9 front cover art glory. You're relegated to a thumbnail glance at the cover (if you're lucky enough to be seen in search or browse results), a split-second decision to click it or pass it by, then, again, if the cover does the trick, a fast read-thru of the top of your book's description/sales copy.

Remember that bookstore buyer that spent time and effort, with the support of their sales reps, choosing titles they should invest in to put on their shelves? There was a lot of manual thought and conscious effort there, and even then, the majority of those titles fizzle and fade into obscurity.

In the case of digital books, either eBooks or print-on-demand (POD) titles, there weren't really any gatekeepers or filters. Pretty much everyone gets in. Which means that there's quite the uphill battle to climb to be seen.

For Amazon, the majority of the visibility of a title is based on algorithms. And Amazon rarely ever shares anything useful about what or how those algorithms work. An entire industry of companies exist whose sole purpose is to profit from analysing and selling services to authors to help decipher and interpret the smoke-and-mirrors of their constantly changing systems. If you've heard the analogy of the only people guaranteed to make money during the Yukon Gold Rush were the people selling shovels, it's even more challenging now. Because these poor folks are constantly having to re-invent the shovels they sell because Amazon keeps changing the landscape and structure between soil, rock, clay, snow, water, and ice.

Most authors have invested in those shovels. But those digging and mining implements have mostly been focused on Amazon, and Amazon alone. It's almost impossible to find any operators who have invested any energy in deciphering the algorithms or structures of the other major retailer sites.

But here's where the glimmer of good news comes for you. I'm glad you were able to bear with me through the scary and realistic portrait I've been painting, because there is some hope. It comes with hard work. But at least there's hope.

While the other major retailers do have algorithms in play, they also have a more direct involvement of human curation. Many call that act "merchandising" which is based upon the "merchandising" that happens in physical retail space.

Yes, their catalogs have millions more titles than could ever appear in the limited space of bookstore shelves. But they have to try to make it easier for their customers to find the right titles.

Amazon bases their "curation" upon an undefined and constantly evolving sophisticated set of algorithms focused on directing the right customers to that elusive "buy" button. They've created an environment with Amazon Advertising and other tools, that is "pay to play." Like in traditional publishing, where the major publishing houses, with millions of dollars to spend on marketing, scoop up all that marketing space, all the highly visible end-caps, tables, and wall displays, so too do the big names, often the ones selling authors on how everyone can make it big, dominate those places.

Yeah, the ones who are flying in first class on the indie-author flight and generously sharing how they did it and how you can do it too, are, also spending hundreds of thousands of dollars on marketing on Amazon in order to bring in those six and seven figure incomes. While I admire and applaud any successful author who wants to pay it forward and help other authors—and truly do believe that they are honestly trying to help others—I'm also a bit leery of that kind of talk. To me, it might be like Penguin Random House (a company valued at €3.3 billion in 2017) telling Kelly Sole Proprietorship how to bid for the same co-op space with their $5 a day marketing budget that PRH is throwing thousands of dollars a day at.

The WIDE retailers, on the other hand, are far more traditional in their approach. Nook and Kobo were both born directly out of the physical bookselling environments. Nook came from Barnes & Noble, a major national book chain in the US, and Kobo was born out of Indigo Books and Music, a major national book chain in Canada. In addition, Kobo has connections with major book retailers in many countries, such as WHSmith and Waterstones in the UK, and Angus & Robertson in AU.

There is some curation. But instead of doing it from the slush pile of millions of manuscripts in their mailroom, they're doing it from the slush pile of millions of books sitting in their live catalogs.

Now, if you're an indie author and you're wondering why I went into such detail about how curation, and marketing, and catalogs, and sales reps, and buying decisions get made, you might now see there was a point to that.

You can, perhaps, understand a bit about what might go into that "publicity and marketing" a publisher does. And how most of those other WIDE retailers operate.

Because it's within those operations that you can begin to differentiate yourself from among the masses.

Now, before we go on, I want you to remember something important. The reality is that retailers and distributors will look to find titles to prop up and put in front of customers.

But at the end of the day, that's all they do. They don't buy your books, and they don't really do much more to promote YOUR books apart from the curation they do to put it into a promotional campaign along with anywhere from 50 to 5000 other titles.

They create promos and landing pages and carousels and emails all kinds of things with selections of titles thinking ONLY of their customers.

They will, quite regularly, push and promote titles that are already selling. (I know, self-fulfilling prophecy).

All the major retailers allow virtually anybody to publish almost anything they want (legally, of course). They do that for free, because for every 100 titles that are published a small handful of them actually make money.

And yes, the retailer and/or distributor (most of them) only make money when the authors sell, so they DO want authors to sell. But they care more about the right book being shown to the right customer than specifically selling YOUR book.

The majority of the non-Amazon platforms use a combination of human touch and algorithms to determine these things. Sometimes one kick-starts the other. That's why behaving and engaging professionally and trying many promotional options (ie, ones the retailer/distributor/etc makes available and other third-party promotional options - BookBub, Written Word Media, Facebook Ads, etc) are a good idea.

And just to be clear, I'm not trying to rain on any parades, just trying to share a perspective of the uphill climb. Selling and promoting and marketing the book takes as much work, learning, effort, and persistence as writing and editing and publishing the book.

But magic can happen when the right customers find the book.

In the next section of this book, I'm going to review some things that you can do, when you understand the wide retailers and publishing platforms a bit better, to help create better conditions for that magic to happen.

# PART II
# RETAIL PLATFORMS

# Direct VS Distribution

You might think that launching one of the direct eBook retailer platforms, as well as the work I do at one of the largest digital distribution platforms is going to bias my perspective on this in an interesting way.

And you're probably right about that.

I do have a bias. We all do. Even when we don't recognize it.

But considering I have a positive bias towards both direct and distribution, how do you suppose that is going to shake out?

It's pretty simple, actually.

And it's similarly complicated.

So, what do I recommend to authors when they ask me for advice on which route to choose?

*It depends.*

Yeah, I know. That's not much of an answer. But allow me to explain.

There are definite pros to publishing direct. There are also definite cons. In the same fashion, using a third-party distribution platform has its own pros and cons. The trick is to leverage those specific pros and cons within the goals, plans, strategies, and tactics you want to employ for every single book you publish.

In the same way that there's no single publishing path for every one of your books, there's no single distribution strategy that works best all the time. There's only that specific project, that book, that particular IP and how you plan on leveraging it.

Let me take a step back.

For every book you write, according to my personal definition of WIDE, you determine how you want to leverage, employ, utilize, license that specific IP in all of its possible incarnations and formats.

One of the many choices you have is between traditional publishing (selling or licensing your rights to a publisher in exchange for money and distribution), and indie publishing (maintaining those rights and choosing your own distribution and keeping a larger percentage of the income from sales).

But even when you're making that choice for a single book, you still have options that aren't necessarily the same. You might:

- license the print rights to a publisher in one country or global region.
- retain print rights in other global territories.
- maintain global eBook rights.
- license the audio rights exclusively to a publisher or retailer.

So, for a single book, you've taken a hybrid approach, ideally based on the calculations you have done based on a combination of maximizing reader reach, unit sales, and revenues earned.

Looking at just one aspect of that book, the eBook, you similarly don't have to take an "all or none" approach. You can choose to publish direct to some places and use a distribution platform for others. How you slice and dice these is completely up to you, assuming you have a basic understanding of how the pros and cons for each work in favor for you and, more importantly, for that specific book project.

Because your goals, plans, and strategies might just be different for different products.

And that's okay.

## Clarification of Definitions

Before going any further, I thought I'd take the time to ensure we're on the same page with the terms DIRECT and DISTRIBUTOR. So, to that end, let me share the definitions I'm using for the purposes of this discussion.

- **DIRECT**—A platform that is owned and managed directly by the retailer/library/subscription service.

Some examples of direct publishing platforms available would be: *Kindle Direct Publishing* (KDP) for publishing direct to Amazon Kindle (eBook) and Amazon (print), and *Kobo Writing Life* (KWL) for publishing direct to Rakuten Kobo, Inc. (eBook and Audiobook)

- **DISTRIBUTOR**—A platform that is owned and managed by a company independent of any retailer.

Some examples of distributors would be: *Smashwords, Draft2Digital, StreetLib, and PublishDrive.*

Of course, even within these simple definitions there are odd hybrid things taking place that I think are important for you to be aware of.

- **ACX** is owned by Audible Inc., an Amazon company, so might be considered a direct publishing platform, but is technically a distribution platform for audiobooks to Audible, Amazon Audiobooks, and Apple iTunes (Audiobooks).
- **Kobo Writing Life** is owned by Rakuten Kobo, Inc. and is, thus, a direct publishing platform. But Kobo itself has partnerships with dozens of bookstores around the globe and is, in many cases, a distributor of eBooks to those platforms. Similarly, because Kobo and OverDrive used to be owned by the same company (Rakuten), Kobo Writing Life can be used to distribute titles to OverDrive. This creates a unique hybrid situation

where KWL is both a direct platform and a type of third-party distributor.

- **Smashwords** is a distributor to multiple retailer and library platforms but also operates its own global web store. So, it's both a distributor and a retailer.
- **Findaway Voices** is a distribution platform for audiobooks to over 40 different retail and library channels (including Audible and Apple iTunes), but it also has an "Author's Direct" option which is, in and of itself, a retail platform for audiobooks.

## Determining Factors

What are some factors that might help you decide direct versus distribution?

Here are a few things to consider. Just remember, there's no one answer for every single project you are publishing. For one book and your goals with it, one element might outweigh the others; but for a different one, that element might not be as meaningful

- **Control**
- **Speed of Updates**
- **Margin/Revenue**
- **Reporting**
- **Marketing & Promotions**
- **Security**

- **Time & Labor**
- **Eggs & Baskets**

Let's break these down and explore them in a bit more detail.

### *Control*

When you publish direct, you typically have tighter control over updates to such things as pricing and metadata. In some cases, there are fields you can enter directly that might not be available on a distribution platform.

When you publish through a third-party distributor, you are making updates to a centralized system that is feeding those updates downstream to the various retail or library channels that consumers interact with. Depending on the relationship that each distribution platform has with specific retailers and library systems, some of the fields you edit/update may or may not affect the downstream channel in question.

There are cases where you may have options available direct that you do not have with a third party, such as when *Kindle Direct Publishing* offered the Kindle Matchbook program (discontinued in 2019) that allowed authors and publishers the option of setting a special eBook price that would be used to combine a Kindle eBook with a print book sold by Amazon. The eBook could be given away for free, or sold for $1.99 or $0.99.

Alternatively, sometimes a third-party distribution platform allows you possibilities that aren't available when you publish direct. For example, you can't price a book at $0.00 when publishing directly with *Barnes & Noble Press* but you can when using a third-party distributor.

Like many things, it's not a cut-and-dry thing. While a platform like *Kobo Writing Life* has the ability for authors to schedule a price update in advance (so that a specific book may, for example, drop to $0.99 USD, CAD, AUD, GBP, EUR on July 1st and then return back to regular price the very next day), *Kindle Direct Publishing* does not offer that. Authors wanting to schedule promos and special temporary sales would have to log onto *KDP* and make the change close to the planned time. With very little precision, since the update time will depend on the "traffic of updates" flowing through that retail system. Some third-party distribution systems offer price scheduling. For example, *Draft2Digital* and *PublishDrive* both offer a price scheduling tool that can pre-schedule price changes to all the major downstream retailers, resulting in the submission of precise scheduled control.

### *Speed of Updates*

Similar to the element of control, when you publish direct, you typically see updates, such as price changes revised covers, and modified descriptions. happening in the quickest time-frame possible. Your update on price or metadata is usually flowing within an internal system that, in most cases, has an advantage over third party systems. Direct updates might take as little as one to six hours to be visible to the customer-facing catalog.

Because third-party distributors are even further removed and in a completely unique ecosystem, updates typically take longer. But this is not always the case.

Just be aware that, because of the typical extra time for data-flow to occur between a third party distribution platform and a retailer or library, that you might need to buffer in extra time to see those changes. One exception, as mentioned in **Control** above, would be platforms like *Draft2Digital* that allow for scheduling price changes. When an author plans those in advance, the metadata is submitted ahead of time to the retailer, and the price change can happen exactly at 12:01 AM local time for the specified date in the update.

### *Margin / Revenue*

It makes sense that when you go direct to a platform, you'll earn a bit more than when you publish to that platform via an external platform. As is the reality in the retail supply chain, the more players and layers between you and the consumer, the more each level takes its cut or share from the margin that makes its way into your pocket.

There is an exception to this, where you can actually earn **more** via a third-party distributor than when you publish directly, but I'll explore that at the end of this section, after I lay out the standard landscape we're looking at.

While these numbers might change slightly, you typically earn 70% of the retail price when you publish direct. Third party distributors usually keep about 10% of that. That is typically the only time they make money; because the setup for most distributors is that you can use their platform for free, and if you sell, they make money. If you don't sell, they don't make anything from you.

It's a decent, no risk option. But that 10% can really add up. Ten cents for every dollar earned goes toward that middle-player in the equation. It's only ten cents. But when you translate that to $100, suddenly you're looking at a cost of $10. And if you're talking $1000, that cost is now $100. (The math is easy, so I'm sure you can continue to extrapolate the 10% at higher numbers) As we will explore in **Time & Labor** that 10% might be well worth it in the end, even when you're talking about earnings of $10,000 and $100,000 dollars; but it's important to be aware of that 10%

I should also pause to clarify that while the default status of the main distribution platforms (*Draft2Digital, PublishDrive, StreetLib, Smashwords*) take pretty much the same cut (approximately 10%), different platforms perform the math differently. *Smashwords,* for example, takes 10% off the retail price **before** the retailer takes their cut. *Draft2Digital* takes 15% off **after** the storefront takes their share. It works out to, within pennies, virtually the same, which is about 10%.

One exception to this 10% is related to a change *PublishDrive* made in September of 2019. Except for a grandfathered clause that some authors can take advantage of, this platform no longer offers royalty share as an option for new accounts. Instead, they introduced a tiered subscription plan that authors pay up front and then keep the full 70% they would get when publishing direct.

As of early 2021, the plans are $9.99 USD/month for a STARTER plan (allowing you to publish up to 2 titles); $19.99 USD/month for a STANDARD plan (6 titles); $49.99 USD/month for a PLUS plan (24 titles); and $99.99/month for a PRO plan (48 titles). These plans are only worth considering if you are earning a particular minimum on the number of titles in question on a monthly basis. One thing to remember, of course, is that, if you publish a book in January, you have to pay $9.99. But you don't earn money on your sales until anywhere from 45 to 90 days later. So you're paying up front, typically with a credit card, and not earning on any sales (if you get any sales) until well after you've been out of pocket for a couple of months on a high credit borrowing system. While this plan ensures you know exactly how much publishing will cost you, you are **always** paying up front regardless of whether sales actually happen. You have to do the math and consider the risk to see if it's worth it for you.

Let's go back to the standard 10% model and the assumption you made that using a third-party distributor will always earn you more. That is not always the case.

Because it's a bit complicated, let's lay out the structure that exists for direct to retailer.

On Amazon *KDP*, if you price between $2.99 and $9.99 USD, you get 70%. If you price above $9.99 USD, your earnings drop to 35%. On *Kobo Writing Life*, and *Apple Books for Authors*, you still earn 70% when you price above $9.99 USD. On *Barnes & Noble Press*, you earn 65% for books priced from $2.99 to $199.99. You cannot price above that on B&N.

If you price anywhere from $0.99 to $2.98 or above $9.99, you only earn 35% on *KDP*. On *Kobo Writing Life* you earn 45%, on *Barnes & Noble Press* you earn 40%, and on *Apple Books Author* you earn 70%.

Pricing from $0.99 to $2.98 through *Draft2Digital* on Kindle earns you 30% (5% less than direct). But, regardless of price point, if you use *Draft2Digital* to publish to Apple, Nook, or Kobo, you earn 60%. This means that there's a benefit in terms of earned margin/revenue for books priced from $0.99 to $2.98 when distributed to Kobo and Nook versus direct.

Yeah, I know, it's a lot of math and a lot of numbers. But it's important that you're aware of the actual numbers and margin involved as part of deciding what's best for you.

### *Reporting*

When you are publishing direct, you typically can see either "real time" or at least close to "real time" sales data. The direct dashboard is often showing you details within the hour of a sale happening.

If you are publishing using a third-party distribution platform, the availability of that near-real-time data is limited. Yes, there are some retailers that can and do provide updates that might appear hours later, but for the most part, sales will be coming in the next day.

There are some benefits and features within direct dashboards that can be useful. For example, the global map that appears on the *Kobo Writing Life* dashboard is a feature that authors appreciate. (You're welcome—I'm very proud that I pushed for it when creating *KWL*—if you really want you can thank me by pushing hard to sell in all 170 countries represented on that dashboard). *Google Play* has, in the latter half of 2020, expanded and improved their online reporting dramatically, with an update to their home screen and the analytics tab.

One benefit you get from using a third party is the possibility of seeing the sales from multiple retailers, library, and subscription service platforms in a single report; making it easier to get a larger picture of your sales analytics. One of the handy reports I've been using in the flexible custom reporting tools (tools that are almost too flexible and powerful so as to be a bit overwhelming to use) in the *Draft2Digital* dashboard include sales by units or revenue from all sales channels.

For example, if I quickly look at the entire "last year" which would be 2020 at the time of writing this, on Draft2Digital, I can see the 9 different sales channels I had sales in on one screen, including the *D2D Print* (in beta at the time of this writing) and easily toggled between unit sales and estimated royalties earned.

There are, of course, third party reporting analytical tools such as *BookTrakr* or *Scribecount*. (You'll notice I didn't mention any of the ones that are *KDP* only. Yep. That's just a reminder that, if you have an actual wide-mindset, anything that's Amazon-only should be less interesting, less important, less prevalent, less useful)

Reporting is important. Understanding which of your books are selling, and where they're selling, and how much you are earning, and all the associated analytics are a critical component of running a successful author business. But I wanted to pause to throw a little caveat out. While it's important to be measuring the results of promotions activity, advertising, and related activities, how much is too much? How often is too often? Are you actually obsessing and wasting time logging onto a dashboard and hitting the refresh button every hour? To what end, other than personal vanity? I mean, with every single view and refresh are you going and adjusting the settings of an ad you're on control of?

I'm not saying that sitting and watching sales go up isn't personally satisfying. There are happy dances, perhaps celebratory drinks, social media boasting, and the like to be had. But let's take a moment to be honest with ourselves and the world. Seeing those sales in "real time" is more for the benefit of your ego and a quick indulgent "rush" or quick fix than it is for any strategic and pragmatic purpose.

### *Marketing & Promotions*

This is a big one. And I doubt that will ever change.

Before I get into the details of marketing and promotion differences between direct versus distribution, allow me to take a bit of an aside regarding the need for engaging in promotional activity.

You might hear some indie authors pining about what they consider "the good old days" of digital publishing. As the legends go, all you had to do was publish any eBook, put it on Amazon, and watch the money roll in.

Perhaps some of that was true. But be leery of such talk.

In those days, you could slap almost any image onto a manuscript with little to no editing and bring in some cash with it because your $0.99 novel's faults were overlooked by consumers who were thrilled to be able to read something on their *Kindle, Nook,* or *Kobo* that didn't cost them $35.

With increased competition came an increase in quality. Suddenly, making your book $0.99 wasn't going to cut it if the cover, blurb, and the quality of the writing itself weren't the best it could be. Because your competition wasn't other digital pulp titles hastily slapped together, but they were carefully edited and polished works that effectively stood on their own against the titles from major publishing houses and were also priced at less than the cost of a coffee.

Consumers expect, and deserve, more than just a hastily slapped together hack job.

But, because anyone can publish virtually anything they want, for free, and get their titles into the catalogs of the world's largest digital and online bookstores, something has to separate the wheat from the chaff. Marketing and promotions are one way to do that.

Many of the platforms have marketing and promotions that you can't get when you publish to their platforms through a third party, or even, when a title is traditionally published to that platform.

*Apple Books for Authors* doesn't have any built-in or DIY promotions available. By default they don't interact directly with authors using their direct platform, but will contact authors when it suits their needs. Among all the retailers, they are the most accommodating and agnostic when it comes to the "direct vs distribution" debate. They work collaboratively with most of the third-party distributors to solicit for promotions and don't care whether an author is direct with them.

*B&N Press* offers authors access to promotions when they are published direct. Authors have to request to have promotion access added to their account, and not all authors who request that access are given it. The team hasn't publicly revealed the factors they consider, but I would imagine they are likely looking at the author's overall professional persona, both the professionalism attached to their books and also the professional (or non-professional) behavior they engage in.

*Kindle Direct Publishing* has a couple of promotional options that are only available to authors who are exclusive within their *KDP Select* program; specifically, they are the ability to make a book free for up to 5 days, or creating a countdown deal with every 90 days of exclusivity. Those options are not available to wide authors. For wide authors publishing direct *KDP* has *Amazon Advertising* (formerly known and often still referred to in many indie publishing circles as *AMS* - which is short for *Amazon Marketing Services*) which (with one exception noted below) is only available when you are publishing direct.

*Kobo Writing Life* has a promotions tab built-in and authors publishing direct can get access to promotional opportunities not available to titles from third-party distributors and most traditional publishers. They also may occasionally email authors who publish direct via *KWL* with other promotion (such as "Buy More/Save More" style promos) that don't appear in their online dashboard.

*Google Play* has the option for authors to create their own promo codes to offer books to customers. You can run up to 3 promotions every month and set a code per customer, or create a single use code with a limit of 5000 redemptions. The coupon codes are flexible and allow for a discount off, or for a free download. They even create a specific landing page that authors can use to direct customers to.

*Smashwords* offers a few annual big sales for direct publishing authors to their retail platform; and they also offer sales to some major retail and library channels that are made available to authors using them to publish to those platforms. And because *Smashwords* is, in itself, also a retail platform, they have a DIY coupon manager where authors can make coupon codes to eBooks. Coupons can be cancelled or reactivated, extended or shortened in terms of expiration dates; the discount can even be changed. There's an option to create public coupons, which appear automatically on your Smashwords eBook page, offering everyone the discount. Books with public coupons will also be listed in the "Special Deals" section of the *Smashwords* catalog while your coupon is active.

*PublishDrive* offers similar promotions, and even has a few built in functions for promotions, including a quick-link to a few of Written Word Media's more popular offerings (FreeBooksy, BargainBooksy, and Red Feather Romance). They also have the built-in ability to run Amazon Ads without leaving their platform, which is pretty slick. This appears to be the only third-party distribution platform that allows an author to run ads on titles that are not published directly to Amazon through KDP.

I was also impressed with how *PublishDrive* allows you to run an ad on a title that isn't published through their platform. **Traditionally published authors also take note here**: this might be the only platform you can use to advertise your traditionally published titles via Amazon ads. You should be aware that, unlike with direct Amazon Ads, you will be out of pocket the full budgeted amount immediately, rather than over the duration of the ad run. If, for example, your budget is $5.00 per day for 30 days, when using Amazon directly, the money is charged on the go and you'd be charged $150 at the end of the cycle. But using this *PD* internal tool, you pay the full amount up front.

*Draft2Digital* has a promotions tab that, at the time of this writing, is used for scheduling price promotions and price changes well ahead of the planned promotion days. In 2020 they hired a full-time person specifically for working on curating titles for promotions with their retail and library partners, and most often get promotions for Apple Books, OverDrive, and Kobo. Much of the curation is done manually through external forms that authors have to fill out, but I'm intimately aware that they are working on longer-term projects that will allow for authors to apply for and nominate titles for promotions within their dashboard.

In the meantime, if you want access to the various promotions or be added to the list of authors receiving promo invites, email them at support@draft2digital.com and request you be added to their currently manually managed lists.

### *Security*

Something to consider, when you are creating an account, is the security of a platform.

A platform that has some sort of enhanced or two-factor authentication might be more secure than another factor to consider. Remember, one of the major retailers (Barnes & Noble) suffered under a massive hack in the fall of 2020 that, as of the time of this writing in early 2021, they are still recovering from. (Note: There is no evidence that any author data was breached in this hack. But it is good to be reminded about security in general).

Beyond basic security measures and protocols, there are two other elements to consider.

*Multiple User Access* and *Connected Retailer Account*.

The first refers to having another person help to manage your account. The second relates to whether or not your publishing account is connected to your purchasing account at that retailer.

When you are setting up an account to use on your own, neither of these may be an issue. But if you reach a point where hiring a virtual assistant or some other professional to help manage your account for you, it's good to understand if you'll need to provide that person with your login and password information, or if the system allows for the assignment of a "child" account with specific roles.

I'll start with the world's biggest bookstore, Amazon, and *Kindle Direct Publishing* to use as an example, because that's cut and dry and clear (at least at the time of this writing).

Your *KDP* account does not allow for you to create any sort of child account to assign roles. Which means, if you use a virtual assistant, you have to give them your personal login and password.

(*I should also note that, in doing so, you may be violating section 4.3 of the Amazon KDP Terms and Conditions agreement, which states the following: "You may not permit any third party to use the Program through your account and will not use the account of any third party."*)

When someone has your login and password, they can see and edit/control your banking and tax information. But not only that, if your retail purchasing account is connected to your publishing account, they can actually make purchases with your connected credit card. And don't forget that Amazon isn't just the world's biggest bookstore, it's the "everything store." There are plenty of large-ticket items available.

I'm not saying that the honest, hard-working, and trustworthy person you hired would ever do such things; I'm just pointing out the potential security issues involved.

*Apple Books for Authors* and *Google Play* are the only direct publishing platforms that offer users the security enhanced option of allowing other people to access your account, with a unique login and password and specifically assigned access. For example, your main author account within iTunes Connect (the platform used to manage your direct publishing) is the main Admin access account. But you can assign other people/emails roles that include: Finance, Technical, Legal, Read-Only, and Sales. This could allow different people or companies you work with (ie, an accountant, marketing expert, virtual assistant, cover designer, etc) the ability to either see or update specific things in your account.

*Draft2Digital* is the only major third-party distributor that offers a similar extremely flexible option. There is an Account Sharing feature that allows authors to assign multiple different people the ability to manage their book data or manage their reporting. One virtual assistant can have access to multiple different author accounts with the same single login, easily logging between accounts without having to log off and log on again. *PublishDrive* offers a similar feature, but a single virtual assistant can only be assigned to one account. So would need to have multiple email logins to work with more than one author.

### *Time and Labor*

One of the factors that authors sometimes don't consider is the time and labor involved in having to manage multiple accounts for a single title. It might not be an issue with one or maybe a handful of books. But what about managing a larger number of titles? What about having to make the same changes on at least five major retail platforms, potentially a few other smaller ones, in addition to the most likely third-party distribution options to get into even smaller retail platforms, subscription services, and the library market.

To update a single title requires potentially having multiple versions of that ePub to manage (ie, with unique retailer/market links in the back of each version—unless you are using some sort of universal book link or only linking back to your own website). So any time you do a price promotion or update, you're making the same update multiple times. It's worth looking at how long that actually takes, and what your time is worth. What if you are looking to update the back matter links in all your previously published titles to include the latest release? Or some other massive overhaul of metadata or pricing?

Does that 10% add up to more, or less, than the time you invested in that work. Consider where else you could have invested that time. Writing, marketing, relaxing?

There is, of course, no one answer.

Just the answer that works best for you.

### *Eggs & Baskets*

Let's not forget the reason you are reading this book: the premise that you're not keeping all of your eggs in one basket.

Yes, I know that, earlier in this book, I talked about quantum eggs and quantum baskets, but let's re-simplify the concept regarding distribution.

If a distributor folds, goes bankrupt, or in some other way, disappears or changes businesses, if you're all in with them, where does that leave you? Fortunately, it's not as if your rights are locked in or trapped, and you'll have the ability to move your titles to another distributor or direct. But that means labor and starting over.

Then again, there are always interesting exceptions where distribution could actually be a benefit in some cases where a retailer is the one who falters. In the spring of 2020, *Barnes & Noble* ran into some cash-flow issues when, because of the global pandemic they had to close most their big box stores in high rent locations across the United States. The result was an expected delay in payments to many of their larger publisher accounts. As *Draft2Digital* shared in an update to their authors, in a demonstration of good faith that *Barnes & Noble* would recover, and requesting authors to not delist their books from *Barnes & Noble* (as that would only make the situation worse) the company took out a line of credit in order to ensure authors were paid 100% of their owed royalties for February, rather than the expected partial payment on *Nook* sales. *Barnes & Noble* pulled through in the end, but one of their business partners was willing to step up and support the authors who maintained their faith in the large retailer. This is evidence that some baskets are made with material much stronger than the standard wicker.

Ultimately, though, perhaps a little bit of diversity in your publishing strategy might be a good idea. It might be worth considering a hybrid combination of going direct to some platforms and using distribution for others which could help circumvent such dependencies.

Personally speaking, I have eBooks direct with several of the retailers, as well as listed through *Smashwords, Draft2Digital, StreetLib,* and *PublishDrive*. This is a result of having been indie publishing since 2004, and my ongoing desire to learn about and personally experience the different platforms to ensure I'm making decisions informed by my own needs, my own experience, and my own preferences.

By default for a new title, I publish direct to Amazon via *KDP*, direct to Kobo via *KWL*, and I use *Draft2Digital* for all the other major platforms and library markets, and then fill in the other blanks with *Smashwords, StreetLib, and PublishDrive*.

Some of my titles, especially the ones where I'm leveraging payment splitting on eBook and print, are all-in with *Draft2Digital*.

Each book might have its own unique setup.

Your needs, your goals, your preferences will probably dictate how this element and others play into your own publishing strategy.

## The Difference Between Distributors and Vanity Publishing/Vanity Presses

This needs to be said, and in no uncertain terms.

I have a personal rule that anyone who calls themselves a publisher should have a business practice where the money flows TO the author, and not FROM the author.

Any company/platform/service offering that charges you money to publish your books to retailers and libraries, is likely a vanity publisher. Yes, they do distribute, but their business model is not to sell books, it's to sell services to authors. They make money regardless of whether you sell a single copy of your book or earn a single penny. And they always make money. Off of an author's hopes and dreams of "being published."

The reason these companies make billions of dollars is because they prey on ignorance.

They also engage in less than honest business practices.

Many will operate under the guise that they are a publisher. In fact, if you ever see a service calling themselves a "real publisher" that's a huge indicator that, to quote Hamlet, "methinks the lady doth protest too much." No real publisher has to call themselves that. Remember the concept of "show don't tell" for writers? The same is true for vanity publishers. Don't tell me you're a real publisher. Show me that you are. Penguin

Random House doesn't have to call themselves a "real publisher." But they pay authors advances and royalties and have warehousing and distribution and dedicated sales reps and catalogs of titles. That's what makes them real. Not false promises of marketing.

Publishers make money from their investment in an author up front, by things such as offering them an advance, editorial, formatting, and marketing support, and book sale royalties. If a book they publish does well, they, and the author, make money.

Distributors make money from their investment in an author up front, by offering free tools that authors can use to publish and distribute, along with perhaps links to trusted services, or additional marketing support, and book sale royalties. If a book they distribute does well, they, and the author, make money.

Vanity Presses make their money by charging the author for services to create, publish, and distribute their book. They make money regardless of whether a book sells.

There are a few notable exceptions to my rule of "author pays platform up front = platform is vanity publisher." Those would be *BookBaby* and *PublishDrive*. And this is because, while both platforms charge authors up front for the services of book formatting (and potentially other services such as editing and design) and distribution, they don't hide behind a false front. They are clear about what they are charging, and they don't position themselves to be something they are not. They also don't keep a share of the earned royalties, since they've already made their money up front. The main difference between places *BookBaby* and *PublishDrive* and *Smashwords* and *Draft2Digital* are that the former make their money from your publishing and marketing efforts, while the latter make their money only when you are successful in selling books.

## Additional Factors: Relationships & Loyalty

Something that I haven't mentioned, but which actually often plays a role in the decision(s) an author makes regarding going direct to a platform or in deciding a third-party distribution system is related to a couple of difficult to measure elements that plays a factor in virtually all business dealings.

Relationships and loyalty.

As authors move about the business of writing and publishing, they cultivate relationships with other authors and industry players. They get to know and like (or potentially dislike) the other people they encounter and communicate with, and those dealings may affect, and in some cases, even over-ride the analytical reasoning behind making specific decisions.

For example, if deciding to publish using method A actually makes more economical sense, but method B involves getting to work with someone you respect and admire, making an unbiased decision is a bit more difficult. Sure, business is business, but relationships and loyalty are definitely strong factors at play.

I'll use a few examples of my own to illustrate this.

I worked at Kobo from 2011 through 2017. I was there to create, launch, and build *Kobo Writing Life* into a successful business-within-a-business. After I left the role at the very end of 2017, I had many authors confess to me that the main reason they were publishing through Kobo's direct platform was because of the personal relationship that we had. Many express thy did it because I was, like them, an author, and because they knew the decisions I made when running that team would always put the author first. Some shared that they migrated from publishing to Kobo via a different method because of that trust and respect.

And that trust and respect came into play in a significant way during the late 2013 cock-up of a mess many know as either *EroticaGate* or *KoboGate*. That trust benefited Kobo and *Kobo Writing Life*. But it also benefited several authors I had positive relationships with.

But it started off a right bloody mess.

It's a day I'll never forget, and not just because it was my wedding anniversary and my wife at the time and I had just moved into a new house that we were still in the process of setting up.

On the weekend of Saturday October 12, 2013, WHSmith, the first retail chain in the world, (they had been around over 200 years) and the one responsible for the creation of the ISBN, shut down their entire website.

This was because their eBook catalog (which was powered by their partner, Rakuten Kobo) had been had let in a few nasty and even illegal types of erotica titles. A number of UK based newspapers posted about this, embarrassing the high street retailer into this act.

I was awoken early that morning by Kobo's CEO, Michael Tamblyn. It may have been 6 AM in the Eastern time zone, but it had already been a most eventful morning in the UK, with newspapers reporting the outrageous discovery of several quite disturbing erotic and pornographic titles. Business leaders in the UK and Canada were back and forth with each other. The minute a title was discovered, and taken down, another two were discovered and reported.

By the time I received my phone call, it had been discovered that the majority of these titles were coming from the self-publishing community, via *Kobo Writing Life, Smashwords, Draft2Digital, and others.*

I leapt out of bed and rushed to the old house we had just moved out of with my laptop because we didn't yet have an internet connection at the new place in order to scour the database and find the offending titles to take them down. But there were more—far more. It was like shoveling water trying to find and unpublish them using the admin tools I had access to. (I should also note that this was a long-weekend in Canada—Canada's Thanksgiving weekend. So getting ahold of anybody to connect and assist was extremely difficult.)

I learned that the titles in question that kept popping onto the radar had been in blatant violation of Kobo's stated content policy. But the systems hadn't been sophisticated enough to catch them. I felt personally responsible, for I had been charged with setting up the direct publishing platform. And I'd missed this crack.

By mid-morning, on a call with the executive team of Kobo to provide another hourly update, I was asked if I could verify that I had found and removed all offending titles.

There were hundreds of thousands of titles in question, and I had not been able to scan or review them all. Nor were the other two or three folks who were assisting me in various ways by offering reports and helping make updates to the catalog.

"No, I can't tell you that there might not be others still out there."

The decision was made, at that point, to pull the plug on ALL self-published titles in the catalog. All titles coming from any self-publishing distributor, and all titles published through *Kobo Writing Life* were shut down. They disappeared from the catalog.

This broke my heart.

I had spent the previous two years speaking and connecting with authors to get them to believe in Kobo and to put their faith in the company and in *Kobo Writing Life*.

And suddenly, all that faith, all that trust, was shattered with the single click of a few keystrokes. And through nothing sinister that I, nor the majority of those authors, had done.

I don't blame the Kobo executives; nor the WHSmith executives. They made the best decision they could for the integrity of their company's reputations. The specific sources could not be properly identified within the channels where the offending titles originated. So those entire streams had to be shut down to prevent the continued contamination of the entire ecosystem.

*Click.*

It was all over.

In a matter of mere moments, no self-published titles were live in the Kobo ecosystem.

But here's where relationships played a huge part for of several authors.

Within the first minute that the entire database had been shut down, I set about turning back on titles that I knew were NOT in violation of the issue at hand. One by one.

Who did I already have a personal relationship with? Who had I met and interacted with at conferences? Who did I know through podcasting and various online virtual author communities?

Joanna Penn, Bella Andre, Barbara Freethy, Tina Folsom, Hugh Howey, Orna Ross, David Gaughran, Patty Jansen, Lindsay Buroker, Johnny B. Truant, Sean Platt, David Wright, Kevin J. Anderson. The list went on and on.

I spent most of the next 12 hours manually turning on individual titles from these accounts and other titles I was manually looking through.

I had support from some of the dev team, where I was able to give them account names and IDs and get them to turn on entire account activations at once.

Let me pause to say that, this was a long weekend where my wife and I had been moving into a new house. The day before we had hired a moving company to get most of the large furniture moved, but we still had possession of our previous home until the end of the month. We were supposed to be spending the Saturday and Sunday with a smaller rented moving van getting the rest of the home's possessions moved.

I sat at the kitchen counter in a house devoid of furniture but with numerous boxes in piles all over, looking up and turning on titles one by one. Because these authors and thousands others I'd never met, had put their faith in me and in Kobo. And I didn't want to let them down.

In the meantime, my wife was continuing on with the moving of those smaller items, and the unpacking, all on her own, while looking after our young son, who was nine at the time. Fortunately, he was helping too.

Because we only had the use of the rental van for 48 hours, I took a break from turning titles back on and loaded it up to do a few runs between the old house and the new one. Then, close to 11 PM, I went back to working on the title curation for a few hours, before driving back home and collapsing into bed.

Only to get up at 6 AM the next day and begin it all over again.

The majority of the weekend was spent in this odd combination of title re-publishing, communications with the author community, and hauling boxes from the old house to the new one. During this time, I was also working on a message to the author community to be 100% transparent about what happened and why, as well as the steps being taken to resolve the matter as quickly as possible. There was a lot of hostility directed at Kobo. It was not a fun time to be the director of author relations.

The personal house move, which was supposed to be over by Sunday night, lasted the majority of the month of October, as much of the free time I had was spent looking at titles and turning back on anything that didn't look like it was in violation of the stated policy.

When the week started up, a huge number of the content team at Kobo stepped up to help, and we were all manually approving *Kobo Writing Life* titles and titles from the distributors who were collaborating on doing their own scouring and vetting to get their author titles turned back on. There were a lot of late nights involved, and plenty of hands on deck. We eventually got to everyone. But the ones we fixed first, the ones I did prioritize were those authors where I had a personal connection or relationship with.

And in that trying time, many of the authors who knew my integrity and the integrity of Kobo, which they believed in because of our relationships, stood up for *Kobo Writing Life*, for Kobo, and for me.

The power of loyalty and relationships.

In a similar matter, my relationships with the third-party distribution platform contacts, with Mark Coker at *Smashwords* and Dan Wood at *Draft2Digital* were strengthened. We all came together, in the interest of the authors we were serving, to ensuring the least amount of down-time for the titles that were not in violation of content policy.

I should note that everyone on the *Kobo Writing Life* team doubled down on efforts to ensure that proper filters and checks and balances were put into place to prevent that from ever happening again. And at Kobo we implemented a rating system for vendor accounts related to trustworthiness and integrity, that, should anything like that ever happen again, there'd be an easy way to say: "Okay, these accounts here, DON'T touch them. They're 100% trustworthy. These ones are probably trustworthy. These we have no idea. And these ones over here, we know for sure based on their standard modus operandi that we can't trust them."

Not every retailer or distributor has such systematic indicators in place. But I can guarantee you that the people who work there are playing attention to their own interactions with authors, and to the things authors do and say in online and public forums.

They're watching, and judging, and calculating your trustworthiness, your perceived integrity, based on everything you do and say. They are also paying attention to your loyalty.

And, in a crisis, I'm pretty sure they know who they'd stand up for without question, who they'd let fall, and who they realize they don't know enough about to say either way.

Let me give you an example. Let's say I'm trying to prioritize fixing or supporting a huge number of authors, and some of have been in and out of KDP Select like a rock star in an out of a rehab clinic, while others have been loyal and publishing wide from day one without wavering. Which ones do you think will always take priority in my book? No, I've never been a fan of the story of the Prodigal Son. Screw that splitter; my investment goes into the unwavering and loyal child.

And, on the flip side, for this is something that has happened in both my role working at a retailer and a distributor, the relationship can come into play in a positive way. A promotional opportunity might come up in which a merchandiser or marketing person is looking for a specific type of book or author and there isn't much time to do any hurting or running complex reports. The answer is needed right away to fill in the element they are looking for. It's the authors who are top-of-mind that get selected. Well, not just top-of-mind, but top-of-mind with a positive impression. Because, trust me, you don't want to be top-of-mind known as a thorn in the side, or pain in the you-know-what.

All this sidebar about loyalty, relationships, and the lengthy personal story shared are to hopefully help illustrate how integral and deep-rooted relationships and loyalty come into play.

And since it's virtually impossible to have relationships or connections with everyone, at the bare minimum, try, at the very least not to be a dick.

Because people **are** paying attention.

# eBooks

## Amazon Kindle

Because there are at least a hundred other books out there that focus 100% on publishing via Amazon Kindle, I'm not going to spend much time here. You can find countless tips in all those other books from folks who have studied Amazon far more effectively than I likely ever will.

But I will not ignore it, either.

I'll attempt to offer a bit of "Reader's Digest" style summary of Kindle Direct Publishing (KDP).

Because, let's be honest here: Amazon is the world's largest bookstore. And chances are that, even if you are very strategic and successful in your global and wide publishing plans, Kindle sales will represent a significant chunk of your author income from eBooks.

Let me skip to a few high-level things that are important to understand and which might not be talked about enough.

KDP is the direct publishing platform.

KDP Select is the optional exclusivity.

You might notice that you can't turn around when navigating KDP without seeing "enroll in KDP Select" buttons and options everywhere. It seems worse than Pepé Le Pew when it comes to accepting a polite "no" from authors who don't want to be locked into such a relationship.

## Royalty Structure

You have a choice between 35% and 70% royalties on titles you publish with KDP.

If your book is priced between $2.99 USD and $9.99 USD, then you are eligible for 70%. The book's list price must also be listed at 20% below the list price for the print version of the book.

Although, you never **really** earn the full 70%, because (and this is something that's difficult to find even in their authoritative help section for publishing), there is a Delivery Cost (they use capitals for that term, BTW, I didn't add them on my own) added to your book.

**70% Royalty Rate x (Promotional List Price—applicable VAT - Delivery Costs) = Royalty**

Amazon rounds file sizes up to up to the nearest kilobyte and the minimum Delivery Cost is $0.01 USD. This means, that, even on a good day with the tiniest of file sizes, you're never going to earn a full 70%.

Delivery Costs are equal to the number of megabytes Amazon determines your Digital Book file contains, multiplied by a schedule of Delivery Costs. On Amazon.com, for example, it would be $0.15 USD/MB.

My latest novel, *Fear and Longing in Los Angeles* which runs around 90,000 words, is 0.61 MB. This means that it's costing me $0.15 USD for every sale.

So, for this book that retails for $4.99, I'm not really making $3.49 USD. I'm actually earning $3.34 USD. That's more like 67% rather than 70%.

In addition, you can't earn more than 35% on sales to customers in Brazil, Japan, Mexico, and India unless your eBook is exclusive to Amazon via KDP Select.

These are a couple of things to be aware of.

But, so that it doesn't feel like I'm crapping all over KDP, let me share some good things that are potentially useful and help. Because I'm not crapping on KDP, I'm just highlighting something that I rarely ever seen mentioned anywhere in author circles or in the dozens of books published every month about how to get rich selling books on Amazon.

If you are enrolled in KDP Select, one benefit of the Kindle Countdown Deal option is that, if, instead of manually changing the price, you use the countdown deal option to set a price below $2.99, you still earn the full 70% rather than the reduced 35%. That's a good thing to know to keep more money in **your** pocket.

## Global Pricing

Although it is more dominant in the US and UK, Amazon is available in 15 global countries. So make sure that you take advantage of the international pricing options. Make sure you optimise your pricing in the main English language territory pricing currencies of AUD, CAD, EUR, GBP, and USD. Unlike many of the other platforms, Amazon doesn't offer a NZD controlled currency. Similarly, there are plenty of international countries where Amazon isn't available. (Hence another reason why publishing wide means you're truly WIDE globally).

### Pre-orders

You can set up a pre-order on Kindle as much as 12 months into the future. And you can set up an asset-less pre-order. Amazon recommends you load the final version of the manuscript several days in advance of the eBook's release, to ensure it's in the system in time for the customers who have placed a pre-order.

But you can only list up to 10 titles for pre-order at a time. You cannot do pre-orders for public domain titles.

Here are some draw-backs for pre-orders on Kindle.

You can move up a release date (i.e., an earlier date than originally scheduled). You need to submit and republish the final version of your book, and all customers who pre-ordered the eBook will receive the content on the earlier release date. This works smoothly.

If you delay a release, perhaps because you need more time to finalize your file, you can delay the release date up to 30 days once without penalty. (This one-time exclusion applies to your whole catalog, not just the postponed book). If you delay the release a second time on a given title, you won't be able to set up a new pre-order for one year or extend release dates for other existing pre-orders. Any update to your release date must be made before your submission deadline. Customers who pre-ordered the eBook will receive an email telling them you delayed the release. As always, maintaining a positive customer experience is important, and part of that experience is releasing the right version of your book on schedule.

Similarly, if you need to cancel the release of your pre-order eBook, for whatever reason, you can unpublish your pre-order eBook just like you would unpublish any other book on KDP. However, if you cancel a pre-order, you won't be able to set up a pre-order for any eBook for one year.

In other words, be VERY careful and VERY sure about any pre-orders you set up on Amazon. Changes that negatively impacts a customer will result in a strike against you or the inability to have this option for a full year. It's like you're in the KDP pre-order penalty box.

### Keywords

This is perhaps one of the most significant places that you want to optimize your metadata at Amazon. Entire books were written, and companies were built upon helping authors understand the importance of those seven fields in KDP where you can enter in keywords.

The fields allow many characters, and, instead of just entering single words, you can enter phrases, multiple phrases in the same single field.

So don't waste that space. Ensure you're entering full and rich details.

For my novel *A Canadian Werewolf in New York* for example, in the seven fields I could enter something like:

1. wolf
2. Manhattan
3. Battery Park
4. reluctant hero
5. vigilante justice
6. humor
7. Spider-Man

This is because my novel is about a man who turns into a wolf, has enhanced senses and strength, and, as a self-professed fan of Spider-Man comics, he uses his superpowers to help others. He lives in Manhattan, the novel opens up in Battery Park, and there's an element of humor to it.

But I could put more relevant phrases that use those keywords. Like this:

1. reluctant hero vigilante justice wolf
2. Battery Park Manhattan Algonquin Hotel

3. Superpowers Spider-Man action humor

This allows me to enter both words and phrases that might be searched into each line, utilizing the real estate offered in a much more effective way.

I also highly recommend Dave Chesson's *Publisher Rocket* as a tool to use in finding relevant keywords that will fit and be useful. (That tool is excellent both for this field and for Amazon Advertising). I typically use *Publisher Rocket* as a start, then maybe tweak the results about 10 to 15% with a bit of human curation to ensure I'm not accidentally attracting the wrong people. (For example, fans of shifter romance aren't going to like this werewolf novel).

## Marketing Resources

There are some other marketing resources under the Marketing tab that include the following:

- KDP Select (exclusivity options)
    - Price Promotion
    - Kindle Countdown Deals
    - (Kindle Unlimited page reads)
- Amazon Advertising
- Author Central
- Nominate Your Books (Beta in early 2021)

I'm not going to go into details about the KDP Select option since that requires exclusivity, but at a very high level, here's an overview of the other three.

### Amazon Advertising

Many authors you talk to might still refer to this as AMS, as it used to be called "Amazon Marketing Services"—so if you hear someone say AMS Ads, this is what they are referring to.

Within this option you can create Sponsored Product Ads and Lockscreen Ads. Options include automated ads, manual insertion of keywords and negative keywords (for which a tool such as Publisher Rocket is an extremely valuable resource), and complex bidding options.

Because there are countless books and resources about Amazon Ads, I will not get into any details, but I will mention a few of them.

Some books you might want to check out on the topic include *Mastering Amazon Ads* by Brian D. Meeks, *Amazon Ads Unleashed* by Robert J. Ryan and *Amazon Ads for Authors 2021* by Deb Potter.

Mark Dawson offers a comprehensive and blow-by-blow Amazon Advertising course within his Ads for Authors course, which is available in seasonally scheduled time-periods at selfpublishingformula.com. There is also a free course from Dave Chesson of Kindlepreneur which you can find at AMSCourse.com.

One last word on Amazon Advertising, and it's a repeat of something I shared in Part I of this book, but you normally have to be publishing direct through KDP in order to access Amazon Ads. However, the one exception I found for this is with *PublishDrive*.

You can create an Amazon Ad through *PublishDrive*, which is the only exception to the "have to be direct with Amazon KDP" rule that I've found. This means that regardless of how a title is published (direct, vis a third-party distributor, or via a traditional publisher), you can manage Amazon Ads through your *PublishDrive* account.

You should be aware, though, that, unlike with direct Amazon Ads, you will be out of pocket the full budgeted amount **immediately**, rather than at the end of the ad run.

### Author Central

This is a great free tool Amazon offers to all authors and which is something you should be taking advantage of. You don't have to published direct to Amazon to have and use an Author Central account.

I, for example, have links to many of my traditionally published books on my Author Central page.

In mid 2020 Amazon significantly improved the experience for authors. Now, instead of having to manually log into a handful of different websites to manage an Author Central presence for the US, UK, and FR sites, you can manage them through a single interface.

It's useful to use this to create a landing page for you on Amazon that can have all your books, your biography, images, videos, and even an imported link to your blog posts.

There are additional tools to help you easily see Amazon customer reviews, sales ranking on your books, and US-based Bookscan sales data.

## Nominate your eBooks

This program was in beta release in early 2021 as I was working on this segment of the book. There are two options available: Kindle Deals and Prime Reading, which are available in the following marketplaces: are available in the following marketplaces: amazon.com, amazon.ca, amazon.co.uk, amazon.de, amazon.es, amazon.fr, amazon.it, amazon.in, amazon.br, amazon.co.jp, and amazon.com.au.

You can nominate two eligible titles at a time for Kindle Deals and one eligible title at a time for Prime Reading. Nominations don't guarantee enrollment, and not all nominated titles will be selected to participate. If Amazon select your nominated title, they'll send you an email with the details and you have the choice to either accept or decline the offer.

Nominations expire after 90 days. You'll only hear from Amazon if they select your book you within the 90-day period. You can choose to have the nomination auto-renew at the end of the 90-day period, or you can choose a new title to nominate.

Titles must be enrolled in KDP Select in order to be considered, but Kindle Deals are open to all authors.

Kindle Deals are limited-time discount deals offered on eBooks, lasting from a single day up to multiple weeks. Customers will see both the regular price and the promotional price on the eBook's detail page.

Books enrolled in Kindle Deals may be eligible for featured placement in the Kindle store or additional email marketing. Amazon states that while the nomination program is in Beta mode, authors will receive royalties on the discounted price for every sale during the deal according to their selected royalty plan. (Meaning, this will be like the 70% earned on Kindle Countdown Deals even if the deal price is below $2.99 USD)

To be eligible for Kindle Deals, a title must be:

- An eBook.
- Not adult content.
- Enrolled in the 70% royalty plan (US marketplace only).
- Available for purchase in at least one marketplace where the primary language matches the language of the title.

## Amazon Affiliate Program

Amazon Associates is one of the largest affiliate programs in the world. Amazon is, of course, an "everything store" in many ways, so the affiliate earnings isn't just on books, but on any products associated with the cookies that come via browse.

If someone buys your book from an Amazon affiliate link, you earn 4.5%. But it goes beyond books. You also get 4.0% if they buy watches or fashion items, an Amazon Echo, or Amazon tablets. You get 3.0% for toys, furniture lawn care products, and more, 2.5% for PCs. And luxury beauty items earn you 10%. In other categories you earn a flat fee.

You earn commission income on any qualifying items placed in a customer's Shopping Cart within 24 hours of their arrival at Amazon.com via your Associates link. A customer may arrive at Amazon.com via your Associates link, add an item to their Shopping Cart, and then leave Amazon.com without placing an order. But as long as the item was added to the customer's Shopping Cart during this 24-hour window, you will still earn a referral commission if the order is placed before the Shopping Cart expires (which is usually after 90 days).

You can enter your Amazon affiliate code into a free Books2Read universal books link.

I only earned about $50 in 2020 from my affiliate account, but already in 2021 I've received a payout of $20. And I'm just fine with that additional trickle of revenue stream that is more passive income.

## Final Thoughts

As I mentioned, there are countless books and resources out there about Amazon that you can investigate, but I'll leave you with one last recommendation.

One of the most comprehensive overviews of the Amazon platform that provides an in-depth perspective about the platform is David Gaughran's *Amazon Decoded*.

## Apple Books

Apple is a global retailer, and the Apple Books app is available in 51 countries around the world. The iOS operating system is the world's second-most widely installed mobile operating system, after Android, and as of January 2020, Apple CEO Tim Cook shared that the number of active Apple devices had grown to 1.5 billion.

Every iOS device in the 51 countries it is available in is pre-installed with the Apple Books app.

So if you want global reach, Apple Books is a place you need to have your books.

One thing that's important to know about Apple is that, unlike Kobo and Nook, where there is an overwhelming internal bias towards wanting authors to publish direct, Apple isn't particular on how a book is published.

All they care about is finding and spotlighting great books.

This means there's not really access to promotional opportunities when you publish direct that aren't available when publishing to Apple through a third-party platform.

The direct-publishing solution for Apple, which has changed named over the years, is, as of early 2021, called *Apple Books for Authors*.

Authors can use this platform to get eBooks into the catalog. Audiobooks are not accepted direct and need to be sent through one of a list of preferred distribution partners. (United States: Findaway, Ingram/CoreSource, ListenUp; Germany: Bookwire, Kontor, Zebralution; Canada and France: De Marque; Japan: OTOBANK).

Apple Books has merchandisers in the major English language markets who are each responsible for the unique storefronts for their regions.

They are constantly curating through the list of existing titles to create compelling carousels of titles recommended based on seasonal themes, new and trending titles, coming soon, special pricing offers, free first in series, and personal recommendations based on previously purchased and browsed titles.

Apple tends to offer solicitations direct to authors they have a personal relationship with. There's no simple way for an author to reach out and get a contact or rep at Apple. It's more of a case of if you and your books start to sell in a noticeable volume, they'll reach out to contact you.

Shy of that elusive direct contact, Apple is content to work with distribution partners like Draft2Digital, Smashwords, and others, and they regularly meet with their partners to take pitches on prominent forthcoming authors and titles that are worth noting.

They also run promotions, many of which are also curated via third party distributors. In early 2021, for example, I'm aware of at least 14 different Apple promotions that were being solicited for through Draft2Digital.

The auto-generated top-seller lists, both the overall bestsellers and the top-selling titles in different categories only show the ranking for the top 20 books.

As mentioned earlier, one of the best ways to get the attention of an Apple merchandiser is to sell a lot of titles there. It might seem like a bit of a chicken-and-egg situation, particularly if you're new to the platform and haven't sold a lot, but here are a few things that might help you with getting the right attention.

### Royalty Structure

Apple Books royalty structure is simple and generous. If you publish direct, you get 70% for books priced $0.99 and above. There is no royalty cap at $9.99 like at Kindle.

You can make a book free but can't enter a price between $0.00 and $0.99.

If you are publishing to Apple through a distributor, that 70% is more like 60%.

### Digital Box Sets

Because of the generous royalty structure, Apple Books is a fantastic platform for what indie authors call a "box set."

This term is used to denote a single ePub file that contains what were originally and also still published as multiple separate volumes of an eBook. Indie authors have liberated and re-adapted a term from the book industry that normally denotes multiple volumes of a physical book (often a series) that come in a cardboard box sleeve. The traditional term for a single volume in the book industry is omnibus. (This is important to be aware of because if you're talking to a bricks and mortar bookseller and use the term "box set" they're likely thinking of a very specific physical item). This is why I like to use the term "digital box set" to distinguish

That tiny soapbox lecture aside, digital

## Pre-Order Power

Apple Books encourages and likes pre-orders. In addition, whether you are publishing direct or through a third-party distributor, you can do an asset-less pre-order for Apple.

You can set a book up for pre-order up to one year in advance. You just need to make sure you upload the final file 2 weeks (10 business days) prior to the release day.

And at Apple, when you have a book up for pre-order, you get a double bang for your buck on that sale. A ranking boost happens on the day that the pre-order is placed. And you get a second ranking boost on the day of release.

This is likely because of the fact they feel if someone is willing to pre-order a book, it's is a good sign of the book's relevance. And then there's a return to that elevated status on the day of the book's release, as if to say: "Hey, everyone, today's the day this book that people wanted so bad they pre-ordered comes out."

Yes, unless the book is in the top 20 of its category the ranking won't be visible. But a ranking boost is a ranking boost, and every little bit helps.

It's amazing that their systems do this. So why not leverage it for your book's benefit?

### Early Pre-Orders

Speaking of pre-orders, Apple merchandisers are constantly looking for titles that are fully polished and edited and up for pre-order anywhere from 4 weeks to several months in advance. They have merchandisers who will actually read the eBook to see if they want to feature it in a special Sneak Peek promotion. This is more than just a "hey look, a new title that looks good" type of promo list. This is a carefully curated and vetted title from one of the people on the Apple Books team who has actually read and recommended it.

Most indie authors don't do extended pre-orders, so if you're setting up longer pre-order windows with an already polished and ready-to-go title, you're going to stand out from the digital masses.

### Custom Samples

Apple has a fantastic option when you're uploading a book. You can not only upload the ePub book file, but you can also upload a custom sample of that book for customers to preview on their web store.

The benefit of this is that, instead of the default first 5% of the book that appears to customers, you, as the author, can control exactly what's in that preview.

Instead of seeing the title page, and other pre-book matter, or if the preview cuts-off in an odd spot, you get to control that.

This is a powerful option not available on most other retailers that is important to leverage.

### Sales Reporting

Apple Books sales are refreshed on a daily basis. Apple is also an excellent partner to their chosen third-party distribution partners, and offers a similar daily reporting.

Reporting includes current sales and pre-order sales.

### Security & Privacy

Apple Books authors can assign people to technical roles to maintain titles without having access to sales reports. You just need to make sure you add the person in a technical role, not into the roles of admin, sales, or legal.

## Be Inclusive

Are you linking only to Amazon on your personal or author website? How about in social media? Guess what, Apple merchandisers are paying attention.

Let's say that they see a title of yours that has garnered some sort of attention. Either it has noteworthy pre-order numbers or it was brought to their attention from a recommendation from a distribution partner or just a book lover.

If they go to your website and they see nothing more than links to Amazon and requests for Amazon reviews, how do you think there are going to react to that? The same goes for your social media posts. Are you being inclusive in your personal promotion, or are you being exclusive to a single retailer that's not them.

You can either link directly to Apple, but remember, Apple is a global company and sells books all over the world. So just entering the US store link might be off-putting to customers who live in other countries and who can't purchase through the foreign version of the site.

Using a universal book link that auto-routes based on a reader's geo-location can work nicely here. For example, a Books2Read.com generated link, which is free to set up, can be used for this purpose. They're not particular about having to have an Apple Books logo on your website, just that your links and your terminology are inclusive and not exclusive.

But just be aware that they are paying attention. You should be attending to this, too.

### Global Pricing

Because Apple Books is available globally, make sure that you take advantage of the international pricing options. Make sure you optimise your pricing in the main English language territory pricing currencies of AUD, CAD, EUR, GBP, NZD, and USD.

### Price Scheduling

Apple Books allows you the convenience of planning ahead and scheduling price promotions. You can set a start and end date for promotional pricing, and can also control that pricing in the multiple currencies that Apple Books uses.

### Apple Books not iBooks

Yes, I know, iTunes was a massive game changer, as was the iPad and the iPhone, and there was a pattern of naming used for Apple products that employed the same pattern. iBooks was the name used since 2010 when Apple launched their eBook reading platform. But it was changed to Apple Books in September 2018.

And, yes, I know, the main digital store is still called iTunes, so it's easy to make that iMistake, but the name changed. So be careful how you refer to the Apple eBook experience. They're paying attention.

Show them that you're paying attention too, so when you mention or refer to them, make sure you use the most recent and accepted terminology. The same would go for any approved logos for links that you might add to your website.

You can download approved official art assets to use in marketing and advertising materials via authors.apple.com.

Apple cares a lot about branding. A LOT. If you're unaware of this, then perhaps you've been living in a cave or on a desert island since 2001.

### Keywords and Search

Apple doesn't have a separate field for keywords, but in a series of virtual workshops that started in late 2020 that they've been giving authors about their platform they did share that they use all the metadata fields when trying to satisfy returns on search results and matching readers to the right books.

This means that it's likely a good idea to ensure you enter relevant keywords into your book's description and that all of your data fields are leveraged to ensure it contains the things your specific target audience would most enjoy.

I do not advocate blatant and haphazard keyword stuffing, because any data field that is visible to consumers can make you and your book look amateurish to both readers and the retailers. But you might want to ensure that relevant and valuable keywords are included in the appropriate ways and places to increase your chance of being seeing by the right customer.

### Promotion Codes

All publishers and independent authors publishing to Apple books receive access to free digital promo codes for every eBook they distribute on Apple Books.

Recipients of the codes can quickly and easily redeem it on Apple Books for a free copy of your eBook. Getting your promo codes out to supportive readers is one of the best way to build buzz for upcoming books still in the pre-order phase, and books that are already available for sale on Apple Books.

If you distribute your book directly to Apple Books through your own seller account, you can access your promo codes directly from iTunes Connect. You can also request, via the distribution company that you use, to have these codes created on your behalf. If you were publishing to Apple via Draft2Digital, for example, you could email support@draft2digital, provide the details (ISBN, etc) for your book, and request the codes. The service team would handle requesting codes on your behalf.

You can request up to 250 promo codes per eBook, and the codes are valid for four weeks from the date you requested them.

### Apple Affiliate Program

Why not earn extra money on the books that you sell at Apple? If you join the Apple Affiliate program, you'll earn extra revenue each time a purchase is made from a link you share — this revenue is in addition to your royalty payment for the sale of your book. And you can enter that affiliate code into a free Books2Read account Draft2Digital offers providing inclusive links

### Final Thoughts

Apple is a global country and Apple Books is available in 51 countries. That's significantly more countries by far than Amazon.

And also remember, Apple merchandisers, who are responsible for a lot of human curation that work in addition to the algorithms, are book loving professionals who care about quality reading, and finding titles they feel will satisfy the needs of their consumers.

## Google Play

Google has been a relative late comer to the self-publishing space. They launched their platform a decade ago, which I was fortunate enough to get into in the early days of eBook publishing, but then they locked it down and seemed to abandon it for several years.

The original platform was glitchy, half-assed, and a tedious hair-pulling experience to use. There was no online sales reporting and the reports themselves were clunky and confusing. It was as if Google had assigned creating the platform as punishment to employees with a track history of not attending to good user experience.

But, since about mid 2019, the platform, and the team behind the platform, seems to have been breathing new life into the Google Play Books Partner Center.

Lately, it's a more robust and easier to use platform, with slick features not available at the other stores, with more to come based on what I've been hearing.

Google Books are, in early 2021, available for sale in 75 different countries. Authors from 43 countries can sign up. Those stats, and also where seller promo codes can be used, which I'm sure are constantly being updated, are available here:

https://support.google.com/books/partner/table/6052428

You can use your own ISBN for eBooks you upload, or, if you don't enter one, Google will automatically assign what they call a GGKEYs, which is a Google-internal identifier.

Updates made in the Google Play Books Partner Center take place virtually instantaneously.

While there are third party distribution options for this platform, you are STILL required to have a direct Google Play Books Partner Center account in order to allow for that.

In my mind, if you're required to have a direct account, then you might as well use that account directly and maintain the tightest control and direct margin.

Here are some features that you get access to with the Partner Center from Google.

- Management of multiple users for your account.
- Control over bibliographic information/metadata.
- Bulk edits by using spreadsheets.
- Scheduled price changes for promotions.
- Distribution of free copies and promotion codes.

Below I'll break down some how-to's and benefits included within each of these areas.

### Multiple User Access

Google's Partner Center allows you to assign other people access to your account through their own unique login to sign in to the Partner Center using their own credentials. This is important because it means you don't need to share your password or any other information associated with your Google Account.

Only users with administrative access can add, edit, or remove users. Any additional users you wish to add must have an existing Google Account. Here's how to add a new user.

1. Go to the Account Settings. If you don't see this option, you may not have administrative access. Contact an administrator for your account.
2. Click Users.
3. Click the Add User button.
4. Enter the email address associated with the Google Account of the user you'd like to add.
5. Click OK. The email address you entered should now appear in the list of users.

Users can use their Google Account email address and password to sign in to the Partner Center. They'll be able to view and edit any settings on the pages they have access to, according to their access type.

There's no limit to the number of users that can be added to an account.

Each user you add has an access type that determines which pages in the Partner Center account are visible. Access types can restrict specific users from viewing or editing certain data. Access types can be edited by anyone with administrative access, and a user can have more than one access type. By default, new users have access to the Book Catalog, so be sure to specify a different access type if necessary.

These are the access types that are available:

- **Book Catalog**: Add and edit books.
- **Analytics & Reports**: Download preview and sales reports.
- **Payment Center**: Manage sales territories and payment profiles (including bank account information).
- **Administrative Access**: This access type includes all the above access types, and the ability to view and edit account settings (such as managing users).

Note: To view and download earnings reports, a user must have both Analytics & Reports and Payment Center access (or Administrative Access, which includes both).

If a user no longer needs access to the Partner Center, you can remove them by clicking on that user and then clicking the Remove button next to the email address of that user.

### Analytics & Reports

The Reports section of the Google Play dashboard is one in which you see, at the top, an Earnings Report section that is broken down by year.

It shows a summary of the payments made in a given calendar year of the month and the dollar amount in your preferred currency. You can download the reports and details, which open in CSV (Excel/spreadsheet) format for your records. If you click onto download and you don't see anything, just be patient. It might take as long as 30 seconds to a minute for the report to automatically download and open up on your desktop computer.

Below that is a Custom Reports option where you can choose from between three types of reports:

- **Sales summary reports**—A summary of net sales grouped by book and country.
- **Sales transaction reports**—Details for each transaction
- **Google Books traffic report**—A review of book visits, visits with pages viewed, non-unique buy clicks, book visits with buy clicks, Buy click click-thru-rate (CTR), and pages viewed

Then you select a custom date or range, and a how you want to organize the report: (Day, Month, or Book).

These reports seem, at first, confusing, but if you experiment with them you can pull out some interesting data that can help you analyse behavior of customers viewing your books and the detailed sales that are taking place.

## Pricing

Currency conversion is an opt-in tool that you control and can disable at any time within the Payment Settings of your Partner Center account. Disabling currency conversion will remove all converted prices, which will remove books from sale in those territories until you provide prices in the local currency.

This is important to understand because if you have currency conversion disabled, Google will not make your book available for sale in a country where you haven't provided a price in that currency.

Just to be clear, accounts created after July 2014 have currency conversion turned on by default. But if you have a Google Play account that pre-dates 2014, like I did, make sure you go and double-check that setting.

## Scheduled Price Changes

Google's Partner Center has the option of pre-scheduled price changes and price promos, which can be a significant time and hassle saver on your part. It means you can set and schedule promos well in advance and not have to (in the way you have to in KDP for Amazon), make the change only on the day it's happening.

You can pre-schedule price changes in two different ways.

One is going into the edit option for a published book, clicking onto the Pricing tab on the left nav, then scrolling down, clicking onto the Add a price button, then, within the Show additional settings option setting a start and end date for a price.

You also have the option to set that currency for a specific territory or to WORLD. I use WORLD by default for all the currencies I use, which basically tells Google to automatically convert that price to the local currency for the other 40+ countries where the book is available if a local price isn't already established in that territory.

This very manual and repetitive process can be tedious, particularly if you follow my advice and manually control the pricing in at least these six currencies: AUD, CAD, GBP, EUR, NZD, USD.

That's where changing prices via the Promotions tab can come in handy.

There's also a benefit of setting up your price drop/change in the scheduled price changes feature of the dashboard, but I'll share more about how that works in the Promotions segment.

## Promotions

There are two types of promotions you can run from the Google Play Books Partner Center dashboard. Scheduled Price Changes and Promo Codes.

*Scheduled Price Changes*

If you set up a promotion to change the list price of your book for a specified date range using the scheduled price change feature your book may be featured on the Google Play Store or in marketing emails that the team sends out.

You can only run promotions for books that are already for sale, so this can't include pre-order titles.

To schedule a new promotion, click Add new promotion. You'll name the promotion, enter a start date, an end date, and then you'll have a choice to manually add a list of books and their promotional prices online or you can load a pre-filled CSV (.csv) template that you download from the Partner Center.

If you are scheduling a one-day promotion, use the same start and end date, as it treats the start date as 00:00 and the end date as 23:59 according to the earliest buyer's time zone. Thus, if you create a promotion for Feb 12, 2021, the price drop will be for the entire day on Feb 12th local time.

The CSV template that you download, fill out, and upload has the following required fields.

- **Identifier** (e.g. ISBN)
- **Title** (This can be left blank as it's meant for human user tracking convenience. Values you enter in this column will not be used)
- **Currency**
- **Amount** (Numeric value. No currency symbol)
- **Countries**

The Currency, Amount, and Countries columns refer to the promotional price and where it should apply. If you list countries that use a different currency, the promotional price will only apply there if currency conversion is enabled.

If you want to apply more than one promotional price to a book during the same promotion period, add a row for each price. For example, you can set one promotional price in the US and a different promotional price for the same book in Canada. Each price would be a separate row in the promotion spreadsheet. If currency conversion is enabled, you can use the keyword WORLD to apply the promotional price to all of your sales territories.

Here is an example of the format of a price promotion I ran in March 2021.

| Identifier | Title | Currency | Amount | Countries |
|---|---|---|---|---|
| ISBN: 9780973568875 | A Canadian Werewolf in New York | AUD | 0.99 | AU |
| ISBN: 9780973568875 | A Canadian Werewolf in New York | CAD | 0.99 | CA |
| ISBN: 9780973568875 | A Canadian Werewolf in New York | GBP | 0.99 | UK |
| ISBN: 9780973568875 | A Canadian Werewolf in New York | NZD | 0.99 | NZ |
| ISBN: 9780973568875 | A Canadian Werewolf in New York | USD | 0.99 | US |
| ISBN: 9780973568875 | A Canadian Werewolf in New York | EUR | 0.99 | WORLD |

The book will be 0.99 to the local currencies in Australia, Canada, Great Britain, New Zealand, and the United States of America. It will also be 0.99 throughout European countries and also use the 0.99 to convert to any other currencies not specified.

When a publisher discounts their book on Google Play Books, the book becomes eligible for additional in-store merchandising and customer notifications. This doesn't mean that every book will receive every promotion, but this discount significantly increases the book's likelihood of receiving more promotion in the storefront.

These discount promotions are driven by Google's algorithm and can include:

- Appearance in a collection highlighting discounted titles, including relevant genre collections.
- Targeted in-app notifications and emails to customers that have wishlisted or sampled that title.

*Promo Codes*

You can give customers a promo code for a free or discounted eBook. You can create up to 5,000 codes per campaign and up to 3 promo code campaigns per month.

Promo codes are available are available only in select countries (in early 2021 there are 30+ countries on this list, which includes all the major territories most indie authors are interested in).

Within the Promotions tab from the upper left nav click the New promotion button and give the promotion a name that you use for personal tracking.

Then enter a Start date, which can be any date from today to a year from today. Your End date can be up to 3 years from the start date. The promotion ends at 11:59 PM on the end date, based on the country you choose.

There are three discount types you can choose from:

- **Free**: Customers can redeem the offer to receive the book at no cost to them.
- **Percentage off** (eBooks only): Customers get a percentage discount on the list price of the book. You choose the percentage.
- **Fixed price**: Customers can get the book at a new fixed price.

You then select the currency and amount. Please note that for fixed price promo codes, you must turn on currency conversion in your Payment Settings.

You can then add one or more ISBNs or GGKEYs. It's important to note that if you include multiple books in a promotion, customers can only use the promotion on a single book.

You then decide what countries you want to make the promotion available in and what countries to run it in.

These are the code types that you can choose:

- **One code**: The same code is used for all customers. Individual customers can only redeem the code once. (You can enter the number of uses per code, which can be up to 5000 redemptions).

- **Multiple codes**: A unique code is automatically generated for each customer. Individual customers can only redeem their code once. (You can enter the number of codes to be generated, which can be up to 5000).

For both types of promotions, there is a downloadable report that will show you detailed transactions of related to the promotion that you run. This is a handy tool for doing post-promotion analytics.

In early 2021 I started experimenting with the use of Google Play coupons for eBooks. One of the things I have planned is offering a limited time offer for an entire catalog of titles to be available at Google Play for 99 cents, perhaps with one book, using a different coupon, for free.

Creating such coupons can be a good way to lift your profile/visibility on the Google platform and potentially start feeding some of those algorithms to get your books in front of the right customers.

### Pre-Orders

As of early 2021 Google's Partner Center doesn't allow for the uploading of asset-less preorders, but they expressed plans to be releasing that option some time in 2021.

Pre-order sales do have a positive impact on the Google Play Books algorithm, but there is no clear indication on if that works any differently than regular sales.

### Content Reviewers (For Pre-Orders)

A stellar perk about the Google Play store is the option, when you load a pre-order, you can use the platform directly to send copies to content reviewers.

Content reviewers get free access to the book for prepublication review, testing, or promotions. They'll be able to read the book on any supported device without having to purchase it. You can grant a book to content reviewers even before it's available for sale.

It's as simple as adding the email address of the requested content reviewers. They will have special early access to the book. It's a fantastic built-in street-team/early reviewer feature.

### Storefront, Ranking & Reviews

The Google Play Books storefront has a merchandised looking storefront, including carousels on features like "Start a new series," "Deals under $5," and other seasonal and thematic marketing generated images and lists that suggest, to me, they are curated by human merchandisers.

One important thing you'll notice about the Google Play store is that many of the category carousels that appear have the subtitle heading "Ebooks for you."

This falls in line with something I was informed about directing by Google representatives. And this is that Google Play Books provides each reader with personalized recommendations, allowing authors to connect with new readers around the world. I'm told that very little merchandising in the Google store is controlled by a human. Instead, it's driven by their algorithm.

As a result, every reader sees a different bookstore based on their previous purchases and demonstrated interests likely through search, browsing, and previews. This benefits authors and publishers in that it supports discoverability and gets their book in front of new potential readers worldwide.

The Google Play Books stores doesn't show a book's ranking, but within the browse functionality of the store, they do indicate the top-selling titles via what they call "Top charts" and spotlight "New arrivals" in fiction and non-fiction. And on those pages they appear to reveal 9 rows of six books plus two additional books, suggesting to me, that it's the top 56 books in that category.

On the right-hand nav of any book you are looking at, there's a "Similar books" feature which, upon experimentation, suggests to me that it's based on a combination of metadata (ie, same author, different title), plus algorithms. For some of my titles, instead of seeing "Similar books" I see a "Continue the series" option.

If you click onto an author name, you get a page showing all of that author's books in large thumbnail with a price (or the word "Free") plus a 5-star average rating/review for the book.

## Search and Keywords

Google is the company that has created the world's most sophisticated and well-known search engine, so, without having any deep insight into the search capabilities on the Google Play store, one has to imagine that their search algorithms are going to be top-notch.

Make sure that your series data is filled out completely and accurately, as Google will connect those for readers to easily find.

And ensure that your book's description includes words and phrases that you want to be indexed and found by the search algorithms.

Just remember, keyword stuffing makes you look amateurish to both readers and the folks at Google. So do it in a way that doesn't make your item page look unprofessional.

## Viewing the Store in Other Countries

By default, Google is going to use automated geo-targeting to show you the localized version of the bookstore in your home country and currency.

If you want to see how your books appear in any country you can update the end of the URL to include a country code.

Add: ?gl=[country code] to the end of the URL.

For example:

https://play.google.com/store/books?gl=us

## Affiliate Program

As an active Play Books partner, you can earn 7% commission when you link directly to eligible products or content in the Google Play Books store.

The Play Books affiliate program is currently available for active Play Books partners. If your Play Books Partner account is eligible, you'll find a link to the sign-up form on the home page of your Play Books Partner Center account.

## Final Thoughts

If you think you know the Google Books platform because of rumours you've heard about their price-matching issues, you have absolutely nothing to worry about any longer. They fixed those.

And if you think the dashboard and user experience is terrible because you tried it five or more years ago, look again.

My experience with Google got off to a slow and rocky start, a long, frustrating ten-year-courtship you might say, but in the past year, it's starting to grow as I've attended to the platform, learned more about it, and spent time running promotions there.

## Kobo

Please be aware that in the fall of 2018, I released a book called **Killing it on Kobo.** This isn't meant to be an advertisement for the book, just an explanation that it's not possible for me to get into the same detail (and the connected back-stories) shared in that full book within this segment of this book. Who knows, maybe I've done a much better job of being concise and to the point here, and the other volume is a hefty doorstop. But I thought I'd at least ensure you're aware it exists should you want an unabridged tome.

Also, I worked at Kobo from the fall of 2011 to the fall of 2018 and created *Kobo Writing Life* so I'm chock-full of biases.

Kobo is an international digital book company (eBooks and audiobooks) with a reach into 170 countries around the world with localization in 16 countries.

Kobo was born in Canada and spun out of the country's largest book retailer, Indigo Books & Music (similar to Barnes & Noble in the US or WHSmith in the UK). Originally launched in December 2009 as *Shortcovers*, a cloud-based e-reading service, in December 2009, the company was spun-off from Indigo into an independent company under the name Kobo, with Indigo as the majority owner.

In January of 2012, Kobo was acquired by and is a subsidiary of Rakuten, a Japanese digital company with an Amazon-sized presence in Asia and other global territories. This acquisition gave the scrappy little Canadian upstart company the opportunity to go head to head with three of the "Big Five Tech Giants" dominant in the US market: Amazon, Apple, and Google.

Kobo not only has free apps available on tablets, smartphones, and desktop computers, but it also manufactures a line of award-winning eReader devices that use an electronic ink screen.

Because of the company's connection to a Japanese company, many assume that the name "Kobo" is of Japanese origin. The reality is that Kobo is an anagram of the word "book."

## Distinguishing Factors

The first important distinguishing factor that sets Kobo apart from its three biggest global competitors (Amazon, Apple, and Google), is that Kobo is only about books and about reading. There's no other "noise" in the system from other products and gadgets, and the people at Kobo, including Rakuten Kobo, Inc. CEO Michael Tamblyn, are book people to the core.

The second factor is that Kobo isn't going this alone. Their strategy includes partnering with dozens of physical and online retailers around the world, including WHSmith and Waterstones (UK), Booktopia (AU),

Mondadori (IT), FNAC (FR), BOL (NL), Indigo Books and Music, Inc (CA), and American Booksellers Association and Walmart (US) to name just a few. In these collaborative partnerships Kobo provides the eBook and/or Audiobook experience, while the retailer provides the physical books and other merchandise.

This means that, when you publish an eBook to Kobo, regardless of whether you do it directly or through a third-party distributor, your book is not just available on Kobo's main website around the world, but your titles, but it's also listed on these partner websites.

This is both a pro and a con, especially if you're popping in and out of KDP Select almost as often as you change your underwear, because some of Kobo's downstream partners aren't as quick to update and delist titles in their catalog. (IE, it can get you "in trouble" with Amazon's exclusivity requirement)

Kobo launched their self-publishing platform, *Kobo Writing Life*, in 2012 and the KWL team is aggressive and adamant that self-published authors should publish direct through their platform rather than via a third party-distributor.

This never made sense to me, even when I worked at Kobo, since the Kobo doesn't earn a single penny more. If anything, Kobo earns far more profit from sales made through Draft2Digital, Smashwords, and other distributors, since those companies bare the labor burden of catalog and title ingestion for them. They do, however, feel like having a direct relationship with authors is more important.

However, it is what it is, and publishing direct to Kobo through *Kobo Writing Life* does come with significant privileges.

## Global Pricing

Because Kobo is available globally, make sure that you take advantage of the international pricing options available. Make sure you optimise your pricing in the main English language territory pricing currencies of AUD, CAD, EUR, GBP, NZD, and USD.

When you enter a price in using your local currency, the KWL dashboard will automatically convert your price using a recently stored conversion rate from the Bank of Canada. The dashboard will also make automated suggestions on localized price-rounding for you and allow you to set custom locked-in prices rather than use the automated conversion.

## Price Scheduling

The *Kobo Writing Life* dashboard offers the ability for you to pre-schedule price changes. There are two types of changes you can schedule: A *price change* and a *sale*.

A *price change* is used when you want a book's price to change from its current price to a different price, at 12:01 AM local time on the date selected.

A *sale* is used when you want to temporarily change a book's price with a specific start and end date, effective at 12:01 AM local time on the date selected for the start, and at 11:59 PM local time on the date selected for the end of the promotion period.

### Pre-Orders

You can set up pre-orders on Kobo Writing Life for longer than one year in advance. The cap on pre-order dates is unclear, but I've seen evidence that it can be multiple years in the future.

You can also change a pre-order date without any penalization.

Since you are unable to set up an asset-less pre-order, the KWL team recommends you upload a file that has at least the first 3 chapters included. This is because all books available in the Kobo store (pre-orders included) have a preview automatically made available for the first 5% of the file.

They recommend that if you do upload an incomplete file for your pre-order, to make sure you upload the final file at least 48 to 72 hours prior to the release date.

Pre-orders cannot be set to be free.

One benefit of pre-orders at Kobo is that they count for double the ranking bonus of a regular sale. This means that if you get any pre-order sales, it'll have a "2 times" bonus effect on increasing your ranking, which can really improve the visibility on the platform for you.

And, if you get a high enough volume of pre-orders, the Kobo merchandisers will see your book come up in reports and might, in turn, feature it on one of the main, more visible merchandised pages or carousels.

### Reporting

The *Kobo Writing Life* dashboard has a simple and easy to read reporting dashboard that automatically defaults to the current month's sales. You can change that to Last 30 days, Last 7 days, Today, Yesterday, or a custom range.

This main/default SALES AT A GLANCE view highlights the total number of eBooks sold (which includes free downloads unless you use the toggle button for turning off free downloads), the estimated earnings for those sales/downloads, the number of titles published in that period, and the number of countries your eBooks have sold in. It also shows an all-time eBooks "sold" and all-time estimated earnings.

If you scroll down, you can see a list of the top 10 eBooks sold in the specified time period showing units and estimated earnings. On the right of that is a bar chart of the purchase activity by day in that period, with call-outs of High, Low, and Daily Average for unit sales.

Scrolling down further you get a top 10 Top Sellers of all time listing and to the right of that a global map that spotlights, in red dots that are sized as a percentage of the overall sales (larger dots for the highest selling regions) with a call-out of the top 8 countries sold in.

You have the ability to click onto a SALES BY BOOK view that allows you to see all those same stats using the same filters for a single book title.

And there's also a SALES BY REGION view where you enter a country name and can get, among bar charts that show the time period, last week, this week, last month, this month, and a carousel of the sales and estimated earnings per title, an auto-generated pie-chart outlining the percentage of each title's sales in that region.

These are all high-level sales details that are estimated and not confirmed. You can download spreadsheets of your sales and payment information from the My Account → Payment Information area of the dashboard.

### Promotions

The *Kobo Writing Life* team works hard to prop up and promote direct published authors. They have a promotions tab that is built into their author dashboard but which is not visible or available to all authors who first sign up.

In order to access the dashboard, authors need to email the KWL support team and request that the promotions tab be added.

Once the promotions tab is visible, upcoming promotions that are being solicited will appear in this tab. They originate from the work the KWL team does negotiating for space for KWL titles in various larger Kobo promotions.

Given that the Kobo merchandisers typically plan out promotions 6 to 12 weeks ahead, the promotions you'll see here will most likely be ones that are available in the forthcoming 3 to 12 weeks.

Sometimes, in the case of promotions that either haven't already been filled, or in which the final decision isn't made until after the submission period, promotions might still be open until the very last day of the submission period.

As of the writing of this book in early 2021, there is no automated or systematic way to be informed of new promotions that are added to the dashboard, so I recommend logging in at least once a week and looking for new promotions.

KWL promotions typically have two types of costs:

- % of Margin Cost
- Flat Fee Cost

Most of the KWL promotions don't cost anything up-front and involve a modification to the percentage of margin earned by authors for each unit sale.

In the % of Margin Cost promotions you don't need to exchange money. If you get into the promotion, the system will automatically subtract 10% from your earned royalties for each item sold during that promo period. (Meaning you'll receive 60% instead of 70% for those sales)

The benefit to this type of promo is that you're never actually paying anything to be in the promotion, you merely earn slightly less for those extra sales.

The potential downside, particularly if the promotion is hugely successful, is that if the volume of sales is significant, the cost increases.

But, again, on the plus-side, it is an easily affordable option, since you aren't paying anything up front and are thus not "out of pocket" to be in the promotion.

The promotions based on flat fees range anywhere from $5 to $100. Those ones you have to pay for up front, and this payment process is usually in place because the promotional space is so limited and highly sought after (such as the *Daily Deal* spot)—this is where "prime real estate" is involved—or for promoting a free title. Because taking 10% margin off a title priced at $0.00 equals 0.

The promotions that tend to work the best, or bring the most value, are usually the following types:

- **Customer Discount Promotions**—Typically these are 30% off or 40% off, sometimes only for Kobo VIPs. They involve coupons and no need to drop the price manually on a book, which means no need to change prices on other retailers and no need to work about price matching.

- **Free Page Listings** (By Genre)—One of the most searched-for terms on Kobo is "free" and that leads to the page these carousels appear on. It's highly visible and great for a free first in series title.
- **Editors Pick Free Spotlight**—The appear above the genre carousel listings and are far more visible, and thus cost more. But are well worth the extra visibility placement if you can get them.
- **Buy More Save More**—Like coupon codes this type of promo usually involves a landing page encouraging readers to stock up and save. It can be a buy two and get a percentage off, or buy three and get one free type of deal. The costs are amortized across the shopping cart, so the margin earned depends, but like coupon codes, they don't require price changes and there's no price matching or updates needed on other retail sites.

Don't take rejection from KWL promos personally. Chances are that they didn't even see your title when they were making selections. The competition is so fierce, that often the merchandisers end up filling up on a promo with limited spaces and end up having to bulk reject the ones they didn't get to.

Kobo doesn't impose rules on how often you can apply for promos, so it's important to apply early and apply often for as many promos as you can.

The KWL team also runs other promotions that might not appear in the author dashboard. They might be special BUY ONE GET ONE sales, or promos related to curated titles for OverDrive. They mail those directly to a list of authors they know are likely to have titles they'll want to use for these promos. You typically get onto such lists by being an active participant with the KWL team.

### OverDrive

*Kobo Writing Life* allows you the ability to opt your titles into OverDrive's library catalog, offering the same percentage (50%) that you would get for the One Copy One User (OCOU) standard library sale license if you were to publish direct to OverDrive. (When I was working in the KWL team I took part in a nine-month negotiation with OverDrive to get that deal in place so if you're benefiting from it, you're welcome. Wink, wink, nudge, nudge). If you get to OverDrive via a distributor, it's anywhere from 45 to 47% that you're earning on most of those platforms.

### Kobo Plus

With their partner BOL in the Netherlands and Belgium, Kobo introduced an "all you can read" subscription service called *Kobo Plus* several years back. KWL authors can opt their titles into this platform and earn money from reads from those customers.

The program launched in Netherlands and Belgium, but was added, in the summer of 2020 to Canada, Kobo's most significant and popular territory.

*Kobo Plus* provides an even larger opportunity for discoverability and earnings because titles are listed in the regular normal a la carte catalog, but also in a special catalog browsable for Kobo Plus readers.

Kobo Plus is a program that allows readers to effortlessly discover new authors and try new genres that they might not otherwise try, encouraging people to read more.

It's similar to Kindle Unlimited, except for the BS of the exclusivity requirement over at Amazon.

There is some worry about how an "all you can read" program might devalue the price of a book, and the potential cannibalization that might happen to their sales, but Kobo has shared stats and reports denoting that the people who are Kobo Plus readers are typically a different or fresh batch of readers and not the same ones who buy eBooks a la carte.

### Affiliate Program

Affiliate income can be an important addition to an author's income, and incremental revenue sources over time do add up.

The Kobo affiliate program is operated through Kobo's sister company Rakuten Affiliate Network (formerly known as LinkShare)

The program allows you to earn 5% commission on eBooks and 10% commission on devices and accessories.

The system is not as easy to use nor as intuitive as the Amazon program, but again, it's an additional opportunity for increasing your revenue earnings.

There are articles about the program on the Kobo Writing Life blog, but you can also email kobo-affiliates@rakuten.com for more details and how to sign up.

### Challenges of Publishing Direct with Kobo

While I'm a fan of publishing direct through *Kobo Writing Life* there are a few cons about their direct dashboard experience that are worth mentioning.

For one, while they accept pre-orders well more than a year in advance, you can't create an asset-less pre-order.

Kobo Writing Life requires that you load eBook content before you publish any book — and that includes pre-order titles. If the final version of your book isn't ready, you can get around this by creating a placeholder file with the title page and copyright, and maybe even a non-final draft of the first few chapters of the book.

Because customers can preview the first 5% of an eBook in Kobo's catalog, I always include a short note or introduction from me to the reader at the very front of the book letting them know the status of the book in this early phase (ie, it's with the editor right now, etc) or some other personal note.

In this note/introduction, I also mention that this is a pre-order draft version and if the customer is reading this particular note after having purchased the eBook either on or after the release date, then something went wrong with the technology. I ask them to email me, as I'd rather fix a poor reader experience than rely on a random customer service rep at Kobo, who might not understand what went wrong and further frustrate my reader.

Here is an example of text that might appear early in the draft "place-holder" file for a KWL direct pre-order.

**NOTE FROM AUTHOR**
**THIS IS THE PRE-ORDER / PREVIEW VERSION**

Please note that if you are seeing this either in preview or as a purchased product, you are reading an early unedited draft version that was loaded to Kobo during the pre-order period while the book was still receiving final edits.

At the stage of this writing, the book is still going through revisions, edits, and upgrades with the editorial and design team.

If, for some reason, you received this as a purchased version, then that is the result of some sort of technical glitch or error. To receive the proper version of the book, please email me at [YOUR EMAIL] and let me know any pertinent details of the purchase so I can first send you the correct file and also work with Kobo to fix the error.

Yours in writing,
[YOUR AUTHOR NAME]

It's also the first thing someone sees if, in the case something goes wrong, they have received the wrong/earlier draft version of the book that hasn't gone through the final edit.

One of the other downsides to the KWL dashboard is that there is no dashboard reporting of pre-orders, or of your OverDrive library sales. Pre-orders are visible for Kobo titles to some of the third-party distributors.

Also, the reporting on Kobo Plus isn't shared on the dashboard or in any live setting. It comes usually mid-way through the following month in an Excel statement. Even when you are publishing through an aggregator, the Kobo Plus earnings stats come in that same delayed fashion.

**Final Thoughts**

The folks on the KWL team are book people. The folks behind Kobo itself are book people. This platform and company is, for many authors, might represent a smaller percentage of their sales, particularly if authors look at the results in giant markets like the US, but it's a market that has incredible potential globally.

So, when you're thinking Kobo, think Canada, Australia, and other international markets. Think about the various book-retail partners that they have; because this is an area where they dominate the industry. They are about partnership and collaboration, and that's something I have always respected about this company.

Kobo and *Kobo Writing Life* are often also the first place where many authors have experienced a true human connection from the amazing people who work there.

Growing your sales on Kobo is not easy, but if you are patient, and persistent, it can be well worth your time and energy. Just don't give up on them, even if it has been 9 months or more since you've seen any traction. Keep at it, keep persisting. I have known very few authors to see strong Kobo sales right out of the gate. For the most part, there's a gestation period of anywhere from 6 months to well over a year.

The biggest issue I remember seeing with authors and Kobo is impatience. That'll probably be your biggest Achilles heel with Kobo, so check your impatience at the door.

## Nook

Nook is the eBook side of Barnes & Noble. It is the name of their eReader device and their eBook store online.

Admittedly, I have long been leery and skeptical of this direct publishing platform for several reasons.

First, the platform wasn't initially available to Canadians. You had to be a US citizen. Then, later, when it opened, you still had to have a US based bank account or address in order to be paid. That created too many hoops.

Second, there was a time in B&N's past where the platform was being run by the same people who run Author Solutions, a giant corporation that operates with a shady integrity, predatory marketing practices, high-pressure sales tactics, and over-priced unnecessary and useless services. Author Solutions companies are listed on the "no-fly" lists of Writer Beware, SFWA's "Thumb's Down Publisher List" and Watchdog Advisories from the Alliance of Independent Authors.

Third, the platform and dashboard, which was non-intuitive and difficult to navigate, changed names, structures, and dashboards seemingly more often than Hollywood celebrities change partners. I'm leery of businesses that do a 180° pivot to their business model overnight on a repeated basis.

Personally, I have long published direct through KDP and KWL and then used Draft2Digital to get my books into the Nook webstore.

However, after listening to me kvetch and whine, Erin Wright, the esteemed leader of the *Wide for the Win* Facebook group spent some time with me to walk through the most recent version of the Nook direct publishing platform. And, given that I try my best not to close my mind to learning new things and embracing fresh perspectives, I have to say I'm quite impressed with what they've done.

Even Erin admits at how awful and glitchy the platform used to be, and how frustrating trying to use it used to be. But it has significantly changed and improved. This ugly duckling of a self-publishing platform might well have grown into a beautiful swam.

## Pre-orders

Pre-orders can be set up as much as 12 months in advance.

You can change your release date without penalty at Nook. And some authors have leveraged this when setting up books that will eventually appear beyond that 12-month window.

Long pre-orders can work quite effectively at Nook.

"If you want a magic bullet for Nook," Erin Wright says, "have a long pre-order."

Whenever Erin has a book that is meant to release more than one year later, she sets the pre-order date to the further it is allowed. And then, as the timeline rolls forward on a monthly basis, she schedules time in her calendar to push the release date out one more month until she finally settles on the originally planned release date.

## Reporting

The reporting on B&N Press is comprehensive, powerful and instantaneous. You can see sales by week, month, year, custom date ranges, pre-orders, and payments. You can also filter by eBooks and Print.

The visual outlay of the reports is quite stunning with easy to see bar characters of royalties earned on one side and unit sales on the other and easy to click Daily/Weekly/Monthly views.

Below that is a "Last 30 Day Sales" line graph that can easily switch between Units Sold and Royalties Earned. You can also toggle on and off free eBook units and between eBooks and Print. By default it shows all books, but you can filter and search by Title, Author, ISBN, or Series.

The Series Sales By Date (which is in beta in early 2021), allows you to easily see how a series might be doing over time. But the Series Sales By Book # (also in beta), is a straightforward way to see the sell-thru volume happening for your series books in the book order.

## Pricing

As of Feb 1, 2021, B&N Press updated their royalty structure from 65% to 70%, and also removed the pricing tiers.

This means that when you publish direct, you earn 70% for all eBooks.

Because B&N is only available in the US, there's only USD pricing. So one of the benefits of publishing here is that you can be US-centric in your thinking. Whereas, being US-centric is not a good idea at Apple, Google, Kindle, and Kobo, who are all international players.

Pricing controls also include price scheduling options. You can choose a start date to make an ongoing price change from that date forward, or you can choose a start date and an end date to create a "temporary price change/promotion." There's a field to enter the price you want to update to on an ongoing basis at the end of that temporary price change period.

There is also a Price Summary view that can show you the historical price changes for any given title. This is useful for when you're looking back at sales data and are trying to understand when different pricing strategies or promotions might have been run.

## Custom Samples Option

B&N shows samples of books to customers. By default the sample that will be shown automatically includes the first 5% of your book as an excerpt on the book's detail page.

But you have customizable options that aren't available on any other platform.

You can upload a specific custom sample that allows you to load a curated and controlled excerpt that you control that will show as available for customers to preview.

Or, you can choose any number of consecutive chapters from your book to use as an excerpt on the book's detail page. This functionality takes your uploaded eBook, shows you the chapters on the left, and allows you to click which consecutive chapters you'd like to appear in that preview. (It's a great option for not having to manually create a custom document/ePub for the custom upload).

### Promotions

The promotions tab at B&N Press is a bit of a confusing beast, because all authors have access to the tab, but not all options are automatically available to all authors who sign up.

So, make sure that you politely request access to the promotions tab by emailing the B&N Press team. It's not clear what criteria they use to grant or deny access to this tool, but I'm willing to be that it's a combination of the professional look and feel of your books, the professional behavior you display in public and on social media, and whether or not your social media and website are inclusive.

In addition, you won't see the promotions tab across the main top nav of the author dashboard where...

PROJECTS
SALES REPORTS
AUTHOR RESOURCES
MY ACCOUNT

...are your main options. (Unlike the *Kobo Writing Life* dashboard). You'll see it inside the PROJECTS tab on the left nav and it appears between the **Create a New Book** and **Manage Series** buttons.

In the promotions area, by default all you will see on a new account that has not been granted "additional" promotion rights, there's only a single option: **Create Coupons**. The other two of the three promotion options don't appear. But, once you have full promotion access, you'll see these three main options available.

- Create Coupons
- Monthly Promotions
- Standard Promotions

The **Create Coupons** option (which, again, is the only one that all B&N Press authors get access to), allows you to create promotional pricing for your books that don't come with the side-effect of having to adjust your price on the other retailers, or the aggressive price-matching from Kindle. That's because your retail price remains the same, but the coupon codes get applied to save customers money during the checkout process.

Both of these types allow you to select multiple titles and a custom start and end date for when the coupons/promotions are active.

- **X% Off w. Coupon Code**
  This allows you to discount your book(s) with a % that you specify, creating a unique coupon code exclusive to B&N readers.

- **Buy One Get One X% Off (BOGO)**
  This allows you to reward B&N readers with a selection of your eBooks available for free or at a reduced-price with a full-price purchase of another item.

If you are having trouble with the sell-thru on a series of books on B&N, one idea is to create a coupon code for the next book in that series at a discount offer (ie, 30% off) and putting a note with the coupon code and a link to that next book immediately at the end of the last chapter of the ePub you publish and upload directly to Nook.

**Monthly Promotions** are one-off or seasonal promotions added to this tab on an ongoing basis and there's no notification from the B&N Press team. So you have to come back and check it out regularly. You might want to put it in your calendar to check this as often as on a weekly basis so that you don't miss out.

When I was talking with Erin Wright about Nook, she admitted that, because this system is similar to Kobo's, when she first got the Kobo Writing Life promotions tab she sat back expecting that the KWL team would email her to let her know when new promotions were added. It wasn't until months afterward that she realized she needed to go in and check on her own.

**Standard Promotions** include ongoing feature spots and promotional lists on the B&N website and might include such regulars as:

- **Top Indie Favorites (previously B&N Presents)**
  Bi-monthly promotion highlighting 100 new and upcoming eBooks. Renews every February, April, June, August, October, and December.

- **NOOK Price Promos**
  Discounted eBooks featured in the "NOOK Books Under $2.99" and "Free eBooks Favorites" collections.

- **NOOK Daily Romance**
  Daily reduced priced romance eBooks featured in NOOK Daily Find newsletter.

- **NOOK Free Friday**
  Weekly promotion featuring a free eBook available on B&N Readouts. Books selected for the NOOK Free Fridays program are featured on Barnes & Noble social channels and B&N Readouts.

- **NOOK Daily Find**
  Daily reduced-price eBook with dedicated newsletter.

There is a Summary tab that also allows you to see an overview of your promotions: which ones are pending, accepted, declined, and completed.

Word on the street is that the **NOOK Free Friday** program includes submissions from a lot of major trade publisher titles (ie, the "Big Five"), and are more likely to accept major publisher titles, so acceptance here is going to be much more difficult. But, perhaps like getting a BookBub Feature Deal, it's worth continuing to apply because if you can get one, maybe the visibility is worth the persistence.

Erin Wright, suggests, when it comes to these promo options, a handy phrase to remember: "The top two are the two you should pay attention to."

## Metadata & Keyword Tips

For some odd reason, there are fields within *B&N Press* that are virtually useless because they're not propagated or used on the B&N website or search indexed.

The **Subtitle** field isn't used at all, so if you have a subtitle and are publishing direct, you might want to enter it using a [TITLE]:[SUBTITLE] format right in the Title field.

There is a field called **Choose Keywords For Search Engines** that is currently useless, so don't spend or waste a lot of time trying to figure out what to enter here. Apparently, the team built that field in without a solid plan on exactly how it was going to be used for website search results, so, as of early 2021, it's useless.

One thing that Erin Wright does, to test and measure whether it's actually being used, is she enters an extremely obscure phrase that's not likely to be used by any sane author. And then, once in a while, she goes to the web store and tries typing in that phrase to see if that book she entered it in actually comes up.

One last thing to note is that the description you enter for your book is not indexed by search at all, so don't waste your time trying to ensure that you have appropriate keywords in this field.

## Subject Categories

B&N Press will allow you to choose up to five categories, so it makes complete sense to optimize this to increase your book's chance of being found by the right readers.

The categories are divided into Primary (which is the first one you choose), and the other four are all ranked as Other.

One of the unique features to allow you to find **more** of the right readers is to leverage some of the "Themes" options that will pop up in the Subcategory selection. This will allow you to transcend the industry standard subject categorizations and get into unique and very specific themes that could potentially resonate with a reader.

For example, under the Category of Romance, if you select Romantic Fiction Themes, you see these options (and more) appear:

- Clean and Wholesome Romance
- Erotic Romance
- Gothic Romance
- Inspirational Romance
- Military Romance
- Romance—Aristocrats and Royalty
- Romance—Captured, Indentured, and Enslaved
- Romance—Disguise and Hidden Identity
- Romance—Former Lovers
- Romance—Holiday Love
- Romance—Love and Marriage?

- Romance—Love and War
- Romance—Rags to Riches/Riches to Rags
- Romance—Rogues, Rebels, and Rakes
- Romance—Unforeseen and Unlikely Loves
- Romantic Comedy
- Steamy Romance
- Steamy Romance—Other

It is well-worth taking some time to scroll through, investigate, and make notes of categories that would be appropriate for you to use. And because there are such different options within the complex category hierarchy, it might make sense to record some of the ones applicable to you in a spreadsheet somewhere.

Because, just within Romance, you'll find different options under Romance > Other Romance Categories that include such things as: Action and Adventure Romance, Multicultural Romance—Other, Romance Anthologies, Romance Sagas, and so forth.

If you go to the website and start scrolling around, you might see how these categories are merchandised. But you have to scroll down to see the detailed options for browse in the left nav.

Using a different example, if you go to the following in the browse on B&N…

NOOK Books > Science Fiction & Fantasy > Fantasy Fiction

…you'll see the following options:

- Adventure fantasy—Other
- Arthurian Fantasy
- Arthurian Fiction—Other
- Comic Fantasy
- Contemporary Fantasy
- Contemporary Fantasy—Other
- Dark Fantasy
- Dark Fantasy—Other
- Epic Fantasy
- Epic Fantasy—Other
- Fantasy—Myths & Legends
- Fantasy—Through the Looking Glass
- Fantasy—Women of Lore
- Fantasy for All Ages
- Fantasy Sagas
- Historical Fantasy
- Historical Fantasy—Other
- Humorous Fantasy—Other
- Light Fantasy
- Mythological fantasy—Other
- Paranormal Fantasy— Other
- Series Fantasy—Other
- Steampunk
- Sword & Savagery
- Urban Fantasy
- Urban Fantasy—Other

I trust you get the point. Just know that there might just be a very specific category that you wish you had on the other retailers that appears within the mystical and complex B&N category hierarchy structure.

## Final Thoughts

Nook might only be available in a single global territory, the United States of America, but Barnes & Noble is a significant retailer and there was a time that the Nook eReader was the top-rated device available on the market.

Though they are no Amazon, Nook is still a pretty powerful force and can represent a significant number of sales for indie authors.

I have never been particularly successful with sales at Nook, but there are plenty of authors who swear by the platform, and many count it as consistently being their #2 earning platform.

And don't forget, as Erin Wright explained to me: "They have some weird-ass quirks, but they also have some awesome kick-ass shit in there, too!"

## Other Retailers & Platforms

I'm not going to get into as many details about the other retailers and wide storefronts that exist, but I will highlight a few things to know about a few of them.

Some of these platforms have direct access. Others don't and they rely on third-party distribution platforms for title acquisition. And some are genre specific.

But I'm hoping this high-level overview helps give you a bit of an awareness of the platforms. Like the "Big Five" it's important for you to have a look at them and perhaps take a bit of time to get to know each one. No, you can't do them all at once, but perhaps pick one, check it out, and see if there's a good fit for you, your books, and their reader base. Because you never know where you'll find that magic.

And, on the flip side, it's good to keep in mind the potential and often inherent instability that came come with some of the smaller platforms. It's great when you can grow *with* a smaller platform, and be there when they're starting off, so that when things take off, you're already riding the wave. But there are platforms that have gone belly up with virtually no warning. Many romance authors and readers alike are still feeling the sting of when All Romance eBooks, went bankrupt, leaving a lot of faithful readers and authors hurt, and confused. And worse, they left a lot of authors unpaid.

So tread with caution. Optimistic caution.

## *Eden Books*

Eden Books, which launched in March 2019, is a romance / women's fiction platform that is the brainchild and "baby" of Robyn Crawford. As shared on their website, it's the simple story of a romance reader and blogger got mad. When a fellow romance writer wrote about a taboo topic and was banned from the main retail sites, Crawford wanted to create a place that would accept such titles without judgement.

Eden Books is dedicated to providing a safe, supportive, inclusive platform that gives authors of all genders, races, ages, or sexual orientation the opportunity to promote and sell their original stories within the romance and women's fiction genres.

It's relatively small within the marketplace but is one that is dynamic and is continuing to grow. It's more than just a storefront in that it's a bit of a hybrid between a webstore and a social media platform.

Authors can create a direct account to sell on Eden Books, and the platform has been described by some authors as a bit "byzantine" to get things initially set up. But I remember the early days of Smashwords and even the very early days of Google, so I know that over time things can improve.

Of course, one benefit of a process that might limit a mass of authors from quick entry is that only the authors with staying power stick around.

And, if you write in any of the romance, erotic, and women's fiction genres, you'll be available on a platform that is likely a lot more inclusive and with better curation and visibility for your target readers.

There are authors within the *Wide for the Win* group on Facebook who rave about this platform, and are looking forward to watching it continue to grow, along with their sales.

### *DriveThru*

DriveThru is a series of connected genre specific platforms operated by OneBookShelf. OneBookShelf is a digital marketplace company for both major and indie games, fiction, and comics and was formed by the merger of RPGNow and DriveThruRPG.

The platforms they operate are:

- **DriveThruRPG**—Their oldest and most popular site, built for RPG (role playing games) stories only. They are currently the largest online marketplace devoted to RPG and RPG-related materials.
- **DriveThruCards**—Connecting card game designers and fans with a marketplace that makes use of high-quality cards custom printed to every order.

- **DriveThruComics**—The first downloadable comic store on the web featuring a wide selection of publishers and creators.
- **DriveThruFiction**—Fiction of all types, although speculative fiction, science fiction, fantasy, horror, crime, and thrillers are likely to reign supreme.
- **DMSGuild (Dungeon Masters Guild)**—Created in partnership with Wizards of the Coast. A community content program where creators use Wizards of the Coast intellectual property to make new content.
- **Storytellers Vault**—A content creation program for World of Darkness, Chronicles of Darkness and Exalted White Wolf games.
- **Wargame Vault**—Wargame Vault has an armory full of wargaming rules, accessories, paper terrain, and other essentials.

Since 2001, the company's platforms reach hundreds of thousands of fans each month, and send millions of dollars in royalties to their publisher/author clients every year. Whether you are an existing publisher with hundreds of titles or an independent creator preparing to sell your first title, this company is delighted to welcome you in and provide a sales platform for selling your creative work.

As a Publishing Partner with OneBookShelf, you choose what titles you wish to list on our site, what the price of those titles will be, when they go live for sale, whether you want your titles included in site-wide sales and promotions, and how your titles are presented on our online store. You can also choose to have your titles available as Print-on-Demand titles, through their platform.

Royalties earned receive either 70% or 65% of what the customer pays, depending on whether you are an exclusive partner with OneBookShelf or non-exclusive, respectively.

Similarly, on print sales, you receive 70% or 65% of the price paid, less the print cost of the book (or cards) that OneBookShelf prints to fulfill the customer order.

The company makes your royalties available to you at any time, via PayPal or by monthly check.

I can imagine, especially for writers within specific genres, that this could be a useful operation to be publishing work to. I'm guessing it could be a dynamic and exciting platform for comic book creators and writers of RPG.

### *Glose*

Founded in 2014, Glose is a social reading platform where people can not only read, but can also highlight text for sharing and engaging and increasing discoverability. The platform's name comes from the Latin *glosa* or *glossa,* which denotes a handwritten annotation made in the margins of or between the lines of a book, intended to clarify for the reader an obscure word or passage. By extension, it refers to any conversation, contribution, or debate around a piece of text.

When I first learned of this company, I was impressed that it was doing something I fondly remember Kobo participating in via their early days.

Here's a brief trivial note of an aside—The *Kobo Writing Life* term was created to be the author equivalent to Kobo's reader-facing gamification platform *Kobo Reading Life* that gamified the reading experience with badges and interactive sharing of notes, annotations, and even (back in the day) special author notes embedded inside the ePub that Kobo readers could explore, and even interact with. It was meant to be a "book club" style engagement right in the digital book on Kobo. However, they let that platform fade into the distance.

Glose was created to make reading more fun, productive, and social with easy access via smartphone, laptop, or tablet. Your books, progress, and highlights are always synchronized in real-time, so no thoughts or comments are ever lost.

Reading sparks emotions, ideas, knowledge, opinions. Whether you're reading a novel for pleasure, an essay for work, or a textbook to study, books always feed your inspiration. Glose is on a mission to help keep that inspiration alive by allowing readers to keep, share, and discuss those moments.

Glose was acquired by Medium in January 2021. This, to me, is a good sign that there are things to come, and I'm definitely keeping them on my radar.

It's not clear how authors can get their titles into Glose, because there isn't a direct upload option and none of the major third-party distributors have access but I'm sure there's something in the works. After all, Medium itself is a company that allows direct publishing. So keep your eyes on this one.

### *Radish*

Radish is a mobile fiction platform for serialized storytelling. Their wide variety of stories are published and read in bite-sized installments optimized for the smartphone reader.

On Radish readers can access thousand of serials across genres and connect directly with their favorite storytellers in live community chat rooms.

Authors can publish their own original stories, revive backlist titles with a young, mobile readership, and pre-release upcoming books to build advanced buzz.

Built to be both user and author-friendly, Radish states that they strive to present the newest and brightest in entertaining, diverse serial fiction to readers while providing authors with innovative ways to build readerships and monetize their work.

You have to apply to get a Radish account and not everyone is accepted. They have a minimum payout of $50 USD and they only pay once per quarter.

Some authors swear by the platform as a great place to earn additional revenue, while others have expressed frustration and anger with it.

### *Scribd*

Scribd is a subscription service platform that allows readers to pay a monthly or annual fee to read eBooks in an "all you can read" way. Publishers/Authors are paid based on how much their books get read.

The company launched in March 2007 as the world's first open publishing platform, allowing anyone to quickly and easily share ideas with the world. In the fall of 2013, they introduced the first reading subscription service. And in November of 2014, they added audiobooks into their subscription services. Sheet music came along in 2015. Magazines were added in 2016, and in 2017 well-known and trusted sources like *The New York Times, The Wall Street Journal, The Financial Times,* were added.

They are considered a bit of a smaller storefront where most indie authors are concerned, but they cater to a wide variety of genres and in January of 2019 they reached a milestone of 1 million paying subscribers.

They even added an "originals" content publishing arm to the company in 2019. They are a site to keep an eye on in your WIDE investigations.

Scribd did run into issues with their all-you-can-eat model when it came to voracious romance readers who were costing them significantly more than their $8.99 USD a month subscription would cover. It's not a good business practice when the goods cost more than you are earning to provide them. They initially pulled romance down, and then came up with a solution and plan where they rotate books in and out of "circulation" or "available stock." This does mean it's likely that not all your titles will be available through Scribd all the time, which makes linking to them and running promotions from third-parties a bit challenging.

You can get to Scribd via third-party distributors like Draft2Digital, PublishDrive, Smashwords, or StreetLib. Typically, if you have a large enough title count and presence, you can contact them to get a direct account with them. But that's more of something that happens on an exception basis. Your path of least resistance is to get to them via a distributor.

I bet you didn't realize that if you have books on Scribd that there's an author page for you. Or that they have reviews.

## *Tolino*

Tolino is a German based eReader and eBook solution.

On March 7, 2013, the first tolino (yes, they use lower case for their device and brand name) eBook reader 'tolino shine' was launched. It initialized a market revolution of bookseller alliance. This is why you might hear references to "The tolino Alliance."

Facing globally active competitors, the German bookselling companies Thalia, Weltbild, Hugendubel, and former Club Bertelsmann decided to join forces with Deutsche Telekom as a technology partner and offer an open eReading ecosystem for digital readers under the common brand 'tolino'.

The alliance managed to successfully establish the tolino brand for digital reading in Central and Southern Europe and to get more partners on board. In Germany, the Mayersche bookstore, Osiander, and Libri also joined the tolino alliance with over 1,500 independent, independent bookstores.

At the end of January 2017, Rakuten Kobo became the new technology partner for the tolino alliance, taking over from Deutsche Telekom. There was no change to this trusted brand, leveraging the best of Kobo's eReader technology, with a trusted and German-born digital reading solution.

As of the spring of 2018, tolino eBook-Readers were selling in more than every third German bookstore and with over 60 million eBook sales since they launched.

This created a proper nationwide alternative to the globally active competition and an important element in the tradition of the German book industry.

Tolino is a dominant force in the eBook space in Germany, and a hearty competitor to Amazon Kindle. You can't really get into tolino directly, but you can get to them via third-party distribution platforms via *Draft2Digital* and *PublishDrive.*

### *Vivlio*

Vivlio is a company owned by large French booksellers and publishers. One way that I have heard them described is as the Tolino of France, because of the unique way multiple parties came together to create this solution.

Vivlio started in 2012 with a mission to provide a comprehensive solution to distribute and sell eBooks. If you check out their website, and pardon my crude translation from French to English, they use the following term to describe themselves: *"Behind your screen hides a team of eBooksellers based in Lyon, on the lookout for new products and curating the best promotions in a catalogue of digital books and audio books from over a million titles."*

The company's partners include Cultura, Mr Decitre (ex CEO of Decitre and Furet du Nord group), Albin Michel, the largest independent French publisher, and Système U, one of the biggest retail chains in the region.

In addition to Standaard Boekhandel, Vivlio is the technical provider of the Cultura group (over 90 retail stores in France), Système U (300 retail stores in France), Actissia (150 stores in France, Belgium, and Switzerland) and Decitre / Furet du Nord (25 stores in France and Belgium).

Vivlio has a line of dedicated eReader devices that range from € 119 to € 199, as well as free computer and mobile apps.

Opting your eBooks into Vivlio gives you the opportunity to sell your catalogue to all these distributors on their websites, eReaders, and mobile applications.

For eBooks, I'm not aware of any other third-party distributor to get your titles into Vivlio than *Draft2Digital*. And via D2D, authors receive 55.25% of the retail price. It's a bit lower than the regular 60% received by all the other retailers, but it's access to yet another global market. Because it is a French-language market, I imagine that the biggest success for authors is for French titles; but you never know, and definitely won't sell anything there if your eBook is not listed with them.

### *Wattpad*

Wattpad is a website and app for writers based on Toronto, Ontario, Canada founded in 2006 with a goal of creating social communities around stories for both amateur and established writers. The platform has an audience of more than 90 million users, who can directly interact with the writers and share their opinions with fellow readers. Wattpad is available in over 50 languages but over 75% of its content is written in English. 85% of the usage traffic comes from mobile devices. In January 2021, Wattpad announced it was to be acquired by Naver Corporation for $600 million USD, but (similar to fellow Toronto-based company Kobo which was acquired by Rakuten) will operate as independently as possible and remain headquartered where the company was founded.

While there is no out-of-the-gate way for authors to make money from their fiction it is a unique heavily reader-engagement community that can be extremely useful for an author looking for feedback and interaction with readers. There are some phenomenal analytics available to authors.

Wattpad has been the platform to launch multiple authors into international success. Anna Todd whose "After" series went on to sell to a large publisher and become a New York Times Bestselling author, is among the most well known, but thousands of other authors have leveraged Wattpad for notoriety and respectable writing income.

There are plenty of experimental and beta options available within Wattpad for earning income and then have launched a publishing imprint and numerous partnerships with global media companies that have gone on to find success on Netflix and other media.

I put a first draft of a NaNoWriMo novel up on Wattpad to test to see if the story had any merit or resonance with readers, and it has received more than a quarter of a million reads. The two most common questions I received early on from readers who loved it were: "Where can I buy the eBook?" and "Can I get this in print?"

### *Additional Platforms*

There are many other platforms that offer differing models of posting and getting paid for your work. I had been trying to hunt down info on many of them, but then had to give up, recognizing I'd never finish this book. Here are just some of them.

I would strong advise, if you are looking for information and following authors who have plenty of experience in this, checking out the *Wide for the Win* Facebook group, or, more specifically, another Facebook group, this one led by the awesome Ember Casey called *Writing and Selling on Fiction Apps*. It is a private group and is for authors only to discuss, debate, and share info about apps they've discovered, and to discuss strategies for selling on these platforms.

- Anystories
- Bravonovel
- Channillo
- Chapters
- Choices
- Dipsea
- Dreame
- Goodnovel
- Love Sick
- iReader
- Kiss
- Lure Fiction
- Plop
- Sana Stories
- Sequel
- Sofanovel
- TailWind
- Tapas
- Webnovel
- Voyce.me

# Print Books

There are two main ways to get a print book. One is selling or licensing your rights to a traditional publisher, and the other is self-publishing your book.

Selling print book rights to a publisher is the easiest way, with the least amount of work on your part, to not only getting a book created, but also getting the book listed, and either already ordered and stocked, or easily available for bookstores and libraries to order with industry standard terms booksellers and librarians prefer.

If you have sold your rights to a publisher, be sure to check the details of the contract and also ask (if it's not already known), if the publisher is a true "traditional" or "legacy" publisher, or a more digital-first publisher.

Traditional/Legacy publishers are publishers that do Offset printing and either have their own warehouse or collaborate with warehouse distribution platforms for making their books available to the retail market.

Digital-first publishers are publishing companies or imprints that have leveraged digital printing and eBook publishing to make their mark, and don't involve themselves with large print runs or the more physical supply chain logistics.

The two main high-level options we are looking at is related to the difference between two main types of printing. If you are well-versed in printing methods and logistics, you'll know I'm simplifying this significantly in order to outline the differences at a really high level.

If your publisher is using Offset printing and warehousing (either their own warehouse or using a wholesaler warehouse and distribution company) this means your book is typically available easily and efficiently for being stocked at bookstores. Bookstores can look up and order the books via multiple different platforms and also listed in attractive glossy print catalogs published either annually, or quarterly to the four buying season cycles. The books are sold at bookstore-friendly trade discount terms (often 40% to 55%) and are fully returnable.

If your publisher is primarily using Print on Demand (POD) for your book, then it might not have attractive discount terms (lower than 40%) and is likely not to be returnable.

In either case, your publisher might allow you to purchase copies of your book directly for a discount of 40% or greater, which means that you might be able to use that for direct print sales or consignment sales via local bookstores. This would be almost no different than the author copies you print and sell yourself through the different POD channels we'll look at below.

### *Examples of Digital VS Offset Printers*

Below are three examples of publishers and explore the use of the two different printing methods with three publishing imprints.

***Stark Publishing***. This is the imprint I created in 2004 when I self-published my very first book, ***One Hand Screaming***. I used *Ingram Lightning Source* to make the POD version available, and initially set it up as fully returnable with the highest discount possible. I have published more than a dozen print books using this imprint, which is mostly used for my own titles. This is an example of self-publishing using POD for distribution.

***WordFire Press.*** This US publisher, owned and operated by Kevin J. Anderson and Rebecca Moesta, is used for many of their own titles, but they also acquire rights from authors, with no advance, but very author-friendly terms and clauses, and higher royalties than you'll ever see from larger legacy publishers. WordFire Press primarily uses POD distribution for their titles. However, they did publish a title with mass appeal in 2019 that needed Offset printing and warehousing, but 99% of their operation is an example of an indie publisher using POD for distribution.

***Dundurn Press***. This Canadian publisher is the largest independent publisher in Canada (Independent means that it isn't owned by any of the "Big Five" publishers). Their contracts are legacy publisher contracts, with an advance and minimal royalties. And their distribution is primarily using warehouse and storing, with UTP (University of Toronto Press) Distribution for warehousing and shipping their books to outlets across Canada. They also occasionally also use POD for some of their distribution beyond Canada.

## Direct Print Options

In English language markets, particularly with a North American centric focus, there aren't many options for publishing to a retail platform direct. I have listed two here.

It's important to note that, while both are US companies, one of them (Amazon) has a huge global presence and is available in all the major English language markets that include the US, Canada, the UK, Australia, and New Zealand, while the other (Barnes and Noble) is a US-only market. Both of these platforms offer POD printing, and they each have their own unique benefits.

The benefit of publishing direct to a retail market is that you will typically earn more because you are eliminating the "middle-man." Essentially, the fewer people who are taking a cut of the pie, the more money there is for you, the publisher.

The downside of publishing direct to a retail market is that it makes your book available **only** to that one retailer.

(Yes, even with Amazon's "extended distribution" which I'll explain below).

## Amazon KDP Print

*KDP Print* is built into the same account you would use when publishing your eBook direct to Amazon. When you log in and go to your bookshelf you will see the option to start with either a paperback or an eBook. If you have an existing eBook, the option to create a paperback for that title will exist.

Given that Amazon is the world's largest bookstore, and one of the largest search engines used on the internet, many authors who are self-publishing will already have their eBook available on Amazon direct through *KDP*. Setting up the print version of their book is that much easier, since much of the same metadata can be used, saving a bit of manual entry time.

The service is free to use, and they only make money from the print book when someone buys your book. And, while it has never been officially stated as a company policy, it does make sense that, since Amazon would earn more from a book published direct from their internal service than they would earn on a POD book submitted to them from a third party, they are very likely to favor books published direct over titles from third party distributors.

Marketing opportunities on Amazon via Amazon Advertising (formerly AMS—Amazon Marketing Services) can only be used for titles that are published directly to Amazon via *KDP*.

It is important to know that, while I have listed *KDP Print* as a direct publishing option, it does come with an "extended distribution" option.

While I believe that *KDP Print* is an excellent solution for direct publishing your print book to Amazon, I also stand by the idea that it isn't the best solution for getting your print books into the WIDE book market.

This is because *KDP Print* offers unattractive and very uncompetitive terms to bookstores; your books are automatically made non-returnable and are given a short discount. You, as the publisher, have no ability to modify these terms that mark your book, in the eyes of most booksellers, as less desirable.

Even though bookstores pride themselves on special orders for their customers, the idea of ordering a book from Amazon, the massive giant that has displaced many independent bookstores, puts them off.

Consider this from the bookstore's perspective. It would be like saying: "Hello proudly independent bookstore. Please support me, a local indie author who is much like you by ordering my book from, and giving your hard-earned money to, the same giant company that fights dirty in trying to put you out of business for the past few decades."

How would you feel if you were in their shoes?

I often refer to Amazon *KDP Print*'s "extended distribution" option as "pretended distribution"—because it gives authors the impression that they are actually reaching a global print market. And, while their books might be listed as available, they are also listed with terms that are good only for Amazon.

You might hear people refer to *Createspace* when talking about using POD direct to Amazon, particularly if their POD experience happened prior to 2019. *Createspace* was originally founded in 2000 in South Carolina under the name *BookSurge*. They were acquired by Amazon in 2005. Beginning in 2018, that operation was slowly migrated and transferred from a separate login and access and merged into the master *KDP* dashboard.

Based on my own experiences comparing *Createspace* and *KDP Print* (and speaking with hundreds of authors who have used both), *Createspace* was a far superior service.

## Barnes & Noble Press

*Barnes and Noble Press* assigns a free ISBN to any book you publish direct to the platform.

Adding the print version to an existing eBook version is pretty easy to do. Much of the metadata automatically copies over for you.

For *B&N Press*, in the most basic of cases, and, as stated on their website, your friends and fans can order your print book from any B&N store across the country—all they have to do is ask, and the store will then place an order and the book will ship directly to the customer. It doesn't even go through the stores.

B&N also comes with unique merchandising opportunities. For example, if you sell more than 1,000 copies of your eBook in a 12-month period, you become eligible to pitch the print version of that book (also published via *Barnes and Noble Press*) to B&N store buyers. If the book is selected by them, it will be stocked in Barnes and Noble bookstores across the country.

Similarly, authors who sell more than 500 copies of a *Barnes & Noble Press* eBook in a 12-month period are eligible to host an in-store event.

*Barnes and Noble Press* also lists various exclusive marketing programs designed to offer authors with awareness and sales via online promotions, monthly themed curated collections, special featured deals and promotions on BN.com, and Email newsletter marketing to B&N customers featuring genres and deals.

Reporting on print titles through *B&N Press* is sophisticated and slick, and nicely merged in with your eBook reporting. And you can bet that the *B&N Press* team are more apt to be a little more enthusiastic about propping up you and your titles when you're publishing direct.

## Print Aggregators

There are hundreds of POD distribution options available. Most of them fall under a blanket "writer beware" category from my perspective, as their goal is to over-charge for services you don't need.

Be warned, dear author, that these are shark-infested waters. Before working with any print service provider, make sure to check the "Writer Beware" website or the listing of approved service providers from the good folks at the Alliance of Independent Authors.

Instead of trying to create any sort of authoritative list, I'm just going to list and talk about a few of them, and, in two groups.

The first group are a couple of full-service POD distribution platforms. I personally don't use these, because I would rather manage the hiring of editors, designers, formatting, etc., on my own. But I recognize that not all authors have the patience or fortitude to find the professionals that can help them.

## BookBaby

*BookBaby* has an easy-to-use website and is up front about the services they offer. Like their eBook services, they make it clear what their basic package services are up front. They do have add-on services, but when navigating through their site, those up-sell items aren't nearly as blatant and in your face as many of the shifty POD service providers on the market.

They also charge for updates to books, but, if you are looking for quality editing and formatting services that can add value, they might be one of the distributors to consider.

And, while *BookBaby* offers eBook distribution at the full royalty you'd get if you were publishing direct, you don't get the same control or marketing options that come with direct or publishing through certain other distributors.

## Lulu

I have known authors who have used *Lulu* and been pleased, particularly about the quality of their print offering. And they offer a range of DIY options as well as packages that start at $99 and go up to thousands of dollars. Authors will have to pay any time they want to make updates to their print books.

Despite some personal recommendations share with me about their services, and the fact the founder is Canadian (what can I say, I'm partial to fellow Canucks), the main thing that makes me leery about a service like *Lulu* are the sheer number of up-sell and add-on services they offer, which appear to be geared towards taking advantage of authors.

And if you consider them for print, please don't even waste a single second of your time considering their eBook distribution option.

## Draft2Digital Print

***[In early beta release as of March 2021]***

*Draft2Digital Print* is free for authors. It includes free title setup, free ISBN (if required), free conversion from Microsoft Word into interior print-ready PDF files, free cover flat PDF creation based on your high-resolution front cover image that you might have for your eBook, and free distribution.

*D2D Print* allows an author to set up and distribute their POD book for free. And with it, you get the same distribution options that you would get when publishing direct with Ingram.

The trim size choices via *D2D Print* are limited to a short list of the most common options, rather than *IngramSpark*'s more extensive offering beyond the standard and typical book sizes. The format, currently, is limited to trade paperback. No hardcover options exist. The discount, while a full trade discount of 40% to bookstores, isn't something an author can edit. Nor can the author choose their distribution options. The books go to Amazon and Ingram. Those might change over time, but at the time of the writing of this book, this is how it stands.

For a beginning author who is trying to limit their expenses and overhead but get the widest possible reach for their POD books, *D2D Print* offers everything they need. It can be done without having to hire a designer for the interior POD or cover files, and also comes with the convenience of using a single distributor for both eBook and POD control.

*[At the time of this book's release,* **D2D Print** *is still in beta release. Yes, I do have personal insights into what's happening behind the curtain, but for NDA reasons, I can't publicly disclose any details. Just know that I'm aware there is a dedicated team of brilliant people hard at work to dramatically improve the author experience of the* **D2D Print** *program. It's my belief that, when it launches, it'll be everything that the eBook publishing experience for authors at D2D has been, and more. Fingers crossed that by mid 2021 the program will be in public release. 'Nuff said.]*

## IngramSpark

Until *Draft2Digital Print* moves out of beta, *IngramSpark* is the best way for an author to get their English language POD book out into the broadest market for English-language books.

They are a more author-friendly front end to *Ingram Lightning Source,* which is the POD service I started using back in 2004 when I self-published my first book.

*Lightning Source* is mostly used by larger publishers and is more challenging to navigate. *IngramSpark* was created to offer a user-friendly DIY option for self-published and independent authors, and does include options for services.

They do have a set-up fee charge per book, and, while they have templates to assist with the creation of your POD book's interior and cover design files, most of the heavy lifting is expected to be done by you (or a designer you hire) in providing print-ready PDF files.

Because Ingram is the world's largest wholesaler, having a book listed in their catalog offers authors the most extensive English language reach into the bookstore and library market available.

If you are looking for the most options in terms of trim sizes (the dimensions of the book, such as 6" X 9" or 5.5" X 8"), and format (trade paperback, hardcover, and even large print), then *IngramSpark* will serve those needs effectively. In addition, the discount you offer to bookstores can be controlled, and you can set a discount of up to 55% to the downstream retail channels, which does make your POD title more appealing to many retailers. (Just a reminder that Amazon *KDP Print* doesn't allow discount control in their extended distribution, and thus offers bookstores a "short" 20% discount).

With *IngramSpark* you are required to have an ISBN for each edition of your book. There are options to buy them, at a discount, via Bowker, but an ISBN will typically cost more than the setup fee for your print books themselves. (Canadians take note. Library and Archives Canada allows Canadian authors access to ISBNs for free).

# Audiobooks

Although I am using the term Audiobooks, please note that I mean digital audio books by default and not the Audiobooks produced in physical CD format, which many of the larger trade publishers still produce.

If you licensed the audio rights to a traditional trade publisher then your publisher has likely already taken care of distribution of your book in digital audio format to the major retailer and library channels. They might even offer a physical Audiobook.

If the publisher did attain audio rights but hasn't actually exploited them and enough time after publication date has occurred, double check to see if there is a clause about that in the contract. The clause might state that rights revert back to the author under specific conditions or timelines. However, even without such a clause, I have successfully negotiated the return of my audio rights to me back from a publisher when, after four years, there was still no audiobook produced. It was simply a matter of the fact that the publisher didn't have the means to produce the audiobook, and, if I was able to, it would create an additional entry point into that book in its different formats, potentially benefiting sales of the print and eBook editions, which the publisher had properly exploited.

If you want to self-publish your audiobook, the two principal routes are the DIY option, or a paid audiobook creation and distribution service.

The DIY option includes having the production-ready audio files prepared to load but might also include a platform that allows you to find a professional narrator to work with.

Following is a high-level overview of four of the DIY distribution platforms.

## ACX

*ACX* is an Amazon-owned platform that allows for direct upload of the finished product and options for finding a narrator to work with using a self-directed RFP-style process. You can determine if you want to pay the narrator up front or to set up a royalty-sharing process. *ACX* will get your audiobook listed with Audible, Amazon, and Apple Books.

It is important to be aware that there is an option within ACX to either be exclusive (with a 7-year commitment), or non-exclusive. There are pros and cons of being locked into a single or limited number of retailers in a continually expanding market.

WIDE distribution is impossible with ACX, so just be aware that if you use their services your audiobook will not be available beyond three retail platforms.

## Authors Republic

*Authors Republic* is a Canadian company which was founded in 2015 and was the first company I ever learned of that offered authors the ability to load their fully produced and completed audiobook beyond Amazon and Apple. At the time of this writing, they distribute to 33 different retailer and library channels.

They offer distribution, and state that they offer the world's widest Audiobook distribution network of more than 50 channels.*

Though they don't offer support with having an audiobook created, they do provide a list of resources for that on their website.

Author's Republic gives you the option to set your own retail price with a disclaimer that they can't promise every distributor will use it. (Audible and Amazon set their own price).

The listed royalties are 70% of what your audiobook earns and they offer payment via a PayPal account or, for US-based authors with 10 or more titles, they allow setup of a direct bank deposit.

[* ***I haven't yet used Author's Republic myself, but in investigating their website, I see that*** **Chirp** ***(owned and run by BookBub) is one of the audiobook platforms they mention distributing to. The BookBub blog shares, in multiple posts, how, if indie authors want to get their Audiobooks listed at Chirp, the audiobook must be available through*** **Findaway Voices.** ***This suggests to me*** *that* Author's Republic *is using some combination of direct distribution to some platforms, and* Findaway Voices *for distribution to others, including* Chirp. *Which also suggests to me that the 70% royalty they claim might be 70% of the royalty received via another distributor—meaning, less money that one might expect. I wonder if it's 70% of the 80% received through any distribution happening via* Findaway Voices *or is it 70%, instead of the 80% received from* Findaway Voices?]

## Findaway Voices

*Findaway Voices*, launched in 2016, is run by Findaway, a US company that has been revolutionizing the audiobook industry since it launched in 2006. You can upload your completed audiobook for distribution, or you can use their platform to collaborate with a narrator, with choices of full payment to the narrator or royalty-splitting options.

In March 2021, *Findaway Voices* lists 42 available retail and library distributors. They constantly add new platforms, but also constantly remove platforms they do not believe are going to bring value for their authors.

Findaway takes a 20% distribution fee for all sales, which means 80% of the royalty receipts from different platforms. Because of the complex nature of the numerous platforms, it's not a clear 80% of the retail list price, like with eBooks. It could be 80% of the anywhere from 25% to 70% receipts as outlined in Schedule C of their distribution agreement. Payments are conducted via direct deposit.

In addition, they have a few built-in promotional opportunities that include an Authors Direct option of selling Audiobooks direct, the scheduling of price promotions to *Chirp* and *Apple,* and giveaway codes for each book published. (If you are in the Voices Plus program of using *Findaway Voices* for all your distribution, you get 100 giveaway codes rather than the standard 30)

## Kobo Writing Life

Kobo's direct publishing platform, *Kobo Writing Life,* launched their direct Audiobook publishing option to their platform in mid 2020. The program was initially offered in a beta release but is currently available to all authors.

Authors receive 35% royalties for audiobooks priced $2.99 or lower, and 45% royalties for audiobooks priced over $2.99.

Publishing an audiobook through Kobo Writing Life will automatically distribute your audiobooks to Kobo.com and the following partner sites: Indigo (CA), Walmart (US), BOL (NL), and Booktopia (AU). While this is 4 countries and partner sites, the distribution is not as extensive as currently offered when publishing eBooks to

Kobo. I'm sure it'll continue to grow over time, and at least, unlike ACX, there aren't any tricky exclusivity clauses.

There is also a possibility that, when you publish direct, you may be eligible for internal *Kobo Writing Life* specific promotional opportunities.

## Final Thoughts

There are also a number of service-oriented audiobook platforms that will, for a fee, help you produce an audiobook and distribute it to the downstream retailer and library channels.

I am not going to list the platforms that offer this, but I do, in the resources section at the end of this book, provide a few online sources where you can find some.

Of the providers in this realm, I have had personal experience working with *ListenUp Audiobooks,* a US company, for both production and distribution. I connected with them via a discounted service offering in a partnership they had with *Kobo Writing Life* (which saved me $100 per finished hour on the production of the very first audiobook I produced). I have also had the pleasure of touring their Atlanta headquarter studios. I can say that my experience working with them has been smooth and consistently professional, and I regularly receive printed checks on a quarterly basis from them.

Some are decent sized. Some come in less than one dollar. (I shared a Feb 2021 image of a $0.62 USD check on the *Wide for the Win* Facebook group, not as a way of making fun of myself, but demonstrating that sometimes wide publishing revenue can be small. But it's about multiple income sources from numerous platforms, that can all add up.)

Just be careful here.

Like with print books, there are plenty of over-priced packages and up-sold services that some companies out there might charge. You should always approach such services with a "writer be leery" attitude, and double check their reputation through online listings from the Alliance of Independent Authors or Writer Beware.

# PART III
# WIDE WITH LIBRARIES

# Libraries for the Win

Libraries should be an important part of your WIDE publishing strategy, as they open up a whole new readership to you and your books.

The first important thing to understand about libraries is that they can be a source of revenue for you as an author, both directly and indirectly.

Direct comes from library acquisition of titles where you are compensated. Indirect comes from the word of mouth that happens when a library patron discovers and talks about your book to other readers, some of whom may purchase by default.

In addition, if you live in a country that has a Public Lending Right program (such as Australian, Canada, Great Britain, etc.) you can also earn additional income from the presence of or circulation of your books through public libraries. (There's an entire chapter on that coming up).

An important thing for you to understand about libraries, is that, while libraries may purchase print titles from online and bricks and mortar bookstores, they typically can't do that for eBooks and digital Audiobook titles.

Your KDP Select title is not available to libraries, which means that being exclusive to Amazon for eBooks prevents you from leveraging the library market.

Something else that is important to understand about the library market, particularly when it comes to digital books, is that, unlike retailers, that are used to quick metadata changes and fast publication and "de-listing" of titles, library systems move at a different speed.

This is **not** the place to be hopping in and out of like one of those annoying little critters in a game of whack-a-mole. I'm referring to either publishing and unpublishing, or even **changing** the distribution method.

If your book is in a library system via one method, I would not recommend that you try to delist it and get it into the system via a different method. The only time to do that might be if there's something broken or significantly wrong with the initial way you got there. The library platforms are nowhere near as quick to respond to such changes, and your update could end up causing systematic issues and frustrations for the library service provider and/or the library itself. I recommend leaving well-enough alone, and, if you desire to change your library distribution methods, using that on your newer releases.

This goes for metadata updates too. I still have titles that, well over a year or more later, are still showing an old and out-dated cover on the library system.

Libraries have always been an important market for writers, and in recent years have become even more important. In March of 2020, when most of North America went into a lockdown, book lovers were not able to go out and browse in physical bookshops or libraries.

But they could very easily open up a library app such as the *hoopla* app or OverDrive's *Libby* and immediately get access to eBooks and audiobooks.

In a twist of fate, people were more worried about the virus that came on a physical print product rather than the digital file.

Digital consumption by readers, particularly library readers, saw triple digit growth in the spring and summer of 2020, the first time growth like that had been seen in the digital book space since the advent of the Kindle and iPad. An OverDrive rep reported to me that sales of eBooks alone through the library market went up as high as 130% in the last two weeks of March 2020 alone.

# Library Platform Overview

There are many library platforms available. Some of them are discussed in more detail in the following chapter, but here is a quick overview to help you get acquainted.

Please note that this is by no means an authoritative list, and it mostly covers general trade library platforms. It doesn't get into specifics on academic, education, and other library platforms.

## Baker & Taylor

Baker & Taylor is a large US wholesaler and provider to the bookstore and library market. According to their website, Baker & Taylor offers the most extensive selection of products and services for public libraries and is the only vendor that can truly offer a one-stop shopping experience for all formats, including print, movies, and music, and digital downloadable eBooks and eAudio content.

*Axis 360* is the app that delivers the eBook and digital audio content to users from libraries.

You can get your eBooks into B&T via *Draft2Digital, Smashwords*, and *StreetLib*.

Audiobooks can be opted in via *Authors Republic* and *Findaway Voices*.

## bibliotheca

bibliotheca (yes, that lowercase 'b' is part of their branding) is dedicated to the development of library management solutions that help sustain and grow libraries around the world. They have worked with libraries for close to half a century, have offices in all major continents and support libraries in more than 70 countries through their dedicated distributors. They partner with over 30,000 unique libraries.

cloudLibrary (again lowercase 'c' is a purposeful branding), is the app bibliotheca uses in support of eBooks and audiobooks for libraries.

You can get your eBooks into bibliotheca via *Draft2Digital, PublishDrive,* and *Smashwords.*

Audiobooks can be opted in via *Author's Republic* and *Findaway Voices.*

## BorrowBox

BorrowBox is an Australian-based digital library download solution for the British Commonwealth powered by Bolinda Digital. The service consists of a website and for most libraries also mobile apps for Apple and Android devices. The BorrowBox vision has always been to create a digital experience for libraries and library members that rivals consumer brands and to create a user experience that is world class—designed to be simple and made to inspire.

Stay tuned for announcements regarding BorrowBox distribution for eBooks and/or audiobooks.

## Gardners Library

Gardners is Britain's leading independent book and DVD wholesale distributor. They work with multi-channel retailers worldwide, both online and on the high street, to supply physical and digital products. Gardners distributes eBooks to independent, chain, specialist, and online retailers and school & library suppliers in the UK and across the world.

*Askews & Holts Library Services* is a sister company to Gardners, and operates the UK's largest library eBook service, powering the eBook checkout systems of 81 public library authorities in the UK comprised of 2,000+ public libraries. This represents over half of the UK library authorities, serving a local population of 17 million people.

*VLeBooks,* another sister company, is used by 400 schools & colleges in Europe, the Middle East & Asia and 78 universities in the UK, with over 200,000 students registered on the platform. More than 16,000 academic librarians and teachers use the platform for their digital and physical book orders.

You can opt eBooks into Gardners Library through *PublishDrive* or *Smashwords*.

## hoopla

hoopla (the 'h' is left lowercase to respect the company's branding) is the digital service of Midwest Tape, a leading provider of entertainment media products and services: DVDs, CDs, audiobooks and shelf-ready solutions, to public libraries across North America for over a quarter of a century. Their purpose has always been to partner with libraries in delivering the best content to patrons in the most streamlined manner possible.

CPC, or cost-per-checkout model is used by hoopla which allows eBooks and Audiobooks to be read by multiple readers at once—no one has to wait weeks or months to check them out.

There is a free hoopla app available on desktop or mobile device that patrons can connect to their local hoopla-enabled library system.

The company does seem to employ manual checking and vetting of titles that are imported, so, even if you are opted into hoopla, it might not mean your title is actually going to be available.

eBooks can be opted in via *Draft2Digital* and *PublishDrive*.

Audiobooks can be opted in via *Author's Republic* and *Findaway Voices*.

## Odilo

According to their website, Odilo is considered by many as the "Netflix for Education." They strive to democratise access to high-quality education, creating a world with unlimited learning possibilities for all, improve literacy levels and critical thinking skills, and empower lifelong learning. They have offices in 7 countries around the world, have a team of more than 100 members, and over 50 global partners.

You can opt eBooks in to Odilo via *PublishDrive, Smashwords,* and *StreetLib.*

You can opt Audiobooks in to Odilo via *Author's Republic* and *Findaway Voices.*

## OverDrive

US-based OverDrive, founded in 1986, is a digital distributor of eBooks, audiobooks, magazines and streaming video titles. The company provides secure management, digital rights management, and download fulfillment services for publishers, libraries, schools, corporations, and retailers.

They are perhaps the best-known library platform in North America. They describe themselves as dedicated to creating "a world enlightened by reading" by delivering the industry's largest catalog of eBooks, audiobooks, and other digital media to a growing network of 65,000 libraries and schools in 84 countries.

In April 2015, Rakuten (the company that also owns Kobo) bought OverDrive. OverDrive temporarily changed its name to Rakuten Kobo. In 2019, private equity firm KKR made a purchase offer for OverDrive from Rakuten. The acquisition was finalized in June 2020, and the company's name reverted back to the original OverDrive.

OverDrive's vision of creating a world enlightened by reading is an accurate representation of what this company does. Having met and interacted with Steve Potash, OverDrive founder and CEO, and many employees there over the years, I can assure you that the very DNA of the company is about the love of reading.

OverDrive's app *Libby* allows for the borrowing and consumption of digital books and audiobooks via local libraries. It offers offline access, sync across different platforms, and car compatible listening via Apple CarPlay, Android Auto, or a Bluetooth connection. In the US market only, *Libby* offers an option to send library books to a Kindle device.

The royalty structure for OverDrive for indie authors is typically one of the two models of OCOU (One Copy One User) and CPC (Cost Per Checkout).

OverDrive rarely works directly with indie/self-published authors. They do have a process by which you can publish direct, but it's extremely manual to get approved, and they usually only do that for accounts with a significant number of titles or an author whose name you'd likely recognize burning up all the major bestseller charts.

If you were to publish direct, OverDrive's terms are 50% on the OCOU (One Copy One User) model. But you get those same terms on OCOU going through *Kobo Writing Life* (those terms were negotiated when Kobo and Rakuten were sister companies), or you can get 45% to 47% via the other distribution platforms.

As mentioned, you can get your eBooks into OverDrive directly, but it's far easier, and a much better author experience to do it via *Draft2Digital, Kobo Writing Life, PublishDrive, Smashwords, and StreetLib.*

You can opt Audiobooks into OverDrive via *Author's Republic* or *Findaway Voices.*

Additional library platforms that might be worth keeping an eye out for include:

- 3Leaf Group
- Axiell
- Bidi
- EBSCO
- Follett
- MLOL
- Perma-Bound
- Wheelers

# The A's of Library Strategy

There are three fundamental elements related to a core library strategy.

First, you must ensure your book is available to libraries. Second, you need to ensure that the library is aware of your book. And third, the library must have the desire to acquire your book.

I call this *The Three A's of Library Strategy*. And I went through them in detail in my book **An Author's Guide to Working with Libraries and Bookstores**. For your convenience, I'll review it briefly, here.

The three A's are:

- Availability
- Awareness
- Acquisition

Let's dip into all three and explore a few of the requirements as we go through each one.

# Availability

## Availability: Print Books

Print is perhaps the most common format we think about when we turn our attention to libraries.

If your books are traditionally published, then that publisher either has warehousing and direct library sales channels or is already set up to sell their books through Ingram or Baker and Taylor, which are two of the English language, world's largest wholesalers of print books. This also means you can skip ahead to the *Awareness* segment, since the availability is mostly handled for you.

If, however, you are traditionally published with a smaller publishing house that uses POD or print on demand printing, then those books might still be available to libraries, most likely via Ingram. It is important to understand this aspect of the publisher you are working with. And I would advise if you have signed the rights to a book to any publisher that you double check and ask your publisher where and how libraries can purchase their books.

So, if you're using some other POD service for your self-published book, check with them to see how their books are made available to libraries.

*A Note of Caution:* Many authors use Amazon *KDP Print*, which is free, and is a great way to get your book in Amazon's catalog. But be aware that their *extended distribution* option isn't as attractive nor as appealing to libraries. This is due to the crappy terms that are offered to bookstores and libraries; non-returnable and short discounts. These terms are much worse than the library would get if you set up the distribution for it via *IngramSpark* or *Draft2Digital* Print.

In addition, some libraries might actually be opposed to the idea that they're ordering books from Amazon. That could actually be something that puts them off. I know it definitely puts off bookstores, particularly independent bookstores that are feeling the competition from Amazon.

It is a case where availability may be there, but awareness and acquisition might be reduced in some cases. And in that same vein, if you are using *IngramSpark* to make your POD book available to libraries, the authors that I know with the most success selling into those channels have usually selected the deepest discount available, which is 55%.

I know it means a deeper hit on your margin, and sometimes it requires having to lift your retail price a little more to compensate for that. But that larger discount can be appealing to the buyers at libraries. And while bookstores are also looking for non-returnable terms, the library purchasing model isn't about returns.

You do stand a much better chance of library acquisition than you do bookstore acquisition. And that's a great thing to consider when you think about the reach that libraries have into different communities.

## Availability: eBooks

Similar to what I mentioned in relation to print books, if you are traditionally published, check with your publisher to ensure they are distributing your eBook to the library market, and see if you can confirm which library wholesalers they are using. At the very least, they should have access to at least OverDrive and Baker & Taylor, two of the larger library distributors.

And, if your publisher is in that continually growing grey zone of calling themselves a "traditional publisher" without having actual legacy publishing warehouse distribution (ie, if they are a born-digital and digital-only publisher), do confirm that they are making the eBook available to libraries.

*Cautionary Note*: If their terms are author-friendly, there is nothing wrong with a digital-first, or digital-only publisher, particularly one that focuses on eBooks. But be aware that some outfits that sell themselves as "traditional publishers" and use a digital-only approach to publishing might be locking your book into exclusivity with Amazon *KDP Select*.

So, if you are trusting either a publisher or a publishing services provider, just double check to make sure they are making the eBook available to the library platforms or library wholesalers.

If you are self-publishing your eBook and are in full control of the distribution, there are several library wholesale distributors that exist and can help you get your books into the library markets.

I'm not going to outline any sort of authoritative list of these platforms, because this is likely to continue to evolve and change, but at the time of this writing, you can use places such as *Smashwords, Draft2Digital, StreetLib, PublishDrive,* and *Kobo Writing Life,* to get your eBook into the various channels that serve the library markets.

OverDrive is the world's leading digital reading platform for libraries and schools, delivering the book industry's largest catalog of eBooks, audiobooks, and other digital media to more than 43,000 libraries in 75 countries. For English language books, there is no doubt that they should be included in your strategy for getting your digital books into libraries.

So, let's spend a bit of time focusing on them. First of all, it is possible to have a direct account with OverDrive.

It is possible, but difficult.

And it is something I would not advise.

Based on my personal experience and from speaking with dozens of bigger name indie authors who were able to establish a direct account with OverDrive over the years, it's not worth your time, hassle, and struggle to establish a direct account. Simply, the systems and the methods to get titles into their systems directly are painful and extremely manual and require understanding and using FTP and Excel files and a whole world of frustration that'll remind you (if, like me, you're of a certain age) of the "Press play on tape one" days of computing.

In all seriousness, the people at OverDrive are among the nicest and most passionate book nerds you will ever meet. They are amazing; wonderful to work with (I've had the pleasure of knowing many of them for years), and they have a long-established wonderful relationship with libraries. But their systems are not optimized for small publishers or indie authors communicating directly with their business. Their systems are optimized to serve the library community, which is their forte and why you want to be in their catalog.

So, from a completely business-minded point of view, there's no need for OverDrive to waste time and resources building out an author friendly front end, because they have no shortage of third-party companies and even sister companies that specialize in getting titles into their system.

When I was running *Kobo Writing Life* (the direct-to-Kobo self publishing platform), I helped to negotiate an aggressive set of terms. So, if you make your books available to OverDrive via *Kobo Writing Life*, you get the same margin (50%) that you do if you had an account directly with OverDrive.

That's right. You get all the benefit of the full direct margin without any of the hassle of the tech stuff that you have to deal with when working direct with OverDrive.

This means, if you set a library price of $10 you would make $5 every time a library buys a single copy of one of your eBooks. This is done under what's known as either a one-to-one or a *one copy, one user* licensing model.

If a library system, New York Public Library, for example, buys a copy of your eBook, they can loan it to one NYPL patron at a time, forever. You get paid a decent amount upfront for the book, 50% but only ever see that money once, because the library now has a permanent copy they can continue to re-loan.

And, unlike a print book, where wear and tear might lead to them purchasing another copy (if a book were so popular that it would warrant that), there is no wear and tear on an eBook.

This *one copy, one user* model via *Kobo Writing Life,* which offers you 50% is the highest margin that you'll make from any third-party provider to overdrive.

If you use *Smashwords,* that same *one copy, one user* model gets you 45%. If you use *Draft2Digital,* you get about 47%.

However, with both *Kobo Writing Life* and *Draft2Digital,* there is an additional model that isn't available. It's called a *cost per checkout* model.

In the *cost per checkout* model, a library is able to get access to the same title for more than one user at a time, and instead of a fixed higher margin of 45%, 47%, or 50% of the library list price, they actually pay one tenth of the eBook's full list price each time the book is loaned out.

Here's how that difference works.

For a book that I have listed with the US dollar retail price of $4.99 I may have the library list price at $6.99.

That would mean that via *Kobo Writing Life*, I'd have the single option of *one copy, one user*, and I would make $3.49 cents per sale to a library market. In that same model, I would make $3.27 via *Draft2Digital*.

In this case, *KWL* nets 22 cents more than *D2D*.

But in a *cost per checkout* model, I'd make 46 cents every time a patron checks that book out.

I would make less up front than I would in that *one copy one user* model, but after more than seven people have checked out the eBook, I would start to earn more than I would for that single sale.

In my own experience, particularly with the *cost per checkout* model from audiobooks, those residual smaller payments can really add up.

Imagine that your book is being read by a local book club. Some people are going to buy the print book, and some are going to buy the eBook. Some are going to flock to their local library for either the print or eBook editions.

If the book club is a library specific book club, then there'd be a higher demand for one particular branch of the library to have more than one copy of the book. So, either the library has to spend their budget on buying multiple copies, or only one lucky reader will have access to it at a time, while the others are on a waiting list and can only read that copy when they finish.

That's not ideal for a book club, where all the members want to be reading simultaneously.

However, in the *cost per checkout* model, an unlimited number of people could check out the book at the exact same time. Let's imagine that there were 20 people in this library branch book club and they all check out the book and rather quickly earn you far more than the single copy sold to a library.

Remember that *cost per checkout* does come with a short-term reduction of margin, but also with ongoing earning benefits of smaller payments that might, in the long run work out to be worth more.

Remember that short-term versus long-term thinking we talked about in the mindset section? This is another area where it pays off.

For my own personal strategy, I am more leaning towards that long-term CPC or *cost per checkout* option. As I've mentioned, I've already seen some decent success in that realm already within audiobooks.

There are plenty of other library distribution options available. Baker and Taylor, Bibliotheca, and hoopla are among the other options that libraries regularly use.

*Draft2Digital* can, for example, get your eBook into those markets and more. Each of these library wholesalers uses either a *one copy per user* or *cost per checkout* model. Some library channels, like OverDrive, use a combination of both.

### *Recommended eBook Pricing Strategy*

Platforms like *Kobo Writing Life, Smashwords, and Draft2Digital* allow you to set and control your library price separate from your retail price.

*KWL* and *Draft2Digital* typically advise that authors set their library price at anywhere between 1.5 to 3 times their regular retail price.

The reason for this is because of the previously mentioned *one copy, one user* licensing model for library sales. In this model, when a library purchases your eBook, they can loan that single copy of the eBook to one customer at a time, forever. This means that, unlike in regular retail channel sales, where you earn money every time a new customer buys your book, you only get paid once via a library sale. That library sale, then, is valued higher.

This strategic pricing strategy also keeps in mind the stark realty that most of the major publishers, whose retail price for eBooks is typically two to three times the retail price for independently published titles, similarly set significantly higher library prices. The average retail list price of a new release from a big publisher can range from $9.99 to $19.99 USD. When it comes to library list prices, those same titles might be priced anywhere between $30 to $80 USD.

While independent author eBook retail prices for full-length books have slowly walked up over the years from the realm of $0.99, $1.99, and $2.99 USD, the majority of retail sales typically happens in the $3.99 to $8.99 USD realm for most of those successful authors.

This pricing strategy is used partially as an obvious value offer for readers, but also as a way to remove the barrier from a reader who might be interested in checking out a writer whose work they are not familiar with.

Personally, while I respect a strategy that makes eBooks more affordable for readers, I still think that self-published authors default to under-valuing their work in the same way that traditional publishers outrageously over-price their books. But let's not get me started on that lengthy and heated discussion, except to say that I believe indie authors can still offer competitive prices on their eBooks without having to practically give them away. A well written, well-edited, and professionally produced book is all a reader wants. And most readers are willing to pay a fair and reasonable price for their six to eight hours of reading pleasure.

In keeping with this type of competitive pricing strategy for the library market, you'd be advised to consider that 1.5 to 3 times your retail price when pricing for the library market. Apply the larger multiplier when your pricing is in the low realm, and apply the smaller multiplier when your regular retail price is north of $4.99.

You should be aware that librarians will often look to see what your regular retail price is on the major eBook platforms. Because, while your library price is most likely significantly more affordable than the pricing of comparable titles from the major publishers, they also don't want to feel like you are ripping them off.

For example, if your regular retail price for a novel is $0.99 USD and your library price is $9.99 USD your pricing model is ten times higher for libraries and might be construed as a greedy move.

If, as a "classically trained" indie author who is most comfortable with significantly lower pricing on your books, setting a library price that is any sort of multiplication higher than the retail price makes you squirm and fidget in your seat, consider this: in the *one copy, one user* library licensing model, you will typically only ever sell a single copy to any library system. This means that library permanently owns that copy and can loan it out, to one patron at a time, forever, and you only ever earn that money once.

## Availability: Audiobooks

In the same way that Amazon is a household name and most authors who are looking at publishing eBooks are familiar with Kindle and *KDP*, they are also familiar with the digital audiobook service Audible (which is owned by Amazon) and *ACX* (*Audiobook Creation Exchange*), the gateway for authors to get their work in to Audible, Amazon, and iTunes (which recently re-branded as Apple Books).

While *ACX* offers a royalty share option that requires absolutely no cash up front (opting to share their earned margin with a narrator), making it easier for authors to break into the audio market, that option comes with a cost of 7 years of exclusivity.

Similarly, even if you pay up front for the narrator's work, *ACX* has a parallel 7-year exclusivity clause that earns authors a higher royalty rate from Audible.

If your audiobook is locked into exclusivity with ACX, then it will not be available into the library market.

There is a way out of exclusivity, if you are looking for one. As of November 2019, the following is true: If the audiobook was completed as a *Pay-for-Production* deal, (meaning you paid for the narrator's work up front), the distribution rights can be changed from exclusive to non-exclusive after it has been on sale in stores for one year. If, however, your audiobook is in a *Royalty Share* deal, the agreement cannot be changed.

If you are interested in getting your audiobook in to the library systems, your two main choices include *Author's Republic* and *Findaway Voices*.

Both of those companies have broad distribution options that include library markets such as OverDrive, Baker & Taylor, Bibliotheca, hoopla, and Odilo.

In my particular case, and the platform that I'm most familiar with for getting audiobooks into the library market is using *Findaway Voices*. So, I will specifically talk about their process; but be aware that *Author's Republic* offers a similar service.

With *Findaway Voices,* you can get your audiobook into the following library markets: Overdrive, Baker & Taylor, Bibliotheca, hoopla, Odilo, Bidi, Ebscoe, Follett, MLOL, 3Leaf Group, Perma-Bound and Wheelers.

These library systems all have either a la carte, which works like the *one copy one user* model discussed for eBooks, or a *cost per checkout* model. In some library markets, such as OverDrive, Bibliotheca, and Odilo, both are available. And, like eBooks, you have the ability of creating a unique library price as opposed to the regular retail price.

This means that you can set special prices just for the library market.

*Findaway Voices* is part of a larger audiobook distribution company called Findaway. Findaway might be considered as the Ingram for the digital audiobook market. Among other things, Findaway boasts the world's largest catalog available for the retail and library market, with close to a quarter of a million titles from over 2400 international publishers.

When you make your audiobook available through *Findaway Voices*, you can leverage this distribution platform, and always have the choice to which specific downstream networks you wish to distribute to via a per-title opt-in process.

### *Recommended Audiobook Pricing Strategy*

*Findaway Voices* allows you to set and control a separate and distinct library price for your audiobook. They have a built-in tool based on details from sales volumes, per genre that can suggest an optimal price for your audiobook.

The pricing strategy algorithm they use is complex and dynamic and is not something that can be replicated here. But it does result in showing you three suggested price range options for your audiobook: Minimum Recommended; Findaway Recommended; Maximum Recommended.

## Awareness and Acquisition

I'm going to cover awareness and acquisition jointly because the two coexist and play well off of one another.

Just having your book listed as available to the library systems does not necessarily mean that libraries will even see or order your book. So it is just as important for you to understand how librarians become aware of books.

Librarians typically order books largely based on reviews. Getting a review into magazines like the following (listed in alphabetical order) can be extremely useful towards awareness exposure into the library markets.

- Booklist (Circulation 80,000 in print; 160,000 online)
- Library Journal (Circulation: 100,000)
- Publishers Weekly (Circulation 68,000)
- School Library Journal (Children/Teen titles) (Circulation: 43,000 in print)
- Voya (YA/Teen Titles—for print and audio)

At the end of this book you will find the URLs for each of these resources along with a bit more information about how to submit to them.

Getting your book listed and/or reviewed in one or more than one of these librarian-centric magazines and online resources can increase the likeliness of the library being aware of and acquiring one or more of your books.

But they are also not easy to get into, and many of them can end up costing you hundreds of dollars, which may take a lot longer for you to earn back.

And, in addition, just having your book listed in such a magazine, journal, or online resource, doesn't mean that there's any guarantee a librarian will actually see it.

So, what does help a librarian find a book?

What other things influence what they might be looking for?

The genre of your book actually makes a tremendous difference. In general, librarians are constantly looking for commercial fiction in order to appeal to their patrons; and that would include any of the more commercially oriented genres such as romance, and mystery and thriller; science fiction, fantasy, and horror also count among these areas, though the popularity of those genres is often related to what is popular in movies and television, as reader demand in an area often peaks during particular seasons, or trends.

In the height of the *Harry Potter* book and movie release period, for example, there might have been a higher than usual search for young adult fantasy novels. Similarly, when the Peter Jackson movies in the *Lord of the Rings* franchise were released, librarians might have seen more demand for epic fantasy. Dystopian fiction (often considered a sub-genre of science fiction), saw growth when *The Hunger Games* books and movies were hot, or with the popularity of *The Handmaid's Tale* television series based on Margaret Atwood's novel of the same name.

Vampire fiction has seen multiple peaks and valleys over the years, from the time when Anne Rice and her ***Interview with the Vampire*** novels and movie created a larger interest in vampire novels, to the increase in public thirst for vampires and other supernatural beings from Stephenie Meyer's ***Twilight*** series.

If you are writing outside of the commercial genres, this doesn't mean that you can't still find a librarian that would be interested in your titles. That is because every library system, and every branch within each library system, has its own unique patrons, its own preferences, its own staff who each bring something unique. In addition, each staff member of a library is going to offer a unique perspective and unique tastes.

Apart from reviews, librarians also acquire books based on customer demand and local interest or special collections. That's where being familiar with the trends, such as the examples just mentioned, can come in handy.

If a particular franchise or type of story is popular, epic fantasy, for example, based on Tolkien movies or the popularity of a television series such as *Game of Thrones*, and you have an epic fantasy novel or series that satisfies the cravings of patrons looking for more in that genre, then you have a relatively easy "in" for getting the interest of a librarian.

Beyond popular culture and trends, libraries in different regions might have a unique speciality or flavor to their acquisitions.

Perhaps there is one particular branch, for example, in a city system that specializes in a certain type of book or genre.

Maybe it's a library in a rural area that specializes in books on agriculture; both non-fiction titles or even fiction titles where agriculture is an important element of the fiction. Perhaps it is a branch that focuses on books for children, young readers, and teenagers.

Or, to use a specific example of a location that I have visited, there is the Merril Collection branch of the Toronto public library, for example. This location, known as *The Merril Collection of Science Fiction, Speculation & Fantasy* is a non-circulating research collection of 80,000 items of science fiction, fantasy, and speculative fiction, as well as magic realism, experimental writing, and writing within what are known as the "fringe" areas that include parapsychology, UFOs, ghosts, Atlantean legends, etc.

Understanding a library's area of specialty or regional biases can help you to understand the likeliness of there being a natural fit for your books and their patron community.

But, apart from default preferences and genre trends, librarians do pay close attention to the requests and demands of their patrons.

Basically, librarians often acquire the books their patrons ask them for. They pay close attention to what their local community is interested in, and the books and authors that they specifically request.

That's why I think it's important to focus on the front-line method of reaching out to local libraries.

There are two fundamental ways to do this.

One is by informing your readers (through your author newsletter, or via your social media presence) that your books are available via the library, and actually telling them to go into their library and request your book. It's actually a great courtesy to your readers and fans of your work. Instead of asking them to purchase your book or books, you're letting them know they can get access to your book for free, just by asking for the book (in print, eBook, or audiobook format) at their local library. I'll walk through a specific method you can use for that shortly.

The other is by spending the time to get to know your local library and the various branches so that you can properly understand more about them, their preferences, their biases, and their staff.

I would advise a strategy of starting with a library local to your town or city. After all, proximity makes it easier for you to spend time there, which is the best way to witness, first-hand, what that library branch is all about. And then, after you have become comfortable with that, you can do the same thing and move on to the larger country, region, or the state or province.

Start as local as possible, then expand your way out. One of the reasons for that isn't just the ease of getting to the local branch for the in person and personal experience. It's for that potential interest in you as a local writer. This can be a significant point of interest for them in general. But also, don't forget to think about the location and setting of your book, whether it's nonfiction or fiction.

Does your novel take place or reference a real-world physical location close to where that library is located? Is one of the major characters from a particular area close to that library?

Either of those can be a local interest element.

And that's just another good "in" you can have with a library.

But before you connect with a library, you need to find contact information.

As always, Google is your friend, but sites such as lib-web.org is a fantastic resource that can help you find local libraries in different regions of the world.

I would suggest that you create a spreadsheet of library contact information so you can keep track of the contact info that you have gathered and who you've reached out to, so you don't have to keep going back to the library website once you find the info that you need.

It's simple if you just stick to local libraries, but it can start to get more complex once you start reaching out to a broader range of library audiences that are beyond your local region.

Your library contact information tracking spreadsheet might be best served with using the following fields:

- Library type (public, academic, public school, etc.)
- Library name
- Library branch
- Website
- Contact name
- Contact title/role
- Email
- Phone number or extension
- Date contacted
- Additional notes

You may have one library where you have multiple contacts, names, and titles. So, you might plan on either having multiple contact name, title, email, phone fields, or organize the spreadsheet to contain multiple listings for the same library or branch.

Additional notes might be a field where you keep track of when you heard back from them or perhaps if you hadn't heard back from them, when and how you might want to follow up.

## Mining OverDrive for Information

You can also use overdrive.com as a way to find local libraries, which is particularly useful if you're making your books available via OverDrive. It's a little trickier to get to the library's actual website, but overdrive.com does offer a handy map that can be very handy for you to see libraries based on region or postal code or zip code.

Once you find a location on the OverDrive map, you can click through it to get to that library's OverDrive specific catalog site. Usually, because it's a default template, if you scroll down to the very bottom, you're likely to find a link to the library's actual website. And it's on that website where you'll be able to find contact information. Unfortunately, every website has their own style, structure and look and feel, so it'll take a bit of browsing around to find what you're looking for.

When looking at library websites, I typically search out three primary contacts. They are:

- The acquisitions librarian
- The reference librarian
- The events coordinator

Titles or roles are going to be different in every library system, so you'll have to pay attention to those subtle differences (such as, for example, a reference librarian being referred to as a research librarian); but in essence, the responsibilities of those three roles are what become important.

Not only will different libraries have different ways of naming the roles for these specific people, but in some libraries the roles might be blended together. Larger metropolitan libraries with multiple branches may have head office folks as well as people at different branches that perform similar and overlapping roles. Smaller libraries might just have a few staff members who perform multiple roles; ie, a really small library, where a single librarian is responsible for everything.

In addition, some websites don't list the names of the people in the roles. In those cases, there's often a *Contact Us* form, which you can use to reach out to the libraries.

I have done both. I've reached out directly to specific people with their names and titles and addressed them personally, but I've also used the contact form and mentioned, in my note that my message was intended for the person in charge of acquisitions or special events or perhaps the reference librarian, depending on the context of my message.

Before you reach out, take the time to learn more about the library. Check out their website, see if they have a blog or community newsletter for events or special activity resources. Sign up for and read their newsletter or their blog. Maybe they have videos. Whatever it is that the library offers or specializes is, understand what they're doing and giving to the community, so you have a better feel for who these people are and what they're up to.

And, while this online contact information is extremely useful and important—we do, after all, live in a digital world—it's important to take some time to get into your local library branch or branches, to visit it in person.

A personal visit to the library can provide all kinds of invaluable insights about the library that might never be evident on their website. Get in there and explore it and understand what they do. Attend an event there. Often the special events coordinator or some other person involved in events might be the person introducing the guest speaker or the workshop.

You might even want to visit your local library as a writer with your own writing research needs, and actually work with a reference librarian to do research for your book. That activity makes that librarian intimately familiar with your book while you're creating it. They have a vested interest because they've helped you along the way.

Imagine a librarian talking to a library patron about your book while sharing the fact that you did a portion of your writing and research for it right there in that branch.

Simply, the more familiar you are with the library and their operation, the more comfortable you're going to be when you reach out to them to talk about you and your book and how you and your book can actually serve the library community.

One of the ways you can best serve the library community comes from having all of the information about your book handy prior to your first contact with them as an author telling them about your book.

## Reaching Out to The Library

Once you have done your homework and learned more about your local library or particular libraries where there is a connection to you and your writing, and you have also found and captured information about your book or books, it's time to reach out to libraries.

As you consider reaching out, keep the following things in mind.

How do you and your book serve library community? What is the uniqueness that either you or your book offer to that library?

If you simply reach out blind to a local library with a "Dear Sirs" style letter that talks about why your book is great and why they should carry your book, you may not get the same reception as reaching out to a local branch where you've already attended an event and you can even comment on, or compliment them on something about their library.

I like to follow a basic structure for reaching out and contacting libraries:

- Point 1: You & your library are awesome
- Point 2: Me and my book are awesome
- Point 3: Here is an awesome thing that me and my book can offer your awesome library

That's a bit of a hyperbole, but remember, people are always quite interested in themselves, so start with something about them.

Then briefly introduce you and what you're about (keeping in mind how it might relate to them), and end with something unique that you can offer them. You can also include some of your experience that helps highlight the offer.

This isn't a sales pitch—it's a note about what you might have that can help them or make their lives easier by assisting with an offering to their patrons.

Here's an example of the type of letter that might work, addressed to a specific person, in this case the person who oversees events at the main library branch.

> *Dear Sheila:*
>
> *I attended the Kitchener Public Library book launch for James Allen Gardener last month, and I had a wonderful time. The event in your stunning atrium was informative and inspiring, and I particularly loved the Q&A interview format with James that made it feel like James was a guest on a late night talk show.*
>
> *I'm an author who recently moved to the region and I have recently published a book for writers that is available in print, eBook, and audiobook. The ISBNs for each format are listed below, as is a link to the book via OverDrive where you can see the eBook and the audiobook versions.*

*I offer workshops that help writers understand the business of writing and publishing, and I would love the opportunity to discuss hosting a workshop for any of your patrons who may be interested in getting started in writing, or perhaps in furthering their knowledge and understanding of the business aspects of writing and publishing.*

*Apart from the aforementioned book, I've written or edited more than 20 books in the past 15 Years with small presses, with Dundurn Press, Canada's largest domestic publisher, as well as indie published titles. I have also worked in the book industry since 1992.*

*I would love to discuss leveraging my experience to help with any writing and publishing programming needs that you have, and I look forward to connecting with you.*

*Sincerely,*

*Mark Leslie Lefebvre*

The letter would include the ISBNs for each format, the URLs to the books mentioned in OverDrive's catalog, perhaps also the URL to my OverDrive author page, and my full contact information, including phone number.

Remember, the key is to be concise, polite and as specific as possible about your book and about how you and your book might serve the library community.

And, of course, following a style that it suitable for you.

I think it's important, when you're talking to the library, to ensure they know you're familiar with them. If you've had a pleasant experience with the library share it with them. It doesn't matter if it's about something on their website, like an article, or blog post or staff recommendation element; maybe it was something in their monthly newsletter; or perhaps it was an event or even some sort of curation that they've done for a book that was recommended to you.

It doesn't matter what it is. Take the time to let them know you appreciate what they're doing in and for the community. Let them know that you're a part of this community. And then let them know what it is that you can do to help them in something that they do to serve the community; that you're there to provide them with valuable content and resources in that mission.

Because that's what a library is. A library is valuable content, valuable resources.

In terms of whom to contact at the library, if I don't already know specific people from my own visits—ie, if the contact being made is mostly due to online research, I try to reach out to the three main contact people I've mentioned earlier in this chapter.

### *The Acquisitions Librarian*

The acquisitions or the collections librarians are typically the ones who do the purchasing. It makes sense to contact them when letting them know about your new or your backlist book.

When you are reaching out to the acquisitions librarian, it is useful if you understand and express how the book you are pitching to them fulfills a particular need for the library patron.

This goes back to the core fundamental of having fully fleshed out your target audience by knowing what comparable titles your book will appeal to. And, the bigger name the author, the more likely you are to get the attention of the librarian.

This is because, with limited budgets, and with the significant costs that most major publishers charge libraries for eBooks (usually anywhere between $30 and $80 per copy, and, often with a limited term), there might be an opportunity for your books to fulfill an important library need.

Let's look at, what to me, is a very obvious example.

Lee Child is the author of the Jack Reacher novels. Reacher is a character who is widely known and loved (you might recognize him as being played by Tom Cruise in a series of movies), and, for avid thriller readers, and, in particular, librarians, Lee Child is a well-known name.

Independently published author Diane Capri, who happens to be good friends with Child, has several novels in *The HUNT FOR REACHER Series* which are the only official authorized Reacher novels. These books are also recommended by Lee Child. In her agreement with Child, Capri doesn't have Reacher actually appear in her books; he is never explicitly seen in them. The series features FBI agents who are on the trail of Reacher and appear in each of the locales he has recently visited.

The first novel in her series, ***Don't Know Jack*** takes place in Margrave, Georgia, fifteen years after Reacher appeared there in Child's first Reacher novel ***Killing Floor***. The other novels follow the agents as they continue to track Reacher's "off the grid" wandering.

For readers who can't get enough Reacher stories and are all caught up on the books by Child, or even for the readers who are on the long waiting lists for the latest Lee Child novels at most library systems, these novels by Capri fulfill an important demand.

And, based on the more reasonable price that I know Capri sets for libraries, a library could acquire all twelve of her *The Hunt For Reacher Series* novels for the price of perhaps two or three copies of the novels by Lee Child, easily satisfying plenty of library patrons looking for a good read that is right in their wheelhouse.

Other authors, who have characters and a series that are similar in style to Lee Child's Jack Reacher would likely also do well with a similar approach.

UK bestselling author Mark Dawson, who writes a series of a Reacher-like character named John Milton, would do well in this environment. Of course, at the time of this writing, most of Dawson's Milton books are exclusive to Amazon Kindle via KDP Select, which means that, while he is earning a significant amount of money from Amazon, that particular IP is not available for library patrons, or for taking advantage of such an opportunity within libraries.

Oh well. More room for other authors who aren't exclusive to Kindle to make their way.

Do you have a police procedural? Maybe even a series of a police procedural? That might fit.

Also, because this is part of a newer series that features Detective Rene Ballard, a newer character, who has teamed up with retired Detective Harry Bosch, there could be a great appeal for an author like Carolyn Arnold.

Arnold, who lives in London, Ontario, has adopted the trademark: *POLICE PROCEDURALS RESPECTED BY LAW ENFORCEMENT*™ and has four continuing series that include cozy mysteries, hard-boiled mysteries, thrillers, and action adventures.

But her Detective Madison Knight series is one that would appeal to readers of this Bosch/Ballard novel and series.

To me, this seems like a ripe opportunity for a local author like Carolyn Arnold to leverage. Because, not only would knowing about and having her books in multiple formats provide a similar reading experience to what the readers get from Connelly, but there's also the "local author" angle that some librarians might enjoy showcasing.

I can imagine a librarian, having to tell countless customers each day that the hot new Connelly novel is on hold, and that the wait time is going to be more than a few weeks, "but we do have stock of an internationally bestselling local author by the name of Carolyn Arnold who has a fantastic police procedural that has been described as respected by law enforcement. Would you like me to show them to you?"

I'm hoping that sharing these examples gives you an idea of how you might leverage this for your own purposes.

The key is to know who your readers are, what other books; especially the more popular books and authors and series, your readers are likely to enjoy, and see if there is a way that you and your books can fulfill those needs.

That is what is important to make sure you share with the acquisitions librarian.

*An Important Cautionary Note*: Whatever you do, **do not** attempt to compare your book in style or content, to a major author if there is no close match, merely because the author is well-known and popular. That will only serve to highlight you as both unprofessional and unreliable.

There is an obvious and direct relation between the novels Diane Capri has written and the popular Lee Child novels. Or between the police procedurals that Carolyn Arnold writes and most of Michael Connelly's novels.

But if Capri were to suggest that her novels would appeal to readers of J. K. Rowling's *Harry Potter* series, or Arnold were to suggest her novel ***Christmas is Murder*** in her cozy McKinley Mysteries series would be perfect for Connelly's police procedural readers, that would be misleading.

Sometimes it can be helpful if you also reach out to the other roles mentioned before, such as the events coordinator or the reference librarian, which I will get to a little later.

But you also might want to ensure that the director or the head librarian or the branch manager also knows about it too, because it never hurts to have more than one person made aware of your book.

Here's one of the reasons it's good to establish contact with more than one person. Perhaps the acquisitions person doesn't like the type of book that you write; or maybe they just received your information on a bad day; such as a day where they were short staffed and had to cover someone else's role, and they received twice as many emails as normal that day, and ended up skipping through half of them, including yours, without really attending to it.

But perhaps the head librarian at that branch is a huge fan of the type of book you are pitching. Or maybe one of the other folks working in a different area of the library resonates with you or your book. It's not all that different from the way that different booksellers in the same store might react differently to you and your book or books.

Connecting with them can make all the difference.

Different librarians have different tastes and different approaches and different styles, and so being in contact with different people at the library or even establishing relationships with them in an authentic and real way could actually work out in your favor in the long run.

### *The Events Librarian*

Reaching out to the librarian who oversees events is typically done when you are offering to fulfill some sort of event.

In my case, because I have written several true ghost story books, letting the library know that I am available to do a talk about local history and local ghosts, and making that offer in mid-to-late summer (about the time they are looking at scheduling their October events, usually events that include a Halloween theme) works well.

I have, of course, done historic ghost talks in the middle of the winter, too. But I have found that the interest in that topic peaks during the lead up to Halloween.

In general, readings on their own don't necessarily work well—except, perhaps, for readings of picture books to younger children. This may be because many authors aren't skilled at readings, or they might go on too long, which can lead to patron unrest. I have found that doing a very brief reading, to give the audience a flavor of the book, combined with a talk related to the book or story, works best.

This is where you have to apply the same creativity that you would have applied to writing your book.

It's easy for me to derive content for a talk about local ghosts; but what if it's a novel, rather than a non-fiction book about that city?

Does anything related to your book or writing connect to a workshop or presentation that you can do at the local library? How about the journey of writing and publishing your book?

I have done workshops on how to write scary stories. I have also done workshops on how to write query letters to publishers, how to self-publish an eBook, how to perform research for a novel. All of these were derived from my own experience as a writer.

Canadian bestselling author Terry Fallis does an amazing talk on his unorthodox journey through publishing, sharing how, when he wasn't able to find a publisher, he self-published the book and began podcasting his novel for free and gained a world-wide audience; then, how his self-published novel won a major literary award, which landed him an agent, a publishing deal, which led to over seven other novels plus a television show based on his first novel—the same one that publishers weren't, at first, interested in.

What is unique or interesting about your own author journey that could intrigue or inspire the patrons of a library who are fascinated with writing?

Perhaps there's something inspiring from the research you had to do. Perhaps the hook from the premise of your novel is something that can draw a reader's attention.

Years ago, I was interviewing UK author Peter James in front of a bookish audience. He ended up sharing stories of how one of his early readers was a police detective who had reached out to correct him on an error he had inserted into his novel. James relayed the tale of how he thanked the man for helping him identify a logistical error to correct and then asked if he would read the early draft of his next book in case a similar error or misperception appeared. The man was honored to be asked, eagerly read and provided feedback on the novel, and a long-term friendship resulted from that experience.

Michael Connelly, whom I interviewed in a similar fashion, also relayed stories about the relationships he has had with law enforcement professionals over the years, and his own background as a crime reporter before he penned his first police procedural crime thriller.

Canadian science fiction author Robert J. Sawyer is a genius at relaying the premise for so many of his novels that usually combine a speculation based on real science combined with a brief "what if" that make for fascinating talks.

For his novel ***Flashforward***, for example, which was adapted into an ABC television series, the basic premise was: *If you could see the future, would you be able to change it*? This premise came from a casual conversation that took place during a high school reunion. In the story, an experiment with The Large Hadron Collider (the world's largest and most powerful particle accelerator) leads everyone in the world to black out for about two minutes where they have a short vision of their future.

In Sawyer's *WWW* trilogy of ***Wake, Watch,*** and ***Wonder*** his premise was: *Given that the world wide web is expected, by the early 21st century, to have the same number of synapses as the human brain, what if, like the human brain, it developed a consciousness?* That came from a combination of an article from *New Scientist,* Sawyer's fascination with chimpanzee sign-language, the nature of perception, and a re-imagination of the relationship between Helen Keller and her teacher, Anne Sullivan.

Without even getting into the details of the plot of either of these novels, Sawyer can hold an audience in rapt fascination, wonder, and speculation just talking about the premises.

So, in that same manner, what, in the genesis of your own novel, inspired you to write it? What about the research that you did for it could be an interesting tale to share? Is there an aspect of the book based on the setting that could be of interest to that local audience? Is there a classic book or movie that relates to your book; or perhaps a combination of two potentially disparate ones? How did you go about the research for your book, and where did you find the information that you needed? What deeply important personal experience led you to writing this novel, or non-fiction or self-help book?

If nothing from those questions work, you can always draw from the experience of writing the book. Often, beginning writers can be fascinated with learning more about the behind-the-scenes of a writer's life. Where did your original idea for the book come from? And how did you adapt that initial idea into the construct of the book? Are you a *pantser* or a *plotter*, or some combination of the two? What sort of environment best suits your writing—quiet isolation, or the hustle and bustle of a busy coffee shop? Do you listen to music when you write—and do different genres or styles of music suit different types of your writing? How much of your personal experience is baked into the various characters in your novels?

The key is that there are plenty of things you can talk about and share about your book that are derived from the content, subject matter, or theme from the book. And while none of those involves an author reading from the text of the book, plenty of them are wider reaching generic subjects that might be interesting to an events librarian looking for content to entertain or inform their patrons.

### *The Reference Librarian*

Contacting the reference librarian can also be critical. Reference librarians are amazing folks and are an incredible community resource. These are the folks who often oversee the main information and archives or resource and research desk in the library. They are typically beautiful data nerds who love collecting and gathering and storing and sharing information.

Their role is to collect and to give out information. Ensuring that they know about you, that you're a local author, perhaps that you're a subject matter expert in a particular area, or a genre author of a specific niche, is likely something they're going to file away and that they may pull out for the appropriate local researcher who comes along.

Like in other more in-depth strategies for authors, it's not a tactic, but rather a long-term investment that you are making in your career.

In my writing journey, I have spent countless hours with different reference librarians when researching for my nonfiction books about ghosts. For example, when I was doing research for my book ***Haunted Hamilton,*** I spent a significant amount of time at the main branch of the Hamilton Public Library where Margaret Houghton, who was the local public library archivist tirelessly filled me with all kinds of information about local history; and, in particular, local ghostly tales.

She gave me access to a wonderful file folder of newspaper clippings, historical articles, and other collected documents that were all related to ghosts and the paranormal and the darker aspects of Hamilton's past. This special file, in the back of the local archives section, is information that I would not have known about or had access to using any of their online systems or even any of the great online resources for the library.

It was through in-person discussions and conversation about the book I was researching for that I learned about all these things. Margaret, who has been described as Hamilton's most beloved chronicler of local history, was amazingly helpful. And I'm pretty sure that up until her retirement in 2016 she likely put my book ***Haunted Hamilton*** into the hands of countless potential readers who came in and were looking for spookier and darker tales of the city; because that's the kind of thing that a reference librarian does.

So even if the acquisitions person might not be interested in your book, or you don't get any nibbles on events that you have offered to the library, sometimes the local archivist or the reference librarian knowing about you, knowing about your book, may be something that they can recommend to different consumers who come in there.

During the school year, for example, children regularly show up at the library and say that their teacher wants them to read a Canadian author. Or their teacher says they have to read an author from their home state of Nebraska. Or a book set in the particular county or region native to the school. Can the library recommend a book? It's usually the reference librarian who is interested in collecting and storing this type of information and they often love having those answers either at the ready, or within their archives of data.

Returning to Robert J. Sawyer, since the aforementioned ***Wake, Watch, Wonder*** trilogy or novels were primarily set in Waterloo and involve the main character's father working at Waterloo's Perimeter Institute for Theoretical Physics, the books have a local hook that could be compelling for local reference librarians in my locale of Kitchener, Waterloo, and Cambridge. And James Alan Gardner, a local Kitchener-Waterloo based author I mentioned in the chapter on bookselling (his "local author" status is already a hook for Waterloo Region librarians), set his two most recent novels, ***All Those Explosions Were Someone Else's Fault*** and ***They Promised Me The Gun Wasn't Loaded*** in the area, with his main characters being students (and superheroes) at the University of Waterloo.

Context, content, and contributor are three things that a reference librarian values; particularly how each of those elements relates to their particular local library needs.

## The Library's Needs

To summarize a common element that flows through the contacts that you have with the library, your focus should always be on how you and your book(s) are able to fulfill a need they have in serving the local community. Whether it's information, inspiration, insight, or just plain entertainment, there is usually something that you are able to offer that might be of value to the library.

Think of it the same way that pundits recommend you engage in your social media strategy. It's an 80% give and share, and 20% ask or request. And if you have to lean or default in any way, make that split a 90 / 10 split, always heavy on the side of providing value and content.

You want the people who manage and work at the library to see their relationship with you as a benefit, not a burden.

# The BIG DEAL about Large Print

Many authors who have their book available in the three formats of print, eBook, and audiobook believe that they have covered all the formats.

But there is another print format that can be a massive thing for libraries.

Large Print books.

Yes, the advent of eBooks means that every single re-flowable eBook is, essentially, a large print book (readers can modify the font style and size directly in their eReader or the app that reads the ePub or Mobi file). But since a huge amount of the population still has not read an eBook, libraries are still on the lookout for large print editions of books.

Creating a large print book is different than the process of creating a standard print book. But you have options that don't require a lot of research and background study. The Apple based eBook creation tool *Vellum*, for example, has some built-in large print creation options. And *IngramSpark* offers large print format options within POD.

There are, of course, costs involved in creating large print versions of your books. But it's also an activity that can set you apart from the competition.

Imagine that a library is looking to fulfill a specific style or type of book for a demographic that only wants these books in paper and in large print format. Your book's availability in that format could be the deciding factor on a sale, or loss of a sale.

# Leaving Your MARC

A detail that I purposely skipped over in this chapter was explaining MARC references and their importance to libraries. And, even so, what I'm sharing here is extremely high level and gets nowhere near close to the full details.

A **MARC** record is a **MA**chine-**R**eadable **C**ataloging record.

A Cataloging record refers to the *Bibliographic* records (containing information about a book), and *Authority* records (containing standardized forms for names, titles, and subjects, providing cross-reference in catalogs). Additional formats include *Classification* records, *Community Information* records, and *Holdings* records, which often have more to do with internal classification and specific product holdings that are location (library) specific.

MARC was developed in the 1960s in the United States as a way for computers to read records about books and other library materials for cataloging. By the early 1970s MARC formats became the library industry standard in the US; and by the mid 1970s, they evolved into an international standard.

While libraries can and do make purchases on titles that lack MARC records, some libraries may be reluctant to create MARC records. This might be from a combination of the labor and setup costs involved.

If your book is traditionally published, chances are that your publisher either has direct account or is using a service to have MARC records created. If you are self-published, a MARC record might not exist.

Some countries have subscriptions, memberships, and services that allow entry of MARC records. Depending on where you live and the resources available, you might have limited ability to ensure a MARC record exists for each format of your book. But I didn't want to talk about libraries without at least briefly mentioning this.

# Public Lending Right Perks

This section is only going to pertain if you live in a country like Canada or the UK, or Australia, or one of the more than thirty countries around the world that have public lending right programs.

And, if you do, then it is very important for you to understand how it works and why it can be extremely valuable for you as an author.

## What Is Public Lending Right?

Public Lending Right is the right of authors and other rights-holders to receive payment for the free public use of their work in libraries.

PLR has been in existence since the 1940s. The very first library compensation program of its type was established in 1946 in Denmark. Norway was second to establish one in 1947, as did Sweden in 1954.

As of 2019, thirty-five countries have PLR programs. Of these, thirty are in Europe. Outside of Europe, only Australia, Canada, Israel, and New Zealand have PLR systems.

Internationally, PLR is overseen by an organization known as Public Lending Right International (or PLR International). The aim of PLR International is to promote international awareness of PLR and inform the PLR community of events, developments, and news from around the world. It brings together those countries with established PLR systems and provides assistance and advice to countries interested in setting up PLR schemes.

You can learn more about PLR international at plrinternational.com.

## How Does Public Lending Right Work?

In most countries, PLR is directly funded by government budgets that are controlled either centrally or regionally.

The currently existing thirty-five programs fall into three broad categories:

- Copyright-based systems where lending is the exclusive right
- PLR as a separate state renumeration right recognized by law
- PLR as part of state support for culture

Some countries incorporate a combination of all three of those approaches.

## How Are Payments to Authors Calculated?

The most common method of PLR is distribution to authors or other stakeholders in the form of payments related to how often their work has been lent out by libraries. Alternatively, payments are calculated to rightsholders via a tally of the total number of copies of their books held by libraries. This method is used in countries such as Australia, Canada, and Denmark. Countries like France base their calculations on sales from booksellers to libraries, with part of the funding coming from the bookstore and the remaining part of the budget coming from the government according to how many users are registered in the libraries.

## Who Qualifies for Payment of PLR?

Writers qualify for payment of PLR. So do other contributors to books, such as artists and illustrators, editors, photographers. In some countries, publishers receive a share of the PLR payments.

## Details from Canada's PLR Program

Because I am a Canadian, and because I am most familiar with, and have benefited from the way the program works in Canada, I will outline how the program works in my country.

I know that the programs in the UK and Australia, for example, are different, such as in Australia, at the time of this writing, the PLR program is only for print books, or that in the UK, there's a 60/40 split on audiobooks for author/narrator. But these things continue to change and evolve.

For the most up-to-date understanding of how PLR works in your own country (including Canada), should you be an author lucky enough to have a program like it, you can learn about it via your country's direct PLR program website, which you can find at the following URL:

http://plrinternational.com/established

Canada's PLR program was established in 1986. In Canada, PLR payments are based on the presence of a title in public library catalogues, as tallied during an annual PLR survey.

The calculation is determined by the PLR Commission, which is an advisory board of the Canada Council for the Arts. The process of paying authors takes a full year and involves four main steps:

- Registration of titles
- Verification of title eligibility
- Sampling of public library collections
- Preparation and distribution of payments

The registration period for Canadian creators is between February 15 and May 1st each year. You must be a Canadian citizen or a permanent resident to be eligible. Writers, illustrators, translators, narrators, editors, and photographers are eligible.

Books in print, eBooks, and audiobooks that have been published in the previous five years are eligible. The print book or eBook must have a valid 13-digit ISBN and must be at least 48 pages long (or 24 pages in the case of a children's book). Audiobooks must be in either a physical media format (CD), or a digital download (MP3) and have a valid 13-digit ISBN.

Fiction, poetry, drama, children's literature, non-fiction, and scholarly work are all eligible.

Practical books, such as cookbooks, self-help, "how-to" guides, travel guides, manuals, and reference works, are not eligible. Educational books, such as textbooks or books resulting from a conference, seminar, or symposium, are not eligible. Periodicals, such as newspapers or magazines, are not eligible.

There can be no more than six contributors to the book, and each creator's contribution must comprise at least 10% of the length of the book.

Sampling of eligible titles is done by including libraries with large collections from all provinces, territories, and regions of Canada. Neither the number of copies found on hand, nor the number of times a title has been checked out are considered; merely the presence of that title in each particular location that is sampled.

At the end of the process of comparing eligible titles to the online or digital copy of library catalogs, a tally of the number of times each eligible title appears is calculated.

Payments for each title are based on the library sampling results, the creator's percentage share of the title, how long the title has been registered with the program, and the amount of money in the program's budget and the total number of eligible titles.

The calculation formula is:

Payment per title = Hit rate × # libraries where title is found × % share × time adjustment

The "hit rate" changes every year. For 2018 the "hit rate" was $58.90. The sampled libraries will be a number between 0 and 7. The time adjustment involves the number of years a title has been registered. If registration was in the past five years, for example, it is 100%. For six to ten years, that drops to 80%.

Only those creators whose library survey results amount to at least $50 qualify to receive a payment. The maximum possible payment varies each year. In 2018 it was $4,123.

## A Personal Example of Canada's PLR

I have been registered with the PLR program in Canada for at least ten years. I can't remember when I first registered. And, because the registration program isn't tracked online via a database, but rather via a printed form that you have to mail, I don't have an accurate record of what books I registered in what year.

All I have are copies of the annual statements that were mailed to me along with an annual check.

In 2019 I began making a photocopy of each newly submitted form, and logging, in a spreadsheet, when the print, eBook, or audiobook was published and submitted; this is to ensure I know which books were submitted, and when.

I remember that the very first payment I received from PLR was relatively small. But, over the years, as I have continued to publish more books, and in more formats

(PLR Canada only added eBooks to the program recently), those annual checks have grown significantly.

My 2018 Public Lending Right check, which arrived in late February 2019, was large enough that it paid for my all-inclusive flight, meal and drink plan for a tropical vacation.

I remember it quite well because, the credit card statement for that particular March Break trip and the check from PLR Canada arrived around the same time.

My 2020 PLR check, which came in while I was still working on this book, was a similar size.

If you happen to live in one of those territories that has a Public Lending Rights program, I strongly encourage you to sign up for it.

# PART IV

## DIRECT SALES & OTHER SOURCES OF INCOME

# Direct Sales

Direct selling is another option that authors can consider. I will not get into any details, but I will outline, at a high level, some of the reasoning behind direct sales and some logistical things to consider.

In order to sell direct, you need to have the rights to sell your own book in eBook or Audiobook format. This means that if you have signed a contract that licenses territorial rights to those formats with a publisher, you may no longer have those rights. Similarly, if you are exclusive to Amazon Kindle via KDP Select, then you are forbidden by the terms of that exclusivity from selling direct.

"Bank over rank" is an important term that has been discussed earlier in this book. So when you sell direct, you're giving up the vanity metrics of seeing your sales rank climbing on platforms like Kindle or Kobo, but, in exchange, you're able to earn upwards of 95% on a digital product rather than the 35%, 60% or 70% via the retailers. (I'm using 95% as a typical number to denote the service charge of the sales provider/credit card company).

The other important thing to consider, when you sell direct, is that, unlike with the major retail platforms, you have a direct relationship with the person making a purchase. None of the big five retail platforms are going to allow you to email or message people who've bought your book. But if a reader buys a book from you, you have a way to contact them and let them know about future sales promotions. That direct relationship is as important in many ways as the larger margin from such a transaction.

For formatting the digital files, there are plenty of free services out there such as *Draft2Digital* that allows you a free conversion from Microsoft Word to an ePub and Mobi and PDF format. *Reedsy* has a free ePub generator. Or you can use tools like Vellum (Mac only), or Atticus (announced in early 2021) from Dave Chesson, the genius behind Publisher Rocket.

As mentioned, there's usually a process transaction fee to handle for the payment method for credit cards and other digital payment formats. There are choices for taking money that include *PayPal, Payhip, Stripe, and WooCommerce.*

*Findaway Voices* offers a "direct audiobook" selling platform called Authors Direct that handles taking and processing the payments.

One of the most challenging things with direct selling is the delivery of the product. That's where, for both eBooks and for Audiobooks, a company like BookFunnel can come in extremely handy.

BookFunnel is an author service that specializes in eBook and audio distribution. It allows the sending of ARCs, reader magnet books, or retail-ready products in a way that is meant to save indie authors time and perhaps even a bit of their sanity.

This is because BookFunnel has created a way for you to deliver the digital product to a customer that has an easy step-by-step process to help your customer/reader get that purchased eBook onto the eBook reading platform of their choice, or available to read directly within a free BookFunnel app.

Not only will the process walk the customer through this step-by-step process, but those customers who are tech-averse can pick up the phone and talk to a patient, friendly, and knowledgeable support person who'll "guide them by the hand" in what the company cheekily calls their special "Tex" support. (BookFunnel is located in the state of Texas).

Plans for BookFunnel start at $20 USD per year, and, beyond digital content delivery, they have a suite of tools to help authors with their marketing.

There are some challenges and downsides to direct selling, such as figuring out and paying taxes for different territories, and the manual set up and even deciding which service provider best works for you and on your website. Some of the service providers have those calculations built in.

But the key, like any decision you make to expand your options for multiple streams of revenue (including this very high margin option), is figuring out what works best for you.

# Other Revenue Sources

## Bookchain

Bookchain® is a Canadian platform built upon blockchain technology that allows authors and publishers the ability to configure security, traceability, attribution, and distribution for their digital publications. It also comes with an option that includes author/publisher compensation for reselling., which is something that doesn't exist for print books. This is a revolutionary concept, because in the used book market, only the reseller earns money on that sale, and not the original creator.

The benefits of this open, yet trackable system are twofold: creators can protect their intellectual property against theft or piracy while rewriting the rules for eBook distribution and management; and readers can enjoy their eBooks using any device with a web browser.

And if you panic when you hear the works blockchain or cryptocurrency, you needn't worry. Because you don't need to. Just like most authors who publish eBooks don't really understand the detailed components of how an ePub is created, the same holds true for this technology.

This user-friendly blockchain solution accepts the cash you already have in your wallet—no cryptocurrency needed.

When you publish to Blockchain, you can personalize your publishing and distribution settings, including price, number of copies available (so you can create special digital limited editions), royalties, resale permissions, and more.

Bookchain charges a small user fee to cover the cost of all the block-chain related transactions. The fees include a onetime activation fee, to add the eBook to their library, validate the parameters of the smart contract, and ensure that your eBook is protected against theft and piracy. This fee is paid per title, not per copy. They charge a small fee for each copy sold. If resale is enabled (which allows you to earn a portion of all resale transactions), an additional small fee is applied.

While this technology currently exists on this platform alone, the company is interested in working collaboratively with publishers, authors, and retailers, to allow leveraging their tools and functionality with their own platforms and spaces.

I've long been waiting for the proper roll-out of such a technology and definitely think it's worth keeping an eye on this and other blockchain empowered technology solutions.

## Bundle Platforms

Bundle platforms that allow users to set their own price and pay what they want for bundled digital products are a solid revenue source. They often rely on two key components:

- **Limited availability** - which creates a sense of urgency to "buy now" before the deal ends.
- **Collaborative/Cross-Promotion Marketing**—creators coming together to promote one another to their existing communities of fans.

Two of the most common of these platforms are Humble Bundle and StoryBundle.

Humble Bundle sells games, eBooks, software, and other digital content. Their mission is to support charity while providing awesome content to customers at great prices. They launched in 2010 with a single two-week Humble Indie Bundle but have grown into a store full of games and bundles, a subscription service, a game publisher, and more.

StoryBundle is a way for people who love to read to discover quality books. They take a handful of books—anywhere from six to nine—and group them together to offer as a bundle. The reader, can take a look at the titles and decide how much they'd like to pay and how much will go to the charity assigned to that bundle. Bonus books are often added to the main lineup and are offered at a set bonus threshold.

Getting into a bundle from a platform like this is not as easy as just signing up. You usually need to be invited to participate in a themed bundle. And that comes from people you might have interacted with either in person or online.

I've been lucky enough to have been invited to several themed StoryBundles over the years, and some years the income from just one or two bundles in a year has represented a significant portion of my annual digital book sales income that can rival the income from the big five eBook retail platforms.

One can call it luck, but it might also relate to the decades of networking that I've been engaging in within the author community.

Evidence of the extreme value of networking with others in the author community.

## Kickstarter & Crowdfunding

Kickstarter and other crowdfunding platforms can allow creators to go directly to readers and let them help decide which books get made. These crowd-funded platforms has not only allowed publication of books that would, otherwise never have been made, but it allows true fans the benefit of knowing that their contribution and participation made the project possible.

Crowd-funding applications have allowed for a much richer and more diverse publishing world in many ways. In a June 11, 2019 article in Forbes magazine, Kickstarter's head of publishing, Margot Atwell, shared that Kickstarter's method of allowing writers to let readers choose which books get made, has resulted in books being published that speak to experiences that often aren't represented in mainstream publishing.

"The Destroy anthology series is one example of this," Atwell explains. "It's a series of speculative fiction and fantasy anthologies dedicated to showcasing the work and stories of People of Color, LGBTQ folks, and disabled people. Mainstream publishers might have looked at these projects and declared them too niche or imagined that there wasn't a market for them, but these Kickstarter projects have proved that there definitely is an audience for stories centering people who don't often get to see themselves represented."

In 2020, on the 10th Anniversary of *The Stormlight Archive* series, Brandon Sanderson created a special leather-bound edition of **The Way of Kings**, the first book in that series. He was able to do this because when he signed his contract, he made sure that he kept special edition rights to the work.

Five minutes after the launch on Kickstarter, it had earned three quarters of a million dollars. And by the end of the run, nearly 30,000 supporters pledged over 6.7 million dollars.

I ran a Kickstarter to help raise funds to pay the authors whose stories I had selected for an anthology I was published could be paid pro rates for their fiction, as well as for audio rights to their stories, and payment to narrators.

I raised more than $10,000 Canadian

Something important to remember is that most books published are going to earn less than $100 in a full year. I know it sounds depressing, but that's based on looking at years of sales stats in the retail and distribution market.

Launching a book on Kickstarter, even for a modest goal like $100 or $500 could end up earning an author more than they might earn in a twelve-month period on the major retailers. But not only that, it's done in a way that gives the reader a feeling of being part of that author's tight-knit legion of fans because they helped make the book happen.

## Patreon & Subscription Services

As mentioned in the previous chapter, having direct access to connect with your fans is an optimal position for an author to be in. A platform like Patreon, or other subscription platforms, allow authors a direct way to communicate with their readers, while providing those fans with early content and/or additional content that they can't get elsewhere.

A fan who is so invested in an author that they are willing to subscribe on a monthly basis to receive access to such exclusive material, is an excellent relationship.

It comes with the perks of direct connection and communication. And it also comes with the perks of a "direct sales" type of earned margin without the hassle of having to figure out transactions on your website.

Simply, Patreon is a membership platform that allows people to pledge money to support creators of all kinds. This would include writers, but also artists, musicians, podcasters, and others.

Patrons pay a subscription amount of their choosing, at levels the creator defines. In return, they are provided with content, or "rewards." Creators have the option of having different subscription levels available, usually starting as low as $1 per month. The higher the subscription level, the greater the access to content, or the more substantial the rewards.

Pages on Patreon can be set up for per month subscriptions (where patrons contribute a monthly amount and receive monthly rewards), or per creation, (patrons pay a set amount for each reward).

Author Blaze Ward not only sells short stories via his personal website that aren't available on any of the retail or library platforms (direct sales), but he also provides his $5 a month Patrons access to content a full year before it is released for anyone else to read.

Many authors, like T. Thorn Coyle, Leah Cutter, do similar things, keeping readers engaged and with access to a combination of early and exclusive content for their patronage.

Canadian science-fiction author Robert J. Sawyer, who originally was exclusively traditionally published, has migrated into a more hybrid publishing approach and his Patreon page has nine levels of support, from $1 a month for those who just want to support him, all the way up to $100 a month (limited to 10) and $1000 a month (limited to 1—this one comes with a bit of a cheeky joke: "All the previous perks plus if I ever have a child, I will name him or her after you.") In early 2021, Sawyer has 159 patrons with a monthly total of $815. This brings in just under $10,000 in a year.

Seanan McGuire has over 3,300 fans on her Patreon page and brings in $13,302 per short story she sells. That's far more than she would ever make even in the highest paying short fiction market, and she regularly ranks in the top realm of authors on Patreon.

And while not all creators will be pulling in giant monthly or per project income, the idea that even a small die-hard core group of fans can get special access to a creator can be a wonderful thing. $25 a month means $300 a year and in a way that's not reliant upon any retailer out there. It also comes with a direct way to communicate with your fans. And, since I've worked in the industry long enough to see the stats of how much the average author earns in a year from digital sales, that $300 would be a gigantic and welcome income to receive.

There are other ways to leverage Patreon that rely solely on your imagination. Lindsay Buroker uses it as a tool to ensure that her biggest fans aren't left out in the cold for the titles that she does publish exclusively to Kindle.

What she has started doing is, prior to publishing a new book into the exclusivity program at Kindle, she offers them to her fans direct via Patreon. She sets up the titles, lets her fans know they are available for a specific time prior to anyone else being able to buy or read them; but that, after a particular date, they'll be launched into the KDP Select program and will no longer be available. That way they can access and download the titles. And they get them ahead of everyone else.

This way she allows fans who are not locked into the Amazon ecosystem to have access to read those books.

## Short Stories/Articles

I'm a huge fan of the idea of recycling content and earning money multiple times off of a single property. This goes back to the concept discussed in the first section of this book related to quantum eggs and multiplying streams of revenue off of a single IP.

It also employs a hybrid approach to selling (or licensing) rights to a short work to a publisher, and then, upon reversion of those rights back, re-selling that work as a reprint, and leveraging it for other projects for revenue and/or marketing purposes.

In 2020, I co-authored a book with Matty Dalrymple that goes through this in detail. It is called **Taking the Short Tack: Creating Income & Connecting with Readers using Short Fiction**.

But below are a few ideas as shared in that book. Please note that some of the ideas in this list can also be leveraged for full-length works. The beautiful thing about digital publishing is that a "book" isn't limited to restrictive definitions such as the idea of it having to be 300 pages bound between two pieces of cloth.

- **Territorial Rights Splitting**—leveraging the option to self publish a work only in specific territories while simultaneously licensing it in other territories with a publisher.
- **Audio**—producing an audiobook for a title that runs less than 10,000 words will cost significantly less than a full-length book. These shorter pieces of content work well on the library and subscription platform "cost per checkout" model in terms of earning back the investment in creating them.
- **Collections** - creating collections of previously published work. They can be full-length books or smaller themed "digital" chapbooks. And, looking back at audio, you can have stories sold on their own and incorporate them into audio bundle collections.

- **Limited Editions**—work sold directly via your own website that's not available anywhere else, or available only to subscribers or patrons, or via a Kickstarter campaign.
- **Foreign Markets/Foreign Language Rights**—(see below when I mention Douglas Smith, who has been rocking this world).
- **Beyond the Book**—Selling/licensing work to apps and game platforms.
- **Reader Magnets**—exclusive content specifically written to entice the right core readers to your newsletter list.

Douglas Smith has a fantastic book entitled **Playing the Short Game: How to Market & Sell Short Fiction**. In it he goes into detail on markets to sell fiction to, as well as the method he has used to get his work sold and translated into many global markets.

Here is one example of how I took a single short story, originally sold the first publication rights to a magazine, and then kept re-cycling that content to earn additional revenue and leverage marketing opportunities.

Here is the publication history for my short story "Browsers" which is a tale of about 5,000 words about a bookstore that acts like a Venus Fly Trap for book nerds. Below I indicate "Trad Pub'd" for where someone else is in control of the "publication" of the work, or "Self Pub'd" where I'm in control.

- **1999**—Sold First Serial Rights to magazine Challenging Destiny for semi-pro rates (Trad Pub'd) (3 cents per word).
- **2004**—Reprinted (Self Pub'd) story in collection One Hand Screaming in trade paperback.
- **2006**—Reprinted (Self Pub'd) in free stand-alone printed "advertising/sampler"
- **2008**—Sold reprint rights (Trad Pub'd) to anthology **Bound for Evil**
- **2009**—Reprinted (Self Pub'd) in **Active Reader** print chapbook for use on an Espresso Book Machine to make print copies to sell direct.
- **2015**—**Active Reader** eBook (Self Pub'd).
- **2017**—**Active Reader** audiobook (Self Pub'd). The use of the narrator, Eric Bryan Moore, brought over a pre-existing fan base of his to discover my work.
- **2018**—BundleRabbit—(Self Pub'd) A digital bundle of similarly themed titles called **Books Gone Bad**
- **2018**—Live video reading of the story on Facebook and YouTube channel as part of my #FreeFridayFrights weekly readings. (Self Pub'd)
- **2019**—Revised print version (Self Pub'd) of **Active Reader**
- **2020** - Excerpt reading of the story as part of a larger Hamilton Public Library Virtual Storyteller feature promotion of local authors. (Trad Pub'd)

Eight of those eleven actions led to direct income off of that single IP product and story. The non-income sources are difficult to measure, but I would count as valuable for author-branding and marketing.

## VoiceMap

This is a smartphone app that combined audio, GPS technology, and storytelling to take people on unique guided experiences. They are like podcasts that move along with the listener you, telling them stories about what they are seeing or standing in front of.

Tours are created by insightful local storytellers, including journalists, filmmakers, novelists, podcasters, and tour guides. Tours can be downloaded and listened to offline, but in the default GPS auto-play mode, listeners can focus on your surroundings with headphones in, and get led by a virtual tour guide on a walking, cycling, driving, or even boat ride adventure.

The built-in GPS functionality ensures that if the person on the tour does wander off in the wrong direction, VoiceMap will play an audio alert, and they can follow the map on their smartphone screen to the next location to get back on track.

In the default basic package for creators, there is no upfront cost to create and upload and sell a tour through VoiceMap. Because it's listed on the VoiceMap app, they work with creators to edit the proposed text and then test the audio samples for quality and consistency. Sales happen on the web and in app and creators are paid 50% of the price they set for a tour.

I did my first tour on VoiceMap in 2019 for downtown Hamilton, ON and it's a half hour 2 kilometer (1.2 miles) walking tour called "Historical Downtown Ghost Walk."

Here's the part where thinking back to the numerous uses for your IP can come in handy. I wrote the book **Haunted Hamilton** for Dundurn Press, Canada's largest independent publishing house, in 2012. The contract I signed with them includes the Audiobook rights. They've yet to produce any Audiobooks, but it was one of the contract clauses they wouldn't budge on. So I have no Audiobooks of the six books I have published with them so far.

But I do have the research notes I had compiled to write the book. So I went back to those notes and also applied new research, to create new stories, written in a different style (obviously, in a oral storytelling style) to generate a new form of IP. Perhaps 50% of the locations and stories will be found, told in a different way, in the book **Haunted Hamilton**, with the other half unique to this tour. It's a unique product, and not a reading of the content of the book, so it's not in violation of any contract I have with Dundurn. If anything, the half hour walking tour probably sells more copies of the book, earning more revenue for me and my publisher.

## YouTube

This popular video channel, owned by Google, is also a robust and dynamic search engine. People use it not just to watch videos, but also to listen to content. Creators with more than 1000 subscribers to their YouTube channel can earn income from ad revenue off this platform.

While hugely successful YouTube creators can earn money from regularly sharing content, there's a use for authors that bestselling indie author Lindsay Buroker has been sharing.

Lindsay initially thought she might just put book one up from each series in order to entice people to check out the series and then go purchase them on other sites.

On Christmas Day of 2020 she got to the minimum subscribers of 1000 where YouTube can allow content providers to earn money from ads. In conjunction with that level of subscribers, there is a requirement of 4,000 hours watched. (This is evident that YouTube wants to make sure the subscribers are likely to represent real people actually invested in watching, and not just fake account sign-ups)

Something she noticed is that there's not as much competition on YouTube for audiobooks as there are on other platforms.

With a single title, **Sinister Magic**, she had more than 90,000 views and earned about $300 USD in ad revenue. She ended up earning more than $1200 USD in January 2020.

Having this content available for free on YouTube also resulted in additional sales on the audiobook platforms.

One user commented they would be willing to listen to an ad after every chapter if it meant that they could "get these works of art on YouTube" - five more users commented that they felt the same.

Two different truck drivers who listens to audiobooks on YouTube while driving commented that they have been enjoying Lindsay's books in that way.

She did note that by having the content on YouTube there **were** more pirated copies of her stories starting to pop up. But she also added that YouTube was actually quick to respond at copyright notification takedowns.

I've put a few shorter pieces of fiction up on YouTube, most of them "live" readings with notes, in a segment I'd run for almost 9 months called #FreeFridayFrights.

I don't yet have 1000 subscribers on my YouTube channel; as of the writing of this book I'm a little over half-way there. And my watched hours are only up to 2,500 of the required 4,000 hours. However, as I continue to put up other content (including the audio-only version of my *Stark Reflections on Writing and Publishing* podcast, which has more than 180 episodes), I'm sure that audience will grow over time. Just like with looking at my eBook sales on the WIDE platforms, I'm patient about the process. I'll keep publishing and watching the numbers slowly increase. And then I'll likely add full-length book audio to that channel and count it as yet another revenue source.

# PART V
# CLOSING THOUGHTS

## A Word About the "The Good Old Days" of Self-Publishing

You might hear some indie authors pining about what they consider "the good old days" of digital publishing. As the legends go, all you had to do was publish any eBook, put it on Amazon, and watch the money roll in.

Perhaps some of that was true. But be leery of such talk. In the way that thinking about and romanticizing the "good old days" of modern society, where things were simpler, also comes with ignoring the underlying principle of what that means. Because in those days, a woman's place was in the home, racial segregation was a fully accepted norm, and you could get away with "locker-room" talk or sharing a joke that rudely mocked a person's culture, religion, skin color, body shape, or sexual orientation, without being judged.

Because a question that's important to consider is, just who were those days good for?

They might have been good for some authors who discovered the power of digital publishing and self-published eBooks early on.

But they weren't necessarily always good for the reader.

Things often look good on the surface. Nostalgia has a way of doing that.

But let's take a closer look at some of what was happening in those "good old days" of indie publishing.

In the "good old days" there was only one main platform that indie authors could publish to. There was Amazon. And, if you wanted to get to *Kobo, Apple, or Nook* there was *Smashwords*. You could get away with a crappy cover, little or no editing, and just slapping up whatever hack-job of a book you wrote and pull in some money. There wasn't as much competition. It was easier to stand out from the $35 traditionally published eBooks with your $0.99 "masterpiece" and readers were, perhaps, so happy to be able to read a book for such a great value that they ignored typos, grammar issues, and blatant plot issues with a book. (Maybe the same way that one might consume fast food to quickly satisfy a need over any properly thought-out nutritional value).

I'm not saying that all self-published eBooks from that era were the equivalent of playing Atari's *Pong* compared to the tennis game on Nintendo's *Wii Sports*, but take the consumer's point of view for a moment. In the mid-to-late 1970s when *Home Pong* was all the rage, it was the only at home video game that existed. I remember standing with a group of friends watching for an hour as others played for my chance to take one of the simple paddles in hand and play that simple game. Hours and hours of thrilling fun in a new era of electronic entertainment. Compare that to the choices and options of much more sophisticated electronic home gaming options that exist now.

The consumer can be more discerning. They don't have to settle on the few cheap titles. They have more than their fair share of free books to read for the rest of their lives if they want. And, sadly, a good number of them do. But, without spending more per book than the price of a cup of coffee, they have more options than even the most ardent reader could ever want.

Would you rather be a mediocre hack pushing out crap as your author legacy for the sake of pulling in more money? Or would you rather have to work to produce the best possible book you can?

Early adopters of a new technology are usually the risk takers. They understand that systems and content will not be ideal, or perfect. And they roll with that. Beta users know there are still bugs to work out. So, they meet less-than-perfect conditions with an open mind, and consider flaws with a grain of salt.

But now that eBook reading is normalized, readers, rightfully so, are more discerning.

Yes, there are now more books publishing digitally than any avid reader can ever consume.

Yes, Amazon is now mostly a pay-to-play system where you pretty much need to advertise in order to successfully rise above the masses. (This is one of a number of reasons why publishing wide is important)

Yes, you have to work harder, focus more on your ideal reader in the writing and marketing of your books.

So, yes, it takes more work, more effort, now. You have to be diligent in producing the best book you can.

Because in the "good old days" the writer could find an easy win, almost regardless of what they did.

But when competition and quality and consumer-focused targeting are three of the main elements for success in the modern version of digital publishing, the reader almost always win.

And when things are good for the reader, we all win.

For, ultimately, when you are thinking wide, are you thinking beyond the platforms, and the systems, and the strategies, and to the reason you are writing in the first place?

It's for the reader.

It's always for the reader.

# Wide Is Being Inclusive

Publishing WIDE is not just a procedural act of putting your books up on multiple channels, but an overall behavior and mindset shift. It's about being open minded and inclusive. And checking your old habits and behavior.

It's important to double check that you are being inclusive in all the things you do, not just in the logistics of putting books up on more than one website.

Because this is something I continue to see, and it can be a bit of a blind spot for authors.

Are you linking only to Amazon on your author website or in social media posts?

It can be, particularly if it has become a habit, something that's almost invisible to you.

But it's **not** invisible to the wide retailers.

Because they are paying attention.

The wide retailers, the non-Amazon platforms really do want to help authors be successful. But they often can only help the authors who are willing to first help themselves.

If a retailer is interested in you or one of your books, what will they see if they go to your website or follow you on social media? Will it be only links to Amazon and requests for Amazon reviews? How do you think there are going to react to that?

If a wide retailer offers you a promotional opportunity, are you just going to assume they'll do all the heavy lifting?

Why would you do that? Because you don't left Amazon do all the heavy lifting. When you're exclusive to Amazon you probably share the hell out of your Amazon links, and you also likely throw money into Amazon Marketing.

And yet, when a retailer includes you in a promotional campaign it's time to sit back and let someone else drive?

The people out there working to help authors find success notice when you do those things.

Be aware that they are paying attention.

You should be attending to this, too.

Because, to reiterate something from the introduction that my dear friend James A. Owen says, if you really want to do something, nobody will be able to stop you. But if you really don't want to do something, nobody will be able to help you.

Ask yourself if you want to take an active role in growing as a wide author, or adopt a helpless, passive stance.

And ask yourself if you want to be inclusive or exclusive.

And behave accordingly.

# Wide for the Fail

I'm an optimist. I am a believer in the power of positive thinking.

But I'm also aware of the realities facing authors and do not want to entertain putting out any sort of misleading thoughts and false hopes.

Yes, you stand a much better chance of long term success in the wider world of publishing.

But also, it's not easy, it takes time, and you will fail.

That's right. You will fail.

Multiple times.

Despite your best efforts, your hard learnings, your expenses of time and money, despite the analytics, the patience, the optimal positioning, all your hard work and planning will regularly result in failure.

The difference between success and failure is giving it one more try.

Now this is a tough thing, because one of the definitions of insanity is doing the same thing repeatedly and expecting different results. That's why there's a fine line between trying again without learning from the errors, from the mistakes, from the failures, and repeating the same mistakes. And it's not always easy to see.

Because sometimes you did everything perfect for the situation and expected goals; but something completely outside of your control happened and took that away.

Imagine the publishers who planned a giant book launch on Sept 11, 2001? Or the billion-dollar budget movies that were premiering in theatres the week after a global pandemic was called in 2020?

I think back to a movie that was premiering on the night of Tuesday Sept 11, 2001 staring Kathleen Robertson. This sticks out for me, because it's about a historic brutal and sensational murder that took place in Hamilton, Ontario, where I was living at the time, and Robertson, the actress best known then for playing the role of Clare Arnold in *Beverly Hills, 90210*, was to play the lead role of Evelyn Dick.

I had researched the murders and had intended on using them in a book I'd been planning on writing. (That book never happened, but some of that research did go into *Haunted Hamilton*, which was published by Dundurn, Canada's largest independent publisher, in 2012). I remember heading in to work that morning and looking forward to seeing the made-for-television movie premiere that night when I returned home.

Later that morning, as the terror attacks happened, that movie was the furthest thing from my mind. I didn't think about it again for months. (Incidentally, the movie was re-scheduled to be released in March 2002 because of the attacks, and Robertson was nominated for a Gemini Award for her role. But I never ended up seeing it).

That's a bit of a long side shuffle to explain a movie that I'd been so looking forward to watching completely disappearing off my radar because of extraneous events.

That can happen. To your book. And to the consumer who was aware of and intended on purchasing your book. You can plan everything perfectly, and something else happens—sometimes known; most often unknown—that impact your plans. Which leads to failure. Timing can be everything.

And that's why it is important to understand the importance of failure on your path to success.

"We are all failures." J. M. Barrie, the creator of *Peter Pan* said. "At least, the best of us are."

Even if you've never heard of Barrie, I'm pretty sure you've heard of one or more of the iconic characters he created: Peter Ban and Captain Hook. And if a writer could have created characters so well known in modern culture, they couldn't possibly have been a failure. Right?

Barrie's first novel, *Better Dead,* which was published at his own expense in 1888, failed to sell. The term "vanity publishing" didn't exist back in the day, but that's what this was. His next two novels were panned by critics and reviewers. Barrie then turned his attention to the theatre, where his first project was also panned by critics and ended up being performed only once. Barrie persisted, saw a few theatrical successes, and eventually, the character of Peter Pan first appeared within the pages of Barrie's episodic novel *The Little White Bird* in 1902 and then was re-adapted into the stage play *Peter Pan, or The Boy Who Wouldn't Grow Up* in 1904, and the 1911 novel adaptation of the same name.

Speaking of names, Barrie is also responsible for the popularization of the name Wendy via the character Wendy Darling, Peter's friend. The name had been previously used as a surname, and potentially was a rare, shortened form for Gwendolyn. In his story, the name Wendy was allegedly inspired by Margaret Henley, the daughter of Barrie's poet friend W. E. Henley. The child, who could not pronounce her R's, reportedly called him "my fwiendy-wendy."

Not a bad legacy for a failure who couldn't sell any copies of his first book.

So, what made the difference?

Not giving up in the face of failure. Persisting. Moving forward and progressing along in the craft. Applying his creativity and imagination to different forms of storytelling. And not giving up.

Let's bring these examples to modern times and examine Hugh Howey, who was one of only a handful of authors to become known outside indie publishing circles for the blockbuster success made within the early days of self-publishing.

In a 2012 interview with Denise Wy, Howey told her that he wished he had started writing earlier in life. "I put it off because I was scared of it," he said. "I should have 30 books written by now, not a dozen."

"The book that took off for me was the one I didn't promote at all. I don't know what that means, but it makes me feel powerless about what succeeds and what doesn't. The reader is the one who does the real promoting by telling their friends, writing reviews, posting on their own Facebook and Twitter accounts. I did everything you can think of: book signings, talking to schools, joining writing groups, going to conferences. But again, it was the book I never promoted at all that took off."

Howey's point about readers being the ones who make it happen can be pretty accurate.

As a writer you produce the book, you put your best effort into writing, editing, polishing it, getting a professional looking and genre-targeted cover for it, and putting it out into the world.

You can employ different marketing strategies and tactics, and sometimes those things can work.

There's quite the degree of luck, of course.

But it's ultimately up to the reaction of readers, and what readers do with the book once they read it. Do they tell all their friends? Do they post and share reviews? Do they insist that people who'll listen to them pick up the book and experience it for themselves?

Things go viral based upon an odd combination of a proper set-up, launch, and flight path, but only if they also happen to hit the right wind-patterns that can carry it further than any power fuel or turbo rocket blaster can take it.

And so many of those things can be out of your control as an author.

I hope you get the point I'm trying to make.

You try. You work hard. You give it your best shot.

And when you fail, or when you don't see the success you had been hoping for, you have two choices.

Try once more (either the same thing or an adapted strategy) or give up.

History is rife with the examples of those who didn't give up.

It's not filled with those who did give up.

I hope you see the difference.

And I hope you make the difference in your own approach to success with wide publishing.

You are ultimately limited, dear author, only by the breadth (or, if you prefer, the width) of your own imagination and mindset.

# Resources

BELOW YOU WILL find a short list of some resources called out in this book, and also others I have found helpful in my own writing and publishing journey.

I also maintain an online listing of these resources, examples, and templates, at:

www.markleslie.ca/wideforthewin

## Books


**An Author's Guide to Working with Libraries & Bookstores**, Mark Leslie Lefebvre, Stark Publishing, 2019.

**Business for Authors**, Joanna Penn, Curl Up Press, 2017.

**Closing the Deal on Your Terms:** ***Agents, Contracts and Other Considerations***, Kristine Kathryn Rusch, WMG Publishing, 2016.

**How to Make a Living with your Writing (3rd Edition)**, Joanna Penn, Curl Up Press, 2021.

**How to Market a Book:** ***Overperform in a Crowded Market***, Ricardo Fayet, Reedsy, 2021.

**Killing It on Kobo**, Mark Leslie Lefebvre, Stark Publishing Solutions, 2018.

**Million Dollar Professionalism for the Writer**, Kevin J. Anderson & Rebecca Moesta, WordFire Press, 2014.

**Mastering Amazon Ads**, Brian D. Meeks, Brian Meeks, 2017.

**Newsletter Ninja**, Tammi Labrecque, Larks & Katydids, 2018.

**Strangers to Superfans**, David Gaughran, David Gaughran, 2018

**Taking the Short Tack:** ***Creating Income and Connecting with Readers using Short Fiction***, Matty Dalrymple and Mark Leslie Lefebvre, William Kingsfield Publishers, 2020.

**The Business Minded Creative**, Diana Wink, Books for Storytellers, 2021.

**The Business of Being a Writer**, Jane Friedman, University of Chicago Press, 2018.

**The Magic Bakery:** ***Copyright in the Modern World of Fiction Publishing***, Dean Wesley Smith, 2017.

**The Seven P's of Publishing Success**, Mark Leslie Lefebvre, Stark Publishing Solutions, 2018.

**The Successful Author Mindset**, Joanna Penn, Curl Up Press, 2016.

**This Business of Publishing**, Richard Curtis, Open Road Media, 2014.

## Podcasts

BookNet Canada Podcast
www.booknetcanada.ca/podcast

Kobo Writing Life Podcast
www.kobowritinglife.com/category/kwl-podcast

Sell More Books Show
www.sellmorebooksshow.com

Six Figure Authors
www.6figureauthors.com

Stark Reflections on Writing & Publishing
www.starkreflections.ca

Story Studio Podcast
www.storystudiopodcast.com

The Creative Penn
www.thecreativepenn.com

The Rebel Author Podcast
www.sachablack.co.uk/the-rebel-author-podcast

The Self Publishing Show (formerly The Self Publishing Formula)
www.selfpublishingformula.com/spf-podcast

Writer's Ink Podcast
www.writersinkpodcast.com

Writing Excuses
www.writingexcuses.com

## Website Resources

**The Alliance of Independent Authors**
www.allianceindependentauthors.org
www.selfpublishingadvice.org/self-publishing-service-reviews

**Blockchain for Publishing** —Joanna Penn
www.thecreativepenn.com/2021/03/12/blockchain-for-publishing

**BookBub Partners Blog**
www.insights.bookbub.com

**Canadian ISBN Service System (CISS)**
www.collectionscanada.gc.ca/ciss-ssci/app

**Kickstarter Best Practices** (Free Teachable Course)
www.wmg-publishing-workshops-and-lectures.teachable.com/p/kickstarter

**Kobo Hacks for Optimizing Sales (Free Email Course)**
www.blog.reedsy.com/learning/courses/distribution/kobo-hacks

**Kobo—Maximizing Your Sales at Kobo (Article)**
www.selfpublishingadvice.org/maximizing-your-sales-at-kobo-by-mark-lefebvre-director-of-kobo-writing-life-author-relations

**Kobo—How To Sell More Books on Kobo (Video)**
www.youtube.com/watch?v=xSZVlEJi5E8

**How To Sell Your Books Directly To Readers And Get Paid Immediately**—Joanna Penn
www.thecreativepenn.com/2020/03/20/sell-direct-get-paid-now

**ScribeCount**
**www.scribecount.com**

**Sell Your eBooks Wide (A Bundle)** – Monica Leonelle
www.theworldneedsyourbook.com/shop/product/sell-your-ebooks-wide-a-book-bundle/

**Selling eBooks Direct: How to Set up A Simple eBookstore**—David Gaughran
www.davidgaughran.com/selling-ebooks-direct-how-to-set-up-a-simple-e-bookstore/

**Universal Book Links**
Books2Read
www.books2read.com
Book Genius
www.geni.us
SmartURL
www.manage.smarturl.it

**Public Lending Right—PLR International**
www.plrinternational.com/

**Wide for the Win (Facebook Group)**
www.facebook.com/groups/wideforthewin

**Writing & Selling on Fiction Apps** (Facebook Group)
**www.facebook.com/groups/2042480162718205**

**Written Word Media Author Blog**
www.writtenwordmedia.com/category/author-blog

**Writer Beware**
www.writerbeware.com

# ABOUT THE AUTHOR

Mark's highly successful experience in the publishing and bookselling industry spans over three decades where he has worked in almost every type of brick and mortar, online and digital bookstore.

The former Director of self-publishing and author relations for Rakuten Kobo, and the founding leader of *Kobo Writing Life*, Kobo's free direct-to-Kobo publishing tool, Mark thrives on innovation, particularly as it relates to digital publishing. He works part-time as Director of Business Development for Draft2Digital.

Mark also writes and mentors authors and publishers about digital publishing opportunities both 1:1 and via his *Stark Reflections on Writing & Publishing* weekly podcast.

You can learn more about Mark at *www.markleslie.ca*

# Selected Books by the Author

## As Mark Leslie Lefebvre

### Writing & Publishing

*The 7 P's of Publishing Success*
*Killing It on Kobo*
*An Author's Guide to Working with Libraries and Bookstores*
*Wide for the Win*

## As Mark Leslie

*Haunted Hospitals*
*A Canadian Werewolf in New York*
*Fear and Longing in Los Angeles*
*Tomes of Terror*
*I, Death*
*One Hand Screaming*

## As Editor

*Pulphouse #10*
*Obsessions*
*Fiction River: Superstitious*
*Fiction River: Feel the Love*
*Fiction River: Feel the Fear*
*Tesseracts Sixteen: Parnassus Unbound*

Lightning Source UK Ltd.
Milton Keynes UK
UKHW020639210421
382364UK00010B/486